Pull up a Chair

Memories of Old-timers

from Armstrong Spallumcheen

British Columbia

by Shirley Campbell

Trafford Publishing

© Copyright 2004 Shirley Campbell. All rights reserved.

No part of this publication may be reproduced, stored in a retrieval system, or transmitted, in any form or by any means, electronic, mechanical, photocopying, recording, or otherwise, without the written prior permission of the author.

Printed in Victoria, Canada

Cover: *Pull up a Chair*
watercolour by the author
Sketch maps by the author
Layout by Trafford Publishing

Note for Librarians: a cataloguing record for this book that includes Dewey Classification and US Library of Congress numbers is available from the National Library of Canada. The complete cataloguing record can be obtained from the National Library's online database at: www.nlc-bnc.ca/amicus/index-e.html
ISBN 1-4120-2466-8

TRAFFORD

This book was published *on-demand* in cooperation with Trafford Publishing.
On-demand publishing is a unique process and service of making a book available for retail sale to the public taking advantage of on-demand manufacturing and Internet marketing. **On-demand publishing** includes promotions, retail sales, manufacturing, order fulfilment, accounting and collecting royalties on behalf of the author.

Suite 6E, 2333 Government St., Victoria, B.C. V8T 4P4, CANADA
Phone   250-383-6864   Toll-free   1-888-232-4444 (Canada & US)
Fax   250-383-6804   E-mail   sales@trafford.com
Web site www.trafford.com
TRAFFORD PUBLISHING IS A DIVISION OF TRAFFORD HOLDINGS LTD.
Trafford Catalogue #04-0294   www.trafford.com/robots/04-0294.html

10   9   8   7   6   5   4

For the *Storytellers*

Contents

Acknowledgements vii

Introduction 1

Chapter One 5
Matthew Seymour Hassen: *Ancient Lies*

Chapter Two 57
Ralph Duncan Lockhart: *Musing with Ralph*

Chapter Three 139
Janet Marion (Hilliard) Coldicott: *A Tribute to Ellie*

Chapter Four 205
Russell Carleton 'Rusty' Freeze: *Poets, Painters, and Ploughmen*

Chapter Five 243
William McLeod 'Mac' Thornton: *Friends and Fortune*

Chapter Six 265
John Rawleigh Boss: *No Time to Rust*

Chapter Seven 309
Martin Houlding Meggait: *Grit and Grace*

Index 364

Acknowledgements

My thanks go first to the seven storytellers who trusted me with their memories of earlier times and persevered with me until we got them right. Their cheerful hospitality and kindness were a lesson in neighbourliness. Wives, too, made important additions and contributed a female perspective. I treasure the hours spent with them all.

I am grateful to Heritage Place Publishing, Surrey, BC, for permission to quote from Hilary Place's memoir, *Dog Creek, a place in the Cariboo*.

Joan Cowan, Curator/Administrator of the Enderby and District Museum supplied a map of Deep Creek settlement and background material written by Janet Coldicott about her early life. Joan was always ready to answer many questions and to offer help.

Ernie Laviolette of Monashee Pictures, Lumby, BC, produced the excellent photographs in this book. He took my 'kitchen pictures' and older photos and made them acceptable for publication.

Archivists Pat Brinnen, Louise Everest, Jessie Ann Gamble and Marion Hope at the Armstrong Spallumcheen Museum found information for me despite the noise and organized disruption of renovations.

Linda Wills, archivist at the Vernon Museum, verified facts relating to that city.

Stan Field, also of Vernon, BC, supplied details of the Fuenfgeld family, including the correct spelling of the name, and was happy to contribute his knowledge to this project.

Rod Drennan, administrator for Spallumcheen municipality, told me what he knew of the history of McLeod subdivision. I appreciated his help and that of the staff.

My friend Lorna Carter provided data the dictionary forgot to include and edited the first proof.

Diana Muir willingly answered questions about health.

Area real estate agents and Armstrong city hall staff were most helpful in supplying house numbers for dwellings mentioned in Ralph Lockhart's milk run. Ralph cheerfully accompanied me on several junkets around town pointing out houses and naming residents in the 1930s. I hope I was sufficiently attentive.

Our painting group – Amy Salter, Helen Riley, Dagmar Watkins, and Linda Neden – supported my efforts to paint the cover for the book. Frances Hatfield and Robert Magenis may recognize the glass door of the stove as their own. Linda, also adept at the computer, readied the disks for the publisher. I am grateful to them all.

Kristen Kane of Spallumcheen read the final draft of the manuscript. As a second pair of eyes she was invaluable.

Mat. S. Hassen willingly contributed his extensive knowledge of Armstrong Spallumcheen. I relied on generous servings of his time.

Finally, I wish to thank my family for their interest and support. My husband, Kevin, encouraged me to write this book, shared the computer, and demonstrated the importance of locating North on my sketch maps. On some of them, however, North flouts the rules of cartography and migrates in the wake of the Lockhart milk wagon. I also thank our children and daughter-in-law for their enthusiasm and hope they find the stories meaningful.

Introduction

This is a book of memories.

Six men and one woman sat in their own homes, usually in the kitchen, and recounted tales about growing up in or near the area known as Armstrong Spallumcheen in the Okanagan Valley of British Columbia. Armstrong is a small city of roughly 4,000. In the municipality of Spallumcheen, which surrounds it, live about 6,000 people. Five of the seven storytellers, presently in their late seventies to early nineties, live here still.

Their stories are full of hardship, humour and tenacity. They grew up participating in a life that included hay and grain crops, vegetable and flower gardens, cattle and horses, pigs and chickens. It was a time when things were largely made "by hand," and substitutes were invented if "store-bought" was out of reach, a time of "making your own fun," knowing your neighbours, and building a community.

The parents of these storytellers arrived in the Okanagan from disparate points of the compass and under unique circumstances. Their experiences were wide-ranging, poignant, adventurous, and sometimes dangerous. Their stories became their children's property and so they are included here.

Family members are familiar with these tales. They have emerged over years of mutual companionship, and they root the family in a common tradition. Our modern community needs to hear them too. They validate the effort that made this area home, and they introduce newcomers to a "history" of which they may know nothing. These stories may help them feel more comfortable here. They may help them value and participate more fully in community life in Armstrong Spallumcheen.

A word about what this book is *not* – it is not a history in the accepted sense of the word: an objective assessment of an assemblage of facts. On the contrary, it is entirely subjective. It is the world as the storyteller perceived it. "How *I* saw it" could be an alternative title to each of these chapters. Each member of the same family may have a different version of events. We cannot truly walk in each other's shoes.

Every effort was made to ensure that the storyteller met no surprises in the published book. Each story went through several drafts, and at each stage the storyteller corrected, enlarged, or eliminated until the final draft was mutually satisfactory. Each person selected the title for his or her story, and each received a copy of the final draft.

The author photographed the storytellers at home. Each storyteller supplied a photograph from earlier days.

The storytellers' words are written in italic print. Their 'voices' are full of life.

Have you ever thought of memory

Have you ever thought of memory
    As a room with pictures hung
Where we can enter and live again
    The days when we were young?

Whenever I enter memory's room
    To view the pictures there,
I find some hidden by years of dust,
    Nearly ruined by lack of care.

As I clean these pictures so laden with dust
    Many lovely old scenes seem to live.
Why should they be hidden by cobwebs of time
    When to me such pleasure they give?

There is a scene of a homestead old –
    The hills with a drifting fog –
Then a sunrise – a sunset – a twilight scene,
    And a pathway my footsteps have trod.

There may be the lines of an old-time song
    A forgotten but haunting refrain –
A boy and his dog – a girl and her doll
    Or a lassie who laughs in the rain –

                      James Russell Freeze

Chapter One

Ancient Lies

Matthew Seymour Hassen

D*ad was 'tail end Charlie,' Mat. says. He had eight older brothers and sisters, and in the patriarchal system the eldest brother would inherit the farm; the others would have to look after themselves as best they could. The girls would maybe marry an eldest son. One brother went to Australia; another one died. Dad decided America was his best bet.*

Matthew Seymour Hassen's forebears were born in the Roe Valley in County Londonderry, Northern Ireland. *Three hundred years before, people used to come over from Scotland, perhaps from around Glasgow, to pick potatoes. Maybe the rough piece of water between Stranraer and Larne [the North Channel] persuaded them to stay in Ireland, where they became known as an ethnic group called the Ulster Scots.*

Shortly after his grandfather married Elizabeth Ferguson, the newlyweds bought a farm with a small store and post office in the Upper Binn area, called Tullintrain, nine miles east of Dungiven. When their youngest son, Matthew Hassen, emigrated, he sailed for New York from Moville at the mouth of the Foyle River, as ocean-going boats were too large to sail farther inland. It was his first trip of any length from home, and he never returned.

An uncle on his mother's side saw him off. He gave him two shillings for the trip. That uncle was another 'tail end Charlie.' He knew how to look after his money. So Dad left home with two shillings in his pocket.

The new emigrant was 'poor' in another way. Matthew Hassen had no middle name. Therefore, he always punctuated a shortened form of his first name with a period. When his own children were born, he made sure they were properly endowed. Son Mat. S. has followed his father's practice, and the name has now reached the fifth generation of use.

On May 8, 2005, Matthew Seymour Hassen is looking forward to his 90th birthday. He intends to live to 100: *I hate Chretien. I want my name to be read out by CHBC television on my 100th birthday.* By then Chretien would be long gone from politics; for Mat., still in operation, a sweet revenge. He is sitting at his kitchen table on Sage Avenue in Armstrong. The room is bright with sun, everything in its place. Mat. wears a neat shirt under his suspenders and dress pants. His navy blazer with its Canadian Legion crest hangs over the back of a chair. He is remembering stories about growing up in Spallumcheen. Images dance into words rich in detail and drama. When he pauses to collect his thoughts, his visions make him chuckle.

Dad found a job working in a bank note company in New York wheeling money around in a warehouse for nearly a year. But he didn't like being out from under the British flag and he moved north to Ontario. He found a job on a farm that raised and showed Percheron horses. Everything was done with horses back then. You walked or you drove a horse. Percheron is a famous 'heavy horse' breed from France, their strength and speed ideal for clearing bush to make farmland, and for hauling loads of logs and grain to mills. Mat. Hassen's job was to show these animals at exhibitions in Toronto and Chicago.

One day at the Toronto Exhibition he struck up a conversation with a young man named Seymour who was admiring the Percherons. Seymour was a teamster, and in horses they had a mutual interest. Mat. accompanied Seymour to Chicago and met his sister, Florence. She was living with a maternal uncle and was employed by a real estate developer with property in the Bitter Root Valley in Montana. Florence wrote brochures extolling the virtues of the real estate. *It was a pretty good ranching and farming area apparently.*

Mat. and Florence were married. After he worked for a period in a feed mill in Ontario, the couple was lured west by the real estate boom then in full force in British Columbia. In April, 1913, they came to New Westminster.

In those days the west was the golden place. In New Westminster Dad was offered a job by a real estate developer running the fellow's branch office in Armstrong. He moved up that month and Mother followed in June. They rented a place on Wood Avenue where the telephone company now has its office. On January 1, 1914, the guy declared he was stony broke, and Dad was on his own. He had a wife and an office but no job and no income. It was a case of 'Root, hog, or die.'

At the office Mat. Hassen had fallen heir to a series of real estate 'options.' An option to purchase a piece of property for a certain amount could generate a profit only by resale at a higher figure within a specified time frame. If the land were not sold within that time, the option expired. Men were not buying land; they were enlisting for war. The options expired and were worthless. Mat. and Florence moved into a place on Thomas Hayes Road, and a son was born in Armstrong's first hospital, 3025 Patterson Avenue. Romley Ferguson was named after Florence's grandfather Romley and Mat.'s grandmother, Elizabeth Ferguson. *I don't know why they didn't call him Mat. Maybe they tossed a coin.*

Since arriving in Armstrong Mat. had recognized the importance of the local agricultural fair, which by 1913 had both a hall for fruit, vegetables and crafts, and stables for livestock. He volunteered to do office work and help keep the books. As World War One approached, the fair's treasurer, Major F.C. Wolfenden, was called up. Mat. Hassen stepped into his shoes as both the secretary-treasurer and the manager. He held the post until his death in 1956. *Dad was the stem-winder of the fair. So naturally we kids got involved – especially if it was free.*

Fairs had been a regular bi-monthly happening at towns in

Ireland. A 'Scot's Penny' (twice the size of a 'toonie') sealed the deal between each buyer and seller, and at 11 a.m. both groups repaired to the local pub to close the transactions. After 11 a.m. stock that buyers did not wish to take home again was auctioned off. In Ireland, Mat. had never acted as auctioneer but he had often seen it done. In Spallumcheen he got his chance. As the war progressed, widows and children of soldiers were packing up and leaving their farms. Mat. sold farms and auctioned the chattels.

He also became an 'estate agent,' a person who looked after a piece of property for an absentee owner until it was sold. He and Florence moved onto a farm at the corner of Crozier and Otter Lake X Road and farmed it for a man named Thompson. Here Matthew Seymour Hassen, born in the same hospital eighteen months after brother Romley, spent the first five years of his life.

Mat. S. Hassen was named for his father and his mother, Florence Seymour. Two prized photographs of his parents, each backed on a six-inch wooden silhouette standing in a grooved base, were produced in Chicago over seventy years ago. They show a dark-haired, dark-eyed man with a small moustache who is facing the camera and wearing a suit, and a composed woman in fine-rimmed glasses looking away to the right, her fair hair in a roll off her face. *I guess you could say Dad was an 'idea man.' Mother kept us busy, and she could give us hell too.*

Mat. S.' earliest memory is of sitting under the dining-room table on the farm at Crozier Road and tying his shoelaces. *I remember getting the laces going the right way and knew I'd never have to learn it again. Another memory is being stung right between the eyes by an American Baldface hornet. My face swelled up. They killed quite a few people, those black hornets, especially if one got stung in the back of the neck. Ed Hoover's eldest boy got stung in the neck and he didn't last a day. Nothing skinny about those hornets. They were as wide as the end of my finger.*

The Hassen boys' favourite spot to play was in the 'Borrow

Pit,' which had been used in building the S and O (now Canadian Pacific Railway) line to Okanagan Landing. If a farmer had a knoll of gravel on his property, a leftover from the retreat of glaciers in the last Ice Age, the highways department could 'borrow' gravel to build roads on the grounds that the surveyed size of the property was not affected by the removal of the knoll. The excavated knoll was called the 'Borrow Pit,' a misnomer, as the gravel was never replaced.

That gravel just spilled out on the edge of the Thompson place from the Borrow Pit area. They used a steam shovel to remove the gravel. I remember how high the walls of the pit seemed. It's now in the Industrial Park off Crozier Road.

Water from Proctor Lake fed Hayes Creek that comes underground and spills out along the west side of Crozier Road between there and the railway track. Dig down two or three feet and you have a good supply of water. Larkin Water District put their well across the track and drilled down 140 feet to the bedrock.

Mat. Hassen continued to sell real estate. He tried to interest one customer in some property in Fire Valley, this side of Edgewood, *but he wasn't going to have anything to do with land that was eighty miles from here across the mountains, and no all-season roads until the 1950s.* Closer to home, his neighbour on Crozier Road, *a fellow called Francis Noel Hales, very English, refused to have one tree on property he bought; he wanted just the cultivated land. He didn't drive his own car – Isaac Harris drove him around in a Model T and broke his arm cranking it. Hales' farming left much to be desired. His cattle were everybody's problem; he didn't maintain his fences. Dad came home one time, got the shotgun and salt-loaded shells and went after this bull and a whole bunch of cows that were scrounging at the straw pile. He got the bull in the tail end with a bunch of rock salt. We kids traced them back home by the blood specks on the snow.*

The Crozier Road place sold. *It's now commonly called the*

Dixon place. Mat. bought the Lauer place off Lansdowne Road just up the hill from Highway 97A. Jake Lauer was an American who left the area. But the log house was too small for a growing family. A larger place on Young Road and Highland Park Road became the Hassen farm where the two boys and their sisters Eileen and Daphne would grow up. *Even fights – two boys and two girls.*

In 1913, the year that Mat. and Florence Hassen came to Armstrong, the town became incorporated as a separate entity within the Municipality of Spallumcheen, which curled like the doughnut around the hole at its centre. The population was sparse. In 1900 Spallumcheen included about 900 people. The 2002 census gave Armstrong and Spallumcheen together a population of approximately 10,000 – a gain of only 9,000 people in a century. Mat. S. Hassen was born in 1915. His memories bring these early years in Armstrong Spallumcheen to life.

Our son, Matthew Robert, was the first one in the Hassen family that ever had a pay cheque. Before he came along, everyone made a living as best they could. Of course, some people get strange ideas about how to do it – like burglary – but, you know, you can make your job. But, of course, that's what Canada was all about. These immigrants came here with certain skills, but what do they do with them? Take A.L. Fortune, for instance – him alone with some Indians. What's he going to do? He can't sell anything to the Indians; he doesn't need to buy anything from the Indians. But he had to grow stuff to eat.

A.L. Fortune, one of the Overlanders of 1862 from the eastern part of the continent, had abandoned the search for gold in the British Columbia Interior in the 1860s and, liking the look of the fertile land along the Shuswap River, had picked up a piece of land near Enderby, called Fortune's Landing.

He figured there was more 'gold' in the ground than he had imagined. I guess, for want of anything better to do, he decided to grow wheat. He didn't have a binder or anything else of the sort, so he got some pigs and used them to harvest the wheat. The pigs just knocked it down and ate it. Of course, inadvertently he drowned a whole bunch of them when they wandered out on the river ice that winter and fell through, but he later sold what was left for six and a quarter cents a pound – ham and bacon, smoked. It was a way of surviving.

Captain Short ran the original boat on Okanagan Lake – a rowboat – and he used to row people up and down the lake. He was called 'Captain' but I don't suppose he had any trade qualifications. He wanted a bigger boat and asked John Hamill to build it for him. John Hamill, an Irishman from Ballymoney who had come out to Spallumcheen in the 1870s, had a carpenter shop in Lansdowne. He built the boat, and B.F. Young, a rancher with horses, hauled it from Lansdowne to the head of Okanagan Lake, a distance of about twelve miles. Captain Short put a little steam engine run with kerosene in the boat, and he used to impoverish the whole population of coal oil when supplies got tight. Left everybody without lights!!

*That was the sort of people that settled Spallumcheen. They didn't just sit and wave their hands in desperation. They got out and **did** something. Spallumcheen was incorporated, for instance, because in order to get any improvements on the so-called roads, they had to write the provincial government in Victoria for permission and possibly some finance. They'd get no answer. The people at Hullcar got fed up with that – the trail to Armstrong was full of mud holes – so they'd do it on their own. That was one thing about Armstrong and Spallumcheen, they did everything on their own.*

Early settlers also knew which breeds of livestock and varieties of produce did well and supplied a market in their home countries. Mat. spoke about lessons learned in Britain:

Lowland cattle accustomed to swampy meadowland and coarse feed in abundance would not do well in the highlands in Scotland – hills, coarse vegetation and rocks – because they would have to eat a tremendous amount of food in order to survive. There were forty different breeds of sheep in England – coarse wool for blankets, fine wool for baby clothes, medium wool for knitted clothes. Horses were either clean-legged or hairy-legged. Horses that worked in rough, rocky conditions produced hair on their lower legs for protection. In muddy country you don't use these horses because mud can cake on their lower legs and the dampness may lead to disease; such as, thrush. So clean-legged horses are better used in wet conditions.

Farming in Spallumcheen, however, was experimental. Although many settlers had brought with them their favourite varieties of grains, fruit, vegetables, and livestock, they often discovered that conditions in the Okanagan Valley produced a different result. Soil, rainfall, hours of daylight and dark, even differences between one side of the valley and the other – all were factors in a crop's development. Living at a subsistence level, farmers had to make progress. They had to find more suitable varieties, grow more volume and get more income. Discovering these answers individually would take too long. The agricultural fair was the answer.

Take apples, for example. Farmers with their different apples from their different locations and different growing conditions would bring in their 'Plate of Five Apples.' Everybody looked at the winners, then at their own soil and climate and decided if they should try these apples. The same reasoning applied to all the exhibits. *The fair meant success or failure. It was not just a merry-go-round. It was real life.*

In addition to managing the fair, Mat. Hassen auctioneered at the Kamloops Bull Sale. In 1923 a 'fat stock' category was introduced at the sale that included a section for boys and girls under the auspices of 'Junior Farmers,' the precursor of 4H in the 1950s. In 1923 Mat. S. was eight years old and Romley nine and a half.

Romley and I each got a calf to take to Kamloops, and we stayed with Junior Farmers right through high school, and went on judging trips. The geographical area for Okanagan children competing in Junior Farmers' activities was east of North Bend, which was located across the Fraser River from Boston Bar; west of North Bend was designated for the Coast clubs. There was a lot of activity up here in chickens, pigs, calves, and sheep. Other clubs would include potatoes, grain, and garden crops.

Mat. S. Hassen began school in 1921. Armstrong Elementary School opened that same year, the first consolidated school in western Canada. One-room schoolhouses in Spallumcheen closed and students were bused into the 'Brick School' on Pleasant Valley Road in Armstrong. The children travelled in the school truck, a Model T Ford, *a very little bigger deck on them than an ordinary pickup today. I swear you could drop the engine in a Japanese orange crate. Of course, that resulted in most of us having to push the darn truck uphill. The municipality was relatively new in those days, and there wasn't a lot of gravel on the roads. Most of them were rutted and muddy. The Hullcar run was about eight miles. Ewart Price lived out there, he had seven children, and his taxes were five dollars a year. Seven kids got hauled to school 200 days a year for five bucks.*

George Game drove the school truck. It had a box with a roof of leatherette laid over laths. There were windows along one side but the holes were empty. An exhaust pipe ran down the middle of the floor and was supposed to provide heat. The kids used to put their rubber boots on top of the pipe and burn them in order to cause a stink. There were no windshield wipers. The two oldest kids, Connie and Allen Game, used to sit one on each front fender with a rag and daub the rain off when the occasion called for it.

Despite multiple opportunities for disaster, Mat. recalled only one fatality. A child jumped out of the truck and ran beside it to climb into the front for a better view. Freezing temperatures had made the roadside slippery, and he fell under the moving vehicle and was killed.

Tom Aldworth was the principal, R. Garner was vice-principal, and J.K. Bell was a teacher. He was a veteran of the air force in World War One, and he was pretty badly crippled up. He walked with two canes. He was the only teacher that came to school in a car – a Model T – and when weather wasn't conducive to walking, he'd bring the car. No other teachers had a car. Most of them were from Vancouver, and they all disappeared for the Christmas holidays. The train used to get in between 7:30 and 8:00 in the morning, and they'd count on coming on that one on the first day of school. The big snowfall used to come between Christmas and New Year's. Quite frequently the train was late because of the snow, so the teachers would be late for school on Monday morning. Of course, they never allowed for that. There got to be a few homegrown teachers who lived here permanently, like Mrs. Dimock, our elementary school teacher, a widow with one child. She taught the grandchildren of her early students. She must have had a soul of iron to put up with that many small kids for so long. Most of my classes were between 20 and 25 because the number of youngsters born during the war would be at a low ebb. It got down to about 12 to 15 in high school.

Winter weather was strenuous. I distinctly remember bright, bright sunshine and cold, cold weather, and you'd come home from school and you'd squint because of the glare on the snow. It was 30-35 below zero every winter – it was expected – and around about the end of January when you were fed up with the cold weather, you'd get the January thaw for a couple of days, and then back to the cold weather for another week or two. Then spring would gradually come. We used to feed steers and show cattle at the Kamloops Bull Sale, March 21st to 23rd. We'd leave Armstrong in a foot of snow, in Kamloops, nothing, and come back to a foot of snow. The water situation was good then.

When winter came, the school truck became a team and sleigh, and a bunch of kids in a sleigh led to the usual hilarity. The sleigh I went on had to go underneath a tree overhanging the road, and when the weather was right, there'd be a lot of snow on the branch. You smartened up quick, you see, and when you got to that branch, you gave it a pull and the snow went all over the rest of them. At the start of an up-grade in the road, we'd all get to the back of the sleigh, and our weight would lift the rack, and George Game would *be sitting up in the air, and of course he didn't get down again until we let him down.*

The occasional Spallumcheen resident avoided winter altogether and became a 'snowbird' before the term had been coined.

Old Thomas Hayes, for instance, used to go to California. His family had come across from eastern United States, landed in California, and worked north after that. So I guess he knew lots of people that had stayed in California, and when he retired, he'd go down and leave the kids running the farm. I remember one time he bought a Deluxe Dodge sedan in California and Harry [a son] drove it back up. But every six months he had to go down to Washington to avoid the duty because it was still registered in California, and he didn't want to import the thing because he'd have to pay it. I think eventually he gave up and registered it in BC.

Winter roads in Spallumcheen were not plowed. Land clearing was the staple winter work and farmers used to haul their logs into the sawmills on these winter roads. The logs were loaded on a bunk and cinched tight with chains, then hauled by horses to their destination. Ruts in the road were packed down on six or eight inches of snow. A continuing controversy existed between the people who wanted the roads plowed and the ones who needed the snowpack in order to haul their logs to the mills.

One solution adopted by Joe Glaicar, who also drove the school truck for several decades, was to adapt his vehicle for winter conditions. *He had noticed lying in the fairgrounds for many years some forms for making concrete culvert pieces. They were half circles. Joe got hold of some of these, put runners under the half circles and mounted them in front of the back wheels of the school truck. The idea was good, you know. It would clear the snow ahead of the wheels that were doing the work – the front wheels, of course, had only three and a half inch tires on them – but his fastening deal wasn't too good, and every once in a while it broke loose and the wheels ran over the culvert parts.*

He had the worst of it up on Grandview Flats. One corner up there frequently drifted with six to eight feet of snow, and Joe would take to the field because the snow had blown off from there. Joe's contraption was the only kind of plowing done in those days.

When Mat. and his siblings got home from school, they were ravenous. Florence would put out a quart sealer of plum jam and bread – fresh bread, if it was Friday – *the house would be full of bread and bread smells – and we'd eat the whole quart of jam. We ate dozens of them.*

Each day of the week had its special flavour. Monday was washing day, and Wednesday was ironing day, as the wash sometimes needed two days to dry on the line. *Friday afternoon all over town was Receiving Day. You had a visiting card and went out visiting. You didn't have to phone ahead – no phones, of course. If nobody was home, you left your card in a tray. I think, though, there were special days when they'd be staying home, and people would know that. There weren't that many people anyway.*

Each day, then, the Hassen children knew what to expect when they got home. After the jam came chores. Gathering eggs and filling the woodbox were *incidental. The main work was with the livestock – pigs, chickens, horses and cattle to feed before supper, and after supper the job of milking the cows and putting them to bed. A cow went dry for a couple of months every year prior to calving, so the solution was to have two milk cows to cover the barren period. Did you know that a thunderstorm sours the milk? Even that evening's milk will be sour before next morning's breakfast. We had a screened cupboard on the shady side of the house to keep milk and butter in. You could also put the cream down the well, where it was cool, but you had to be careful you didn't slop the stuff over and spoil the water. That was a job then – you'd have to pump the water off until it was clear.*

Dad was a director of the Armstrong Creamery, and the cream would come in from the farms and there'd be mice in the damn cream! They'd have to use a screen or – I don't know – wipe the cream off the mouse – or wring it out. There were lots of people around here – Brits – that were a long way from being tidy. The upbringing in England, and in many other places, was less exotic then, and they were casual about sanitation. We had a neighbour, a Yorkshireman, who used to milk in the summertime wet-handed on the manure pile. The cows would come in and stand on the manure pile, and he'd get a bucket and stool and sit beside them. He'd squirt some milk on his hands and milk wet-handed. (A cow was something that smelled like a cow – no nice, neat, tidy udders. Some of the teats were the size of a cob of corn – maybe a cow had suckled calves at one time.) It was easy if the teat was wet to get the pressure from the top to the bottom, [but contaminating the milk was more likely]. I didn't like wet-handed milking, but that family all lived to a good age. You eat a peck of dirt before you die.

I remember Romley and I with the neighbour's kid went over to his place to pick a peck of windfall apples. They had a kind of press for squeezing the juice. We used to take a sack from the barn – God knows what had been in it before – and we'd put a bunch of apples in it and smash them with the flat of an axe. Then we'd put the sack in the press and squeeze the juice out of the apples, filter the juice through the sack into a two-gallon stew kettle – along with dirt from the barn floor, the axehead, the ground. We'd get a fair bunch of the stuff, and we'd drink the whole lot going home. There must have been several spoonfuls of dirt in the bottom of the kettle when we finished. We didn't bother about those things. We didn't know anything about disease or microbes or germs or anything like that. Eat anything that might eat you first!! They didn't have the hospitals that we lack today!

Florence kept her boys busy. Rom and I used to have to do the dishes as well as farm chores. The girls didn't have anything to do – they were younger, you see. I'm mentally alert – I'm sure of that – one night I realized that my sisters were older than we were when we started doing dishes. I brought this up at the Family Conference and we immediately shed this responsibility and the girls had *to assume it. I don't know why my brother didn't catch on – he was eighteen months older than me and should have figured it out a lot sooner. There was a certain amount of opposition from the Opposition, but it didn't hold any water.*

One of their evening chores was to crank the cream separator. Two milk cows gave three to four gallons of milk a day. Some was set aside for household use; the remainder was separated into cream and skim milk. Turning the crank on the cream separator, especially at the start, was slow, strenuous labour. Once it got going, the crank took on a life of its own: *You knew sixty revolutions a minute as well as you knew your own name. You could turn a cream separator for hours on end and never miss a cycle of sixty revolutions a minute.*

The cream separator was as important an item in some Spallumcheen farmhouses as the stove or the kitchen table. From early in the century farmers had supported a local creamery, which was situated on the highway east of Armstrong. When a fire destroyed it in 1927, Vernon and Salmon Arm creameries filled the void. However, some local people wondered if the fire had been an accident. The speculation swirled around the sighting of a butter churn.

In those days the churns were wood, and they had to be soaked in water for a week before they could be filled with cream for churning. Otherwise, the cream would stick to the insides. The creamery burned at noon on a Friday. The town was out there watching – kids on their bicycles – I was about twelve at the time, and I went with Dad in the car. At one o'clock while the fire was burning, Nels Griffith was there loading the cream off the deck to take to Vernon. It was churned that day. On the previous Friday an empty 500-gallon churn had been sent through Armstrong on a CPR flatcar to Vernon.

It was the job of the Hassen children on Saturday afternoon to churn into butter the cream that had been saved up over the week. Florence had a barrel churn, which is mounted in a frame, a cork in the side for draining. A person turned the handle until the motion coagulated the butterfat in the cream into clumps of butter. Waiting for that magic moment could tax the patience.

Sometimes it doesn't come very fast and sometimes it does. My brother and I were churning this particular time, and I guess the cork in the barrel got a little bit loose, so that led to "Let's make it a little looser." The barrel was going around and we had cream over the floor, ceiling and walls in a nice, straight line.

Their mother taught them the correct way to make butter. Mat. is scornful of commercial butter. He points to the butter dish on the table. *This stuff here isn't butter – it's grease – it smears – real butter will break like good cheese. When you are making butter, you must never smear it. It comes out of the churn like wheat, in granules, and you get cold water and wash all that buttermilk out of it, and then you get your paddle and you work it and you turn it, but you don't ever rub it – that breaks down the grain in it, you see. There was a butter printer that was a box with a handle on it and you filled it up, and it held a pound of butter – still not smeared – and then you pushed the handle down and let the butter come out on wet parchment paper and wrapped it up.*

The colour of the butter was related to the type of feed the cows ate.

Originally, cows were fed clover; horses were fed timothy and clover. Then alfalfa was introduced and the cows received alfalfa. That gave the yellow colour to the cream and butter. And in the summertime they were on grass – yellow again – and it also gave yellow fat to the cow when you butchered it. However, if you put the animal on dry feed for thirty to sixty days before butchering it, that fat became white. There was a demand for white fat. So the ideal became to pasture cattle late in the fall on dry grass to get this preferred white fat. Yellow fat was associated with ex-dairy cows. There was no meat grading here until the 1930s, and every worn-out milk cow became beef on your plate – rather, stew. In the Interior here they could sell good grass-fed cattle with white fat. Then there got to be opinions as to whether grass-fed cattle or grain-fed cattle gave the most flavourful beef. They still argue that point.

I worked at Douglas Lake Ranch in the early '30s, and they couldn't sell cattle without thirty days of grain in them – preferably sixty days – but that area wasn't grain-growing country. Yet cattle on dry grass feed were beautiful meat. I remember 1100-1200-pound steers going down the road after sixty days of grain for $27 apiece – less than five cents a pound. Frank Ward was manager of the Douglas Lake Cattle Company. I remember him saying at one of the bull sales of some Ranch cattle in railcar load lots at $3.25 per 100 pounds: "If cattle ever get back to five cents a pound, we'll start to make money." Now it's a buck and a half a pound at auction. It was Depression time, of course, and people couldn't afford to pay any higher.

A similar controversy surrounded the breed of milk cow to be used on the farm. The two Hassen milk cows were crossbreeds. Jerseys, however, were the early choice of many farmers in Spallumcheen.

There's a lot of difference in the makeup of milk. A Jersey is the highest butterfat-producing breed, and the fat globules are large. In Holstein milk, the fat globules are scarce – they said the milk was just like water; you could see to the bottom of the pail! The Ayrshires are in between – they have a good butterfat test, but it is a finer globule and more easily digested. You could easily get sickened on Jersey milk, it was so rich, but in the early days the breed of choice was Jersey because the by-product of the milk business was creameries – butter – and the skim milk went for pig feed. Then when the cheese business began, the Jerseys went out because the volume wasn't great enough, the butterfat test was too high, and dietitians and doctors were promoting their ideas of two percent and one percent milk. So if you were going to have a family cow, you wouldn't go for a Jersey.

There was a philosophy behind chicken production, too. Chickens were fairly easy to care for – chicken 'scratch' was minimal feed, and chickens knew all about 'scratching for a living.'

Lay in the summer and freeze in the winter. They were a natural animal – born in the spring, raised in the warm weather, then quit laying in the winter when it got cold. So if you wanted eggs in the winter, you'd have to store them covered in waterglass in five-gallon crocks. Along about March, Mother would send you down cellar for some eggs, and you'd be up to your elbow in waterglass feeling for eggs in the bottom of the crock. There was nothing wrong with those eggs except they weren't good for frying because the yolks would break, but they made good scrambled eggs and there was nothing wrong with them for cooking.

Accommodation for chickens wasn't elaborate. *You might have a chicken house but it wouldn't be heated or insulated – maybe one side would be open with chicken wire stretched across it. The poor chickens would be up on the roost with their heads under their wings, and some winter mornings probably some chickens would be staying there – frozen solid – especially the older ones. At other times of the year the hens would run loose and lay everywhere. They'd hide their nests, and you'd have to go hunting for eggs under bushes, and if you weren't careful, you'd get some very ripe eggs!! So to be sure you weren't using eggs that had been sitting around for a few days, you'd break them individually to check – because if you were baking a cake that called for five eggs, and you broke the fifth one in with the rest and it was rotten – you'd have to throw out the lot.*

A Leghorn rooster gave Romley some bad moments. *Whenever he entered the chicken house, that bird would jump on his back and peck at his head. We were about four or five years old at the time and had a little toy klaxon horn. You'd crank the handle and it would blare. We got the bright idea of using it to scare off that rooster the next time we had to go into the chicken house. It worked. It filled the air with chickens and feathers flying, and we caught hell for it because a day later all the eggs had bloodspots in them.*

That was the second rule: "Don't frighten the chickens because they'll lay eggs with bloodspots." The first rule was "A thunderstorm sours the milk."

When Mat. S. grew up, his own young son, Matthew Robert, came crying to him one day because the rooster had chased him. Mat. found the bird and booted him into the pond. When he fished him out, he axed him. It was justifiable homicide – a satisfying retribution.

Mat. will allow Leghorns the prize for egg production – but only that.

For the farm, the utility bird is a real asset, right down to the old hen. One thing that they don't have today which is absolutely out of this world: two- maybe three-year-old, meat-style birds canned in sealers, and when you opened one of those jars, it was full of jelly, ideal for a hot summer's supper, beautifully tender and flavourful. If you cooked a Leghorn, you might as well cook a ball of string – all legs and no meat on them, and if they were two years old, you had to be careful because you could actually cut yourself on a broken bone – they were just like flint. The Wyandots and the Rocks were the favoured meat birds then – Barred Rocks, Plymouth Rocks, and White Rocks. No one has them anymore. Some have been bred to laying birds and now they have no meat on them. You can buy Rocks that are the same colour as the old breeds but you can't cook and eat them – no, no, terrible! Now the meat business is supplied with six-weeks-old chicks, raised for fryers, which is not chicken. Chicken has to be matured.

All meat has to be matured to taste the best. In the early days cattle weren't usually killed until they were three years old, entirely different to today. When you cook today's beef, the fat and dripping that comes off the roast is scarce, and hard like glass when it cools. Fat from a mature animal is larger globules. A favourite thing for kids' lunches was bread and dripping – the brown mixed with the white. The white stuff was granular, something like cream of wheat, and you'd mix the two together and spread it on your sandwich and it was wonderful stuff.

Pig-killing day was replete with its own excitement – all the squealing and screaming that was the prelude to the death and the butchering that followed. A large cauldron of water was brought to the boil over an outdoor fire, and a rope and pulley rigged up above it to lower the carcass into the water.

They had to scald the pig to get the hair off, and if the darn rope broke, the pig would be half cooked before they got it out of the barrel. Blood pudding was a favourite of several European countries – oatmeal and blood and garlic. My dad liked it, but us kids didn't go for it much because of the look of it. Bacon and eggs was standard fare. They hung the hams in the attic.

They had lots of varieties of food then and all of it with flavour. Today there isn't much variety and none *of it has flavour! There are a lot of apples now that are not worth a damn. I bought some a while ago – I don't even remember what they were – and I baked them. I might as well have baked that book!! And there was brown sugar and butter and spice with them too – everything – but they were no good.*

That's another place where man has got in where Mother Nature was doing well by herself. Apple trees were grown on poor soil – what they called well-drained soil – rocky, sandy soil so they had deep roots and were big trees. Lots of colour, flavour and juice. When you brought four or five apples into the kitchen, you could smell them all over the house. But a big tree meant a big, high ladder to get at them and forty trees to the acre. Now there are 120 trees to the acre, a shorter ladder so the picking is less laborious, and a shallow root. But no flavour and no juice, not the same apple at all – even a McIntosh grafted on root stock tastes nothing like the original. Espalier planting is flat – pick from both sides and sun and air gets in from both sides. They're easy to pick and you don't need a ladder. But you can pick the apple up and put it right against your nose and you smell nothing. Old apples, even a Transparent, had a nice odour to them.

Crabapples were Transcendent or Hyslop – one was reddish and one was yellowish. Growing them was an outcropping of the Depression years on the prairie. Somebody started canning crabapples in gallon cans, and they went like wildfire. They brought them here too – used to put them on the table in restaurants with a clove in them – darn good eating. And Transcendent makes a wonderful jelly – real red stuff – and, of course, it jells to beat the band. As a matter of fact, people used crabapples for jelling preserves. If you wanted to jell something, you put in some crabapples.

There were eight packing houses here when I was a child – all along the railroad tracks. Armstrong was the best express point in BC for the [fruit and] vegetable packing business. R.W. McDonald used to go out in February every year to the prairies and call on all the produce businesses there. That was when the railroad was good. He'd put [the orders] on the train here at night and they'd be in Calgary the next day, and probably in Saskatchewan the next night. Tuesday was the big shipping day so they'd have it in their stores for the weekend. Gullivan was the agent here when I was a youngster. [It was said] he never touched his pay. He didn't need to – he saved it and lived off express commissions. He got a commission on express items that went to the prairies. There would be a [rail] carload going out of Armstrong every evening in the growing season. The passenger train would wait here for an hour lots of times loading the express. Up to twenty-five cars of [fruit and] vegetables left in a day from here. McDonald also used to harvest fir and cedar branches – twigs – and package them up and send them out there for Christmas decorations – the aroma was a big deal.

Along with the disappearing varieties of produce, Mat. deplores too the loss of basic knowledge about food among the general public.

People are not going to know how to survive pretty soon. Their food, which is an essential deal, is all prepared for them. You go to the grocery store and it's all packaged. Even if you go to the butcher's, the meat is pre-cut; you don't order it and watch the butcher cut it from the carcass. You can only buy what the stores want to sell, which means what the wholesale manufacturer wants to produce for sale.

But you don't have to eat any of that stuff; you can buy the real stuff in this area here. And there's no comparison between the real stuff and the stuff they want to sell you. There are people so ignorant that they wouldn't think of eating a naturally raised egg. They don't like the looks or the taste of it – the orange yolk is terrible – they've got to have that pure white yolk. And the difference in cooking between a store-bought egg and the other! There's a different flavour and a different appearance.

[Nowadays] you don't have to learn to cook. There was a lady who used to help my wife with the cleaning. She was White Russian – a German that had moved into Russia. There were nine in her family over there and the meat supply for that family was half a pig a year. She made cabbage rolls that were out of this world. Nothing was wasted. Everything went into the pot that was always simmering on the back of the stove. That's how a lot of soups and other dishes were developed. Of course, they had a solid fuel stove! You can't afford to do it on an electric stove. But you can make soup with things, some herbs out of the garden, lots of onion and lots of garlic. People had these skills years and years ago. But they have forgotten or don't bother. It's no-effort cooking now – the Depression brought that along – both parents working in an office.

Threshing was responsible for a lot of tremendous cooks in Spallumcheen. Ten or twelve men gathered together to thresh the grain, and they'd be fed a hot meal by the woman of the house. They weren't old fellows – many were single men who lived in boarding houses and were gone [around the countryside] for two or three weeks' threshing every fall. At dinnertime they'd comment about the fine roast or pie they were eating or, worse, rave about the meal they'd been served at the previous farm. They were just doing it to get a rise out of them, but it put some of the women at loggerheads with their neighbours. The competition for best cook was fierce! Generally, if you went to any of these houses, you'd get a wonderful meal – well cooked, lots of it, and lots of flavour. You still get that quality at church-catered meals, the ones at the fair, for instance, or Legion meals. Mat. doesn't have much good to say about hospital meals. *They have the latest modern equipment and technology, but they couldn't boil water without a manual.* It was definitely not the Armstrong Spallumcheen way.

The Armstrong Spallumcheen way meant self-reliance and community participation, and included making your own fun.

A bit of bare ground shows up in the spring and that's all you need to play marbles – the south side of a building in all the mud; and the knees of your pants would get soggy and wear out from kneeling, and the toes of your boots would wear out from scraping on the ground. Everybody had clay marbles and maybe a couple of glass ones called agates. You'd put a couple of marbles a few inches apart on the bare patch, and with your 'shooters,' you'd try to hit them and knock them away. A fancier version was played inside a big ring on the ground.

A game called nobbies called for ingenuity and equipment: a shoelace, two pieces of the family's garden hose, and a hazel stick.

A hose didn't come the way it does now – in lengths with fixtures on the ends. You bought the fixtures yourself and attached them to the hose. So it was easy to undo the fixture from one end of the hose and cut two pieces off, each about two inches long. You punched a hole through the centre of the first piece and pulled one end of the shoelace through and tied a knot in it. Then you pushed the other end of the lace through a similar hole in the second piece of hose and knotted it, making sure that the distance between the two pieces of hose was about three inches.

Nobbies was played like lacrosse. You cut a hazel stick at the roadside, making sure it had a fork in it, and then cut off the branches about two inches above the kink to make a lazy L or a 45-degree angle. You'd throw the nobby and use the kink to catch the shoelace. With a partner you could both throw and catch the nobby with the hazel stick. For years you could see lost nobbies hanging from wires strung up overhead. I made some when our Mat. was young and the neighbour kid was over playing. They got the idea pretty good. But nobbies didn't catch on. Nobody's played with them for fifty or sixty years. But it cost nothing except two pieces of your dad's hose – which he'd never miss. Mat. didn't play lacrosse on the town teams because he had regular chores. He felt the game was mainly for the Armstrong crowd.

Other than his brother and sisters, Mat. found his playmates mainly at school. *Like us, they had work to do on the farm when school was out. There was a family connection to the Birds. Dorothy Bird worked for the Pea Growers for years and years. A son of Donald Bird was a friend. The Grintons were related to the Birds. Walter Grinton and Harry Collins were playmates; they're dead now, I guess.*

There was no ice rink at school, but where Hassen Memorial Hall now stands, there used to be the Agricultural Hall. *Behind it was a building with no floor and, of course, at 30 to 35 degrees below zero there was no trouble keeping ice in there. We used to flood that place every winter. There was playoff hockey here in Armstrong until late March or, the odd time, early April. Of course, when a crowd got in there, the ice got rather wet because the air warmed up. Vernon didn't have indoor ice, just an outdoor rink, and they didn't last long in the skating and hockey business. Lumby was the next most prolific supporter because it was colder there. So Enderby, Armstrong and Lumby were the three main hockey towns.*

You had to take part to make things go. We'd have house dances in the wintertime, and it would be 30 below, and even the damn stove was taken out of the room and put on the verandah. Open the bloody windows and have a dance in the empty house and have a good time. The next morning they'd have to put everything back again. It didn't cost anything except for the fifty or seventy-five cents a man would donate for the fiddler, and a woman would take some sandwiches or cake. Of course, there was one bed left in the house and all the coats and babies were on that bed. You'd have to move all the coats to find your baby.

A violin has five strings and a fiddle has four. Billy Glen used to fiddle for lots of dances in the north end of the municipality. He would stand by the edge of an open, double-sashed window, sawing away and chewing tobacco and spitting over the top of the sash – ffffttt. That stuff wouldn't go these days. So many things don't go these days.

Churches were another important source of entertainment. *Lots of people pretty near wore out the sidewalks going to church. They used to traipse off to church morning and night, winter and summer, day after day. (Some never paid their bills either.) It was a different age. That was probably the only entertainment they had in their life – going to church – and they walked.*

Then there was the type of guy who was kind of up-and-coming ('upwardly mobile' might be today's term), and he'd come at top speed in a buggy, or a team and a democrat – making a real splash – checkrein on the horse – its head high. He'd tear up the street and rear to a halt at the church door. The ladies would get out of the buggy or the democrat, and he'd go round to the tie-shed at the back of the church to tether his horse. He'd not necessarily attend the service though – a congregation inside and another one outside.

The cemetery was half a mile up from our place. On Sundays there was a solid stream of people going up Highland Park Road to the cemetery for their Sunday stroll. A funeral procession was quite a sight. A horse-drawn hearse carried the body, the driver sitting up front wearing a black suit and a black top hat, and driving a black team wearing black rosettes. They hired this outfit from the livery stable. It looked pretty smart going up the road.

It was all horse and buggy in those days. A buggy has four wheels and a seat. The early models sometimes had a trunk on the back of the seat, but mainly a buggy had just a front seat. A democrat had four wheels, a longer body, a front seat, and often a back seat. So you could carry more people. A governess might drive a basket arrangement on two wheels so she could take the children out for some fresh air behind a genteel pony. There were so many variations. Some styles had a low fender curving up from the back wheels over the front wheels to make getting into the buggy easier for the posh passengers. Another type had a footman riding on a step at the back. The Royal Coach is the fanciest buggy there is. Watch a Royal Procession and you'll see all kinds of vehicles, all horse-drawn, of course, and anywhere up to eight horses pulling them. Nowadays the wheels have rubber tires, but the wheel is the same. Mainly in my day they had iron tires, but a fancy buggy had rubber tires. But they weren't too useful around here because of the gravel or dirt roads. They would chew the rubber up pretty fast, but in the city rubber was quieter, perhaps smoother too. You see all these buggies today at horse shows; they are manufactured to order.

The inventiveness of the modern automobile industry in producing elaborate vehicles for everyday use, however, has Mat. shaking his head. *It's got out of hand. When I was a kid, Ford and Chev cars were less than $1,000. Mind you, they were a seat and four wheels, and a little knob up in the front to make the wheels go round. Today they are* parlours, *and you pay $30,000 to $40,000. Well, you can't pay that if you grow a few rows of carrots. I can remember when it was a real thrill to get a ride in an old, oak touring car. Oh, boy, a ride in a car! And that was all it was – a ride. Now there's more stuff in the damn car than there is in the house.*

And there's nothing you can do to keep the darn thing running either. You see somebody at the side of the road with the hood up. He can pour water in the radiator if he knows how to take the cap off without getting hurt – nothing else he can do underneath that hood – nothing. Nobody can do it on the side of the road – it has to be taken into a garage and a component part replaced. We used to be able to cut a piece of wire from the fence and fix the car and get it going again.

What do we need the present car for? I watch the morning traffic report on TV and see people in Vancouver going to work. And what are they doing with that car? Finding a place at an exorbitant price to park the bloody thing! So then a worker is in an office in front of a computer and his $45,000 is sitting parked somewhere. And that's another thing about this parking, you know. If you can't stop right in front of a place, you don't want to go in there. You don't want to park around the block and walk back – no!

In the 1920s and '30s, Canada's population was mainly located in rural areas, farming was a viable occupation, and, despite jokes by outsiders about 'country yokels,' young men felt a closeness to the land. Mat. S. Hassen was one of these.

When I was a kid, everyone [from the Coast] considered us second class, backward people because we didn't know which streetcar to take when we were in Vancouver. We didn't know any of those kinds of things and they did. But they didn't know anything else!! But this was a wonderful place to survive, particularly in the Depression; you couldn't get the variety of food anywhere else. So anybody who lived here was actually lucky.

Farming is tremendously interesting because there are so many things to learn, to try, and if you get embarked on something that is more successful than something else, then you want to pursue it to get more production, more perfection. One thing I am quite convinced about – doing away with the walking plough did away with some good farm management. When you're behind a walking plough and a team of horses, you hear, you smell, and you see the soil. When you're eighteen feet up on a diesel-powered tractor, you don't know what the heck is going on down there behind you because you can't hear, see or smell. I used to enjoy walking behind a team of horses because as you go on, the sound is different – each amount of humus content in the soil makes a different sound, a different smell, a different feel. When the plough hits a piece of hardpan, it's like ploughing a highway. When you get that personal contact, you know how to treat each part of the field.

I watch 'Prairie Farm Report' on TV on Sunday, and I'm amazed at the contraptions people have built to handle these huge acreages. One program showed an eighty-seven foot wide seeder that was a combination of a whole lot of grain drills on a hitch with a great big tractor pulling them. The driver was seeding eighty-seven feet wide with each swath. What did he know about what was happening? On the old-fashioned seeder, you were standing on the back of the grain drill, and you watched the seed go into the ground.

The weeds we kill are not necessary. When you walked behind a plough, you'd see weeds in a little spot and know to do something about it. Nowadays fellows treat a whole field the same way, or they have a field of weeds before they realize it or get busy on it. When they are combining, they find there is no grain there!

I know the way the economy is today, you can't make any money farming with a team of horses – volume is dollars – but at the same time how much is a person making for himself? The machine companies and the banks are getting all the money. I remember we used to have early business closing on Thursdays, but I had gone back to town to work in the afternoon. An Indian whom I knew from Head of the Lake was in town for a funeral, and he summed the situation up: "There's no difference between a white man and an Indian. They're both working for the bank."

Even though farmers learned by experience, either their own or someone else's, events occasionally caught some by surprise. Haying and baling could be problematic, particularly because these jobs required a lengthy process and depended on the weather. A sense of humour and some ingenuity in rescuing a bad situation were indispensable.

In those days hay was in demand at the Coast because they had lots of horses there – drays and every other use of horses – and not enough of their own production to satisfy the need all the time. So growing hay here and shipping by train to the Coast was an economic possibility. The hay had to go through two 'sweats,' first in the coil and then a thirty-day sweat in the stack. Those stacks were out in the field. There were three baling outfits around here, and they spent the whole winter going around (like a threshing crew) baling hay out of these stacks. They didn't bale ordinarily when it was subzero – if it was above zero or even if it was freezing, it wouldn't be too bad.

I remember one time Dad was at the Coast, and he phoned home that he wanted two [rail] carloads of hay shipped down to somebody or other. It was around 30 below zero here, you see, but they went and baled Bob Wood's hay and loaded it. As the train went down the [Fraser] Canyon, the temperature became more moderate, and by the time the hay got to the delivery point in Vancouver, the water was pouring out underneath the doors. The condensation was so great that the bales were wet through. So in order to salvage something out of the hay, Dad had to make a deal with Burns Meats because it could be fed to cattle that were up for slaughter.

Some of Mat.'s acquaintances, however, had a more jaundiced attitude than he to the adventure of farming. They drifted off to town. Some became merchants. They would open a store akin to what they knew about.

A butcher, you see, might not be interested in raising animals, but he'd know his meat and could sell it. I'm thinking of George Murray. He and his family lived in Lansdowne but started a butcher shop in Armstrong when the town moved. Fred Murray followed in his father's steps, and Mike, too, a bit. Jimmy Phillips was in the air force in World War One. When the war was over, he started a gro-

cery store. Maybe life in the air force had convinced him he didn't like pitching hay. So he'd be selling five or twenty cents' worth of candy or sugar or flour. He went back to farming, though, when he retired because farming was in his blood. At the last he was raising purebred Herefords.

Mat., however, had no doubt about his love of farming. After high school graduation he was enrolled in Olds College, Olds, Alberta, from 1932 to 1934.

It was a vocational course, not university standard, but students were supposed to have a practical knowledge of farming in order to go there – although some Calgary kids went too. When the Department of Agriculture began the College in 1913, there were naturally a lot of people in Alberta that had never finished school. Some were immigrants. A lot of farm boys on the prairie, especially, had come out from Britain with imported livestock and they didn't have the education to go further. But they had time off from chores in the winter, so they would attend. At that time it was a two-year course, and a third year would give them their junior matriculation. So, if they then entered university, they could enroll in second year agriculture, or if they were entering pharmacy or medicine or some other profession, that third year gave them their university entrance.

The first president of the Food and Agriculture committee of the United Nations was a graduate of the Olds School of Agriculture. It's a wonderful opportunity for people even today – I think they offer fifty-six different courses. My granddaughter took horticulture there. Neil Bosomworth went there too – John Shepherd – Rich McCallum. The valley is full of people that attended the Olds School of Agriculture – they move out here because of the better climate. Actually, Olds graduates are all over the world.

Since population in the Okanagan Valley was sparse, young men were in demand for many labour intensive jobs; such as, threshing grain, and picking fruit and vegetable crops. In the South Okanagan crops reached maturity earlier, and workers could pick up some wages here before they were needed farther north. In addition, since everybody rode or drove a horse, some signed on as cowboys.

Roddy Crozier's father was an Irish policeman that enlisted in the Northwest Mounted Police and settled in Armstrong. In time Roddy became the town's entire board of works. As a young fellow he used to ride down to Spokane and work his way back to Armstrong on round-ups. In his later years Roddy was very round himself and didn't look like a cowboy, but he was more cowboy than all the others put together.

A cowboy would make fifteen to twenty dollars a month. For five days he'd get his food and five dollars. But a saddle cost only fifty to sixty dollars and a horse around twenty. You took what you could get for the animal.

Mat. opted to discover the pleasure and pain of a working ranch. In the break between his first and second year at Olds College, he worked as a farm labourer at the Harper Ranch for $20 a month. By the end of his second year at Olds, he had decided against returning for the third year, as the prospects for a person with a degree in agriculture were not promising.

The best job in BC was the position of supervising district agriculturalist, of which there was only one; he was located at Williams Lake. He supervised a limited number of district agriculturalists; one at Kamloops, another at Chilliwack, for example. The supervisor received $175 a month and the district agriculturalists, $125. The next best job prospect was as a junior in a bank, which paid $35 a month.

Instead Mat. worked a year on the Douglas Lake Ranch, the largest cattle ranch in BC. *I worked at 65 below zero and at 110 above – I guess they're both alike. The cattle were standing out there and had to be fed. We took the hay out on sleighs at 65 below for a week. The temperature broke on a Sunday afternoon and it started* to snow. There was three feet of snow when it stopped. A Chinook blew up, and on Friday afternoon we had to go back to using the wagons.

I lived in a tent by myself in winter. A tent warms up fast. I'd keep a four-gallon can of water boiling on the stove for ablutions before meals mainly, and at five o'clock in the morning there might be a quart of water in it. I'd keep the kindling ready to hand, and when it was really cold, I'd light a fire with one arm stretched out of my sleeping bag. Then I'd go out and look after the horses. Breakfast was at six, of course, in the cookhouse. On that part of the ranch there were ten permanent crew – the Home Ranch had more. In the summertime two other guys from Armstrong came and stayed with me.

Romley, on the other hand, had no interest in ranching, farming, or the family business; instead he had gone into selling bonds and securities for Pemberton's in Vancouver, and advising clients on their financial portfolio. Mat. worked around Armstrong in other farm jobs and, when the Depression eased, began to help his father sell real estate. When the old fellow who had been keeping the books for his father moved to Vancouver, Mat. took over his duties.

The advent of a municipal poll tax, however, sent him along a different road. This tax was an attempt by the local government to ensure that young men in the community made a financial contribution toward the costs of infrastructure. Thus anyone twenty-one years of age and not a landowner (and therefore not subject to property tax) was ordered to pay a poll tax of five dollars a year, the most common local exemption being a serving member of the Militia of Canada. Since five dollars represented a week's wages, Mat. decided in 1937 to join the militia.

It was a turning point for me. I wouldn't have met my wife otherwise. I was a member of 'C' Company in Armstrong, with headquarters in Kamloops. In those days the pay was $1.10 a day for the allowed ten days' annual camp, but the pay went to the Regi-

mental Fund and [these] were the only funds available to the unit except if it had a wealthy patron. That is how Canada prepared for war and produced trained soldiers and sailors. Airmen were more a product of World War Two.

World War Two was, in fact, the third war for some local residents. The earlier wars had been the Boer War in 1899-1902 in South Africa, and World War One.

A combination of things sent people of this area into the services. The people in the valley here were staunchly supportive of World War One and Two, more than of the Boer War, which was kept going by the British influence in the population. The people who were born and raised here were not so much connected to Britain in the Boer War as they were to cavalry [units] because everybody used horses.

The settlers in this area were mainly from Britain – Scotch, English, Irish, Welsh – so especially in the years before World War One they came, got their feet muddied, and all of a sudden joined up and were back over there again. There was a natural attachment to Britain. It was the thing to do to go into the services. Some of them detested the idea because they had got so damn seasick coming over here that they didn't want to face up to going back. Some of them had been six weeks in transit depending on what kind of boat they could get. Many had accompanied livestock that had been bought in Britain and shipped over here to the new country as seed stock. So these fellows were mostly farm boys, as they would be the only ones of any use in looking after the livestock on the boats.

Lack of establishment was another reason these fellows enlisted in the services. Having come over here, they were pitching hay and bundling sheaves on the prairie. They worked for this farmer and that farmer, in this town and the next town – it didn't matter. They didn't have any money accumulated to get married because you <u>had</u> to be established somehow or other, even if it was working in a sawmill and living in a shack in town; otherwise, how were you *going to get married and support your wife?* "What the hell, let's go back home."

There were also Reservists all over North America who had been discharged from the British army. When World War One came on, for example, they were being hauled by trainloads out of the US to New York to ship overseas. However, when German Americans started to protest this obvious favouritism for Britain, the train was pushed across the border into Canada at Windsor, Ontario, and these fellows were stuck there. My batman had been one of them. He had come from San Francisco to Windsor – nothing in his pocket, of course – so, like a lot of the others, he had joined the Canadian army as a means of keeping on going. He had enlisted again in World War Two. *He had been a veteran of service in China in 1910, so he was really too old.*

For some, military service presented an escape from the interminable battle to earn a living. *Poverty was another reason for joining up. They didn't know anything about birth control – that's why the average family seems to be nine. I look at my own history and they are nine… nine… nine. On a homestead farm, these kids were a necessary evil to clear land and harvest crops. And infant mortality was an item in those days. A common cold could carry them off or an injury could kill them.*

In an adult a broken leg or a broken arm could be fatal if he didn't get it attended to. An injured man stuck back in the bush somewhere is going to die – that's all there is to it – if nothing else, he'll starve to death. He doesn't need to get an infection in the broken limb – he just doesn't eat!

Yet life wasn't considered hard because there was nothing better to compare it to. You froze to death in the wintertime, but you did that back in Britain or wherever you came from – no central heating, no home comforts. They had these darn little fireplaces that hold about a pound of coal. You had long johns on in the house and plum duff to eat – suet pudding – because you needed the heat from

39

it. These people weren't comparing distances to today's plane rides to Britain in five hours. A trapper walking from Hudson's Bay to Montreal would take most of a year!!

Sometime during his pre-war training with the Militia of Canada, Mat. was persuaded to go on a blind date with another couple and met Evelyn Rice, a nurse from Vancouver. In June, 1940, he was called up on mobilization and, when a move came, ordered to New Westminster. Evelyn asked him to deliver a box of dishes to her home in Point Grey. Mat. accepted the commission, knocked on the door of the Rice home on October 9th, 1940, and Evelyn's sister, Rose, answered. On November 13th, Rose's employer, a lawyer, conveniently died. Mat. proposed, Rose accepted, and on December 9th they were married. *I got an income tax exemption that year – a big deal in those days.* They were married for sixty years.

Before I went overseas, Rose and I were planning to buy a house in Vancouver. It was a brand new, two storey with full basement and an unfinished second level, hardwood floors, fireplace, many extras, and selling for $3,750. Today it would go for $250,000 - $300,000. I was going to use a car for the down payment, but tire rationing came in, and people were leery about buying a car if they couldn't get tires for it. No hindsight! Just prior to that time in the '30s, all kinds of property were being foreclosed on; people couldn't pay their mortgages. Les Needoba bought a place [in Spallumcheen] from a guy named Howe, who got it from Canada Permanent, which was taking over foreclosed properties and cleaning them up – weeds were growing and fences were falling down. Prices were starting to pick up a little bit when Needoba was in the market, but they were still pretty flat.

When Mat. S. went overseas in 1942, Mat. and Florence Hassen invited Rose, who was pregnant, to stay with them in Armstrong. It was a happy arrangement, but the loss of the little girl in infancy was a cruel blow. In subsequent years Matthew Robert and Patricia Adele completed their family.

Mat. S. came home on leave, and after he went back, Rose bought a house in Armstrong. *If I were still alive after the war was over, I'd write the civil service exams – veterans were guaranteed a job – we'd be moving somewhere, and we'd sell the house.*

In 1944 Mat. S. transferred to the Seaforth Highlanders of Canada, the First Infantry Division, which was in Italy; one of five Canadian divisions in the war, the fourth and fifth being armoured divisions. *I took a draft of 500 men from England to Italy when reinforcements were very scarce, thanks to that draft dodger of World War One, Mackenzie King, the source of most of Canada's troubles since then.*

Consequently, Mat. S. participated in the liberation of Europe. V-E Day was his thirtieth birthday: May 8, 1945. He spent it in Holland, a country that supplied him lasting memories and lifelong friendships.

Arie de Groot was my interpreter – we had three – he had finished high school and wore the Canadian army uniform. I still phone him two or three times a month. He has a letter of reference I wrote for him when Canadians were being reassigned to units closer to their homes. He was applying to enter university that fall and needed proof that he hadn't been a Nazi collaborator. When he showed them my letter, he was accepted. He became city planner for Amsterdam and held this post until he retired. In 1990 he showed me my letter, which was just as pristine as the day I had written it. Two hours ago [July 10, 2003] the phone rang and it was him. I wrote that letter on July 10, 1945, and he had phoned me up to remind me of it.

Another friend is Frits Reurekas, a photographer. He photographed Colonel Bell-Irving coming through the barricades on the Amstel River in May, 1945. So, you know, these were people of consequence.

Some Canadian veterans who had participated in the liberation of Holland returned to that country to take part in national ceremonies commemorating the event. Mat. and Rose went four times.

Rose and I used to take this trip every five years during the 1980s and '90s. Quite a few couples went, and we were all billeted. If you admired something in their home, you'd find it in your luggage, so you had to be careful what you said. You know, the connection between Holland and Canada has never been duplicated in history, and when we went there in 1980 and did a re-enactment of our advance into Amsterdam, there were a million people out on the sidelines watching the procession, which could barely crawl. Lots of old people had been given seats along the road, and we'd stop and get out and say something to them; the tears would be streaming down their faces, and all they could say was, "Thank you, thank you." They had been victims of German domination for two sessions [World War One and Two], and felt real gratitude.

Girls who wouldn't have been born in 1945 held their babies up to be touched as if you were the messiah, and when you touched the baby – salvation. They teach that history in the schools. We went to a church service on Sunday – a big line-up – and a fellow said, "You come along with me." We went in through the back of the church, through the preschoolers' Sunday school, and the story of the Canadian liberation of Holland was on their desks. They were being taught what we had done and why we were at church that day.

The Canada-Holland bond is apparent in the care of the Holten Cemetery on the eastern side of the Ijssel River in Holland.

It's a Canadian cemetery, the one I know best – a beautiful place on a hillside and totally enclosed by trees. It's the only place where members of all five Canadian Divisions are buried. We came up from Italy with the First and the Fifth, and the Second, Third, and Fourth were already here, and they all contributed in the end to this cemetery. A few other nationalities were here, air force guys in particular; if a plane came down, they'd bury them where they landed. There are 1354 graves in all in Holten.

A Finnish woman was visiting Holten Cemetery in 1991 or '92 and noticed a Finnish name on a headstone. They have a custom in Finland of putting a lighted candle at the gravestone of a friend or relative on Christmas Eve. So she thought she'd do that for him, as it was unlikely somebody from Finland would be there on that date. Then she thought it wouldn't be fair to the other 1353, so she sent to Finland for the candles and, with the help of local schoolchildren and some parents, put a lighted candle on every one of those graves. She paid the shot for five years, and then a local organization took it on and still keeps up the custom. It's quite a sight.

With the assistance of Dick Lonsdale, a history teacher from Pleasant Valley Secondary School in Armstrong, his grade 11 class, and members of Canadian Legion Branch #35, Mat. introduced this custom to his hometown. On Christmas Eve they place at the cenotaph in Memorial Park a lighted candle for each of the thirty-nine Armstrong Spallumcheen boys who died in World War Two. *These people were my schoolmates or younger.*

Mat. had persuaded Dick Lonsdale to add Holten Cemetery to his annual school field trip that includes visits to World War sites in Europe in which Canadians participated. He provided Dick with names and introductions to people in Holten and Amsterdam who would be helpful in setting up this aspect of the trip. Thus the friendship of Armstrong students with their counterparts in Holland strengthened the original connection. The Christmas Eve candle-lighting ceremony in the park is one result.

Aside from the extraordinary occasion of war, people in Armstrong Spallumcheen did not travel far. Neither did Mat.'s relatives in Britain.

The tail end of that life was still here when I went to high school. There were kids born and raised around here that had never been to Vernon [fifteen miles]. Everybody didn't own a car in those days, there was no occasion to go, and that was that. With the one exception I mentioned, I don't suppose many of the teachers ever went to Vernon. They were mainly women and lived in boarding houses. They walked.

In 1942 I went to Ireland and visited Dad's mother's place, Elizabeth Ferguson's, where Dad grew up. It was a stone house with a thatched roof and a dirt floor that you wouldn't know was dirt because it was so smooth. The table and chairs were three-legged so they would balance on the uneven floor – four legs won't do it. There was a big fireplace at one end of the room with a large kettle hanging above the fire. A visiting cousin asked the housekeeper what was cooking in the kettle. "Some for the men, some for the calves, and some for the dogs." Everybody was getting the same mush.

When I got back to Armstrong, I was telling Dad all about my visits in the area, and I could tell darn well by his reaction that he'd never been anywhere near these places, and they were within fifteen or twenty miles of his home. Even in World War Two they were still walking and still sweeping the roads – nothing very fast or very far. You limited your exposure to walking distances. Of course, Dad was 'tail end Charlie.' There was no reason for him to go anywhere.

It was the same with Mother's people. They were Londoners and I used to visit them too. It was fifty miles from Brighton where we were stationed to their place. I'd get there about 10 a.m. having had my breakfast, travelled the fifty miles, and got from the train station to southeast London where they lived, and my aunt, married to my mother's brother, would practically throw me into bed – I must be exhausted.

The screwball part of it all was that Mother hadn't heard from her family in a long time, and when the war came on, she didn't know what had happened to them. I thought I'd check the records of bombing deaths and see if they were still alive. I myself had been writing to a cousin, Harry Seymour, the son of Mother's youngest brother, and remembered his address. When I knocked on the door, I was told he had moved, but a passing neighbour took me to the shop where a friend knew where 'Mrs. Seymour' was holidaying in Essex.

I got a bus to the train station, got out at a certain station, took a bus, got out at a certain corner and hiked across a pasture to some cabins. The people were sitting in the sun as I came over the hill. I discovered all these relatives in less than a day, and didn't travel any distance really, but it was something they might do once in a year. But when you walk everywhere, you're not going to go very far.

Mat.'s wartime travels gave him the chance to see the harsher aspects of food rationing, part of the war effort in both Canada and Britain, but probably less severely felt in a rural area; such as, Spallumcheen. Quotas were fixed for each kind of food product, and the bureaucracy was formidable.

An aunt in Londonderry used to visit the Hassen farm at Tullintrain, always carrying her sewing basket. She'd go back home with eggs underneath her sewing. Each egg was supposed to carry a Ministry of Food stamp on it the size of a dime – MF – and if the garbage inspector found eggshells with no stamp on them, there was big trouble. A farmer was allowed for his own use what he could grow on the three-foot perimeter of his property. The rest of his produce was subject to quotas.

Mat. and Rose's visits to Holland always included a trip to Ireland, where he enjoyed the rural peace. He recognized in the landscape a feeling of his own childhood.

The road divided the house from the farm buildings. As far as I know, they are still there – old stone buildings of no use today. You can't get through the doors with a tractor or other farm equipment – too narrow and too low. They were fine if you were just using a fork to farm or packing things on your back. You see all-steel buildings too, fine for hay storage, usually with red-painted steel roofs, nothing picturesque about them, unfortunately.

Even the fanciest houses have a big heap of peat outside. Going there in the fall is the most spectacular because as it gets cool, you smell the peat smoke all over the town. It's lovely.

When the war was over and Mat. S. came home, Rose had sold the house in town, since their prewar plan had been for Mat. to find a government job, which would probably entail a move. Mat. did write the civil service exams for a placement – *if you survived the war, you'd get a job* – and there were some opportunities for veterans to go to university – *I was thirty years old with a family and no income.* Not surprisingly, Mat. chose a third option: to acquire his own farm under the auspices of the Veterans' Land Act.

This Act replaced the Soldier Settlement scheme that had followed World War One. In the earlier case the government acquired blocks of land and settled returning veterans on it. Under the Veterans' Land Act a person could choose, within a certain monetary limit, a piece of property, a small holding or a business, and the Crown would buy the land or holding with a right of purchase to the veteran. He had to stay on the property and make payments for a period of ten years. After that time he could sell it. If he sold before the ten years were up, he had to repay the full price. However, when prices rose, some found they were better off to get shut of the deal and move on to better prospects.

Mat. and Rose selected a ninety-acre farm on Davis Creek east of town. The land that straddled the creek had been owned by the Davis family and ran between the mountain and the railroad. *That was before the celery business dug out the creek from the railroad to the [Shuswap] River, and this piece was called Fortune Creek.*

In addition to farming, Mat. S. became fully involved with his father in all aspects of the family business: selling real estate and insurance, and auctioneering. Perhaps naming their second son 'Matthew' had been an auspicious decision, after all.

Very few people in these parts could get by on only one endeavour. You had to do what you had to do to make a living. That's the way the world was in those days. At certain times – like seeding – I'd come home from the office, get some supper, change my clothes, get on the tractor, get down off the tractor at six in the morning, change my clothes, have my breakfast, and go to work at the office. You had to do that because the dollars didn't come easy. What you could do at night, you did. That's fine and dandy because it's for yourself.

For haying and such I'd hire somebody to help me. You had to find a mature man to do the job – a man forty-five to fifty years old – and you'd pay him $1.25 to $1.50 an hour. Some young guys would ask for more than an experienced man, but that was how things went.

Generally, business was conducted in town six days a week and Saturday night. Some stores in Armstrong opened at 6 a.m.

I remember a fellow dug a ditch for a water line for my dad – an Italian. He used to come to work at seven o'clock in the morning and always brought the same lunch – a loaf of bread, a pound of cheese, and water in a sealer. At twelve o'clock he'd sit on the edge of the ditch, tear the bread and cheese apart with his hands to eat, and take a swallow from the sealer. He bought both bread and cheese on his way through town in the morning because as he quit work at six o'clock, the store would be closed on his way home. The sawmill worked a ten-hour day from 7 a.m. to 6 p.m. with an hour off for lunch. That was the standard. Farming started at 5 a.m. or earlier and didn't quit until 8 or 9 at night. So the sawmill was easy – you only worked ten hours!

For the ten years until his father's death in 1956, Mat. S. was also directly involved with him in managing the Interior Provincial Exhibition (IPE), the local agricultural fair that had grown and thrived. In 1956 he became the fair's manager and, with Rose's support as office clerk, held the post until 1972 – a Hassen family contribution that had begun in 1913 and lasted for fifty-nine years.

When their insurance and real estate business could sustain them, Mat. and Rose sold the farm and moved into town on Sage Avenue.

The first piece of land I sold was forty acres for 500 bucks. And that was only because I sold it to a guy from the prairies who had been hauling his water for eight miles! The place I was selling had a hydraulic ram in the Steele Springs pushing water up to the house, and he couldn't believe that water could be obtained in that way. So he was happy to buy it. The original owner had gone to England and died over there, and the place had been vacant for two or three years. It was also very dry out Hullcar way in the '30s so there was nothing to attract anyone to the property except that one guy who was starving for water. He then sold it to a fellow who went into the chicken business.

Land is probably $3,000 – $4,000 an acre now. In my early time in the real estate business, $100 an acre was the maximum and would include buildings too. The formula was 40 acres for $4,000 and a house and barn for the price. I forget what I sold your place for – a German couple – I think his name was Weber. She was a good cook and did some catering. I remember being up there and the wind damn near blew us off the front steps, and not a breath of air down in town. W.F. Brett first owned that farm along with another one on Highland Park Road and a place in town. He was in the Home Guard in the First World War and stayed on around here. The Weber farm became the Thompson dairy farm, then the Arkinstall Morgan horse farm, and in 1976 the Campbell beef and alfalfa, then grain and tree farm.

The people of Spallumcheen came here with one thing and ended up with something else. That's what life around here was like for me. I never was in one thing forever. I've done every damn thing. Life has been wonderful in this area. There are so many opportunities and have been all over the years. You didn't do much that you didn't like to do. I took part in the things that I enjoyed – the things I didn't like I stayed away from. It was a really good community – a good class of people – down-to-earth people – you might say 'farmer type' – they weren't 'city type' – they weren't hollow. And that makes an awful difference. So many people, it seems to me, are looking for accolades, but they don't really want to put in much effort.

In the course of his work, Mat. had occasion to fly CP Air between Williams Lake and Kelowna. He was fascinated by the geological formations that he saw out the plane window – in particular, the results of glaciation.

You see these potholes all around the country, and you see in them these concentric circles of different kinds of growth. In a pothole pine will be in the highest, driest part; below that will be spruce; then willow and birch. And hay land, meadowland, will be right in the bottom of the pothole. The oldest ones still have a pond in the middle. All this growth will be in concentric circles. Thousands and thousands of people will fly over this area and never notice it. But it hits you like a bat in the head.

The Rocky Mountains, you see, were pushed up by another continent to the west. Its western boundary was about the eastern side of the Rockies. Coal deposits there, like down in Fernie, were marshlands that were buried – the same in the States. We have no idea what the shape of that smaller continent was that pushed up against this one, but it accounts for the striated levels of mountain rock that are on the edge of the part that was pushed up, formed in the ocean bottom, tipped up on edge. I often think about that – was there any **sound***?*

Take the trees. There wasn't one planted by man. At one time or another this was all grey rocks – desert-like sort of stuff. And then it all got planted without our help. I often wonder what it looked like – all grey. I've been to the bottom of glaciers. You can take this ground-up kind of sand in your hands, and it doesn't leave any, what you might call, 'dirt' in your hand. You can rub it in your hands and nothing shows – it's pure, ground rock. And the next thing a bit of moss grows on it, and more, and more, then brush, and the first tree is a spruce. Where did the seed come from?

Mat.'s curiosity, fertile imagination, and attention to his environment are readily noticeable. When he was a boy, these qualities dispatched him on a hunt for Bill Miner's treasure, and he still feels the excitement of that dig. Bill Miner was a stagecoach and train robber who lived for a time in the area under an assumed name and had a history of prison and escape.

The story was that Bill Miner had a cabin down in Sleepy Hollow in the gully where Deep Creek crossed the road. Kids can imagine anything. Anything looks to them like the remnants of what they are looking for. I remember there was a hole there and a couple of pieces of log, and we figured it must be the remains of Bill Miner's shack. At eight or nine years old you don't ask too many questions.

We started digging alongside the creek at this place; first grass, then sod, and down about three inches we struck steel!! OOOOhhh, boy! Palpitations!! We dug some more – still *steel –* <u>still</u> *steel –* **still steel.** *We started clearing off some of the sod – heart beats banging. Bill Miner's cache in a steel vault!!!!*

We got to the edge of the thing and it was a broken circular saw blade. There was once a sawmill down there, and the blade must have bound in a log, and the log shifted and broke it. It can't be fixed, so they just discarded the blade there – buried it with a little sawdust on top – and in time grass grew over it. The darn thing is probably still there. But, boy, was it thrilling!

Nowadays Mat. says his eyesight is so weak that he can't see three feet in front of him, but he can see a bird in a tree a mile away.

I was standing at the sink looking out yesterday, and it seemed to me all the shrubbery was sticking up outside the window, and I looked again and it was a buck deer eating right against the house – his horns were sticking up when he raised his head. I watched him, and a car came by and he paid no attention. Then he wandered over the lawn and walked across the street. They have bird feeders over there, and he ate the stuff the birds had thrown overboard. Then he walked back again – a whitetail. We didn't used to have whitetails, just mules, but lately the whitetails are coming. They don't run to-

gether though. One time I had four or five whitetails out here and two mules down over there.

A whitetail has quite a white rump on the very back, and the tail is about ten inches long with a black tassel on the end; a mule deer has an erect tail. Nobody bothers them in town here and they love vegetables and roses. There are 125 rosebushes on this property and last summer I picked three. There's one rosebush right by the door. I go outside and one's standing there eating the roses. I talk to her – she looks at me – and grabs another rose – never runs away. But, you know, they have to be somewhere, and we have moved into their 'somewhere.' And there's no malice in them at all. Some guys were doing some work here a couple of years ago – they came to work at nine o'clock and there were five deer on the lawn. They stood for fifteen minutes watching them. They were flabbergasted that there'd be deer in town.

When Mat. reached middle age, he decided to attempt something different. *When I was fifty years old, I thought I probably couldn't learn anything new. So I said to myself, "I'll see if I can," and I went to Kelowna for flying lessons. And I could learn! Then I bought a little plane, a Cessna 172. The airport was out at the Spallumcheen Industrial Park – we developed that area as an airstrip before the municipality got too fussy. At first, though, I used to keep it at Kelowna (again, that's fifty miles). We had five or six planes in Spallumcheen when we got it going.*

The Cessna had four seats. I'd take Rose and fly to Castlegar – four and a half hours by car – we'd have an hour for lunch, fly back, and go out for dinner that night. We flew to Quesnel. One time we were socked in at Smithers for two or three days. On the question of his flying expertise: *We always went up and we always came down.*

I had it for ten years. I sold it for fourteen or fifteen thousand. Piper and Cessna don't make that size anymore so I wish I'd kept it. There were a lot of these small planes on the farms in the prairies

– they could fly anywhere and land anywhere. Here, mountain flying is quite a bit different.

A J3 Cub, for instance, would take off around 25 mph and land about 25 mph. Three guys I knew over in Lumby had J3s and they used to fly over Greenbush Lake, Thor, and Woden mountaintops this side of Revelstoke. The snowpack would be on there all summer long, and it was attractive, it looked a good place to land. A guy would decide to take a trip up there – well, he'd have to fly with a second plane – and he'd take some rocks about as big as a squash and fly over the glacier and throw a rock out. If it sank, he wouldn't land, but if it bounced off, then the snow was hard enough to land on. The other guy meanwhile was still up in the air, so that if his partner came a cropper somehow or other – landed on a hard spot but then rolled into a soft spot – then someone would know he was down there. These J3s were great for that kind of flying. The Procter boys in Lumby had them too.

Mat. is a cook and enjoys discussing and preparing food. He has a red clay garlic roaster that bakes four garlic bulbs to tender perfection in an hour at 350 degrees. He spreads it over a meat paste on crackers and drops a bit of colour on top. Baked acorn squash are delicious – the orange flesh thick and firm. His recipe for a turnip dish is a surefire delight. Vegetables, fruit, meat are long-time acquaintances. In his case the old saw holds true: "You can take the boy away from the farm, but you can't take the farm away from the boy."

About fifteen or twenty years ago, Rose and a friend got some chickens from somebody or other because they got the idea they were going to can them. Well, the damn things were Leghorns!! Two year old Leghorns!! Dangerous to take apart, damn sharp bones – they were awful!! It was a big disappointment. Mat. would have to continue to dream about summer days and jellied chicken or do the thing right himself. So this spring he did, and he lined a basement shelf with sealers of chicken as he remembered it.

Another interest is politics. Mat. is reading a Christmas gift: <u>Bastards and Boneheads</u> by Will Ferguson, a denunciation of Canadian prime ministers who may fall into either category. He is fuming.

Mackenzie King was the worst politician Canada ever had. He did a terrible injustice to the Japanese. McPhail and Smith hardware was at the corner of Okanagan and Railway Avenue. Smith was in the Seaforth Highlanders in World War One, and he knew Ian Mackenzie from the war: a no-account Scot who came back to Canada and mentored Mackenzie King. He was feeding King with incorrect information about the Japanese.

Some of the Japanese were Rose's personal friends; two of them had the Order of Canada. George Hirayama and Tommy Ogata were real good local farmers. They weren't incarcerated because they were outside the 100-mile limit [around Vancouver]. Ogata had a family. Sakakibara brothers at Vernon Toyota are his grandsons.

Mat. also takes a lively interest in aging. He has watched people grow old around him and has definite opinions about what happens to them and to their caregivers.

You know, I think it's wonderful if somebody gets in their nineties and they have all their faculties and take part in things, but if they get to be that age and they don't know what's going on, and two or three people have to be around to keep them breathing, that's different. People are dead above ground and dead below ground. That's stupid.

In the old days people kept their parents and grandparents in the back bedroom, raised their kids, said nothing about it and just kept on going – no life for the old people and no life for them either. Mind you, it wasn't heart attacks or anything like that – it was just dementia. They could go on like that for ten or fifteen years.

A good army buddy of mine has a bad heart and now he's down in a hospital in North Vancouver. First he worried about people forgetting him. Now his brain is going too, and his family and friends have to be continually visiting him. The only time he shows signs of understanding is if two of his army buddies talk about the same thing in front of him. You can't write to him because he can't get anything out of the letters. That's not living. Giving him pills or something keeps him going. If he didn't have them, he'd be long gone. Then they could have a real good visit over the funeral, and everything would be fine. And he'd be better off too.

You know, people were only engineered to live to half our bloody age. You go to England and visit some of those old churches that go back three, four, five hundred years, and you see that most of them died around forty. If they are 'right' upstairs and physically taking part in things, then good! But on pills? Not for me!

Instead Mat. is sticking to a good supply of healthy food from the area, fresh fruit and vegetables nicely cooked, and a good dose of 'the news' and non-fiction to keep him up to date. He can read for only a short while each day, but his forte is conversation, anyway. And he now has the time to indulge his sense of wonder at the beauty and mystery of the natural world.

When asked to record his memories of growing up in Spallumcheen, he chuckles.

Let's tell a bunch of lies, he says.

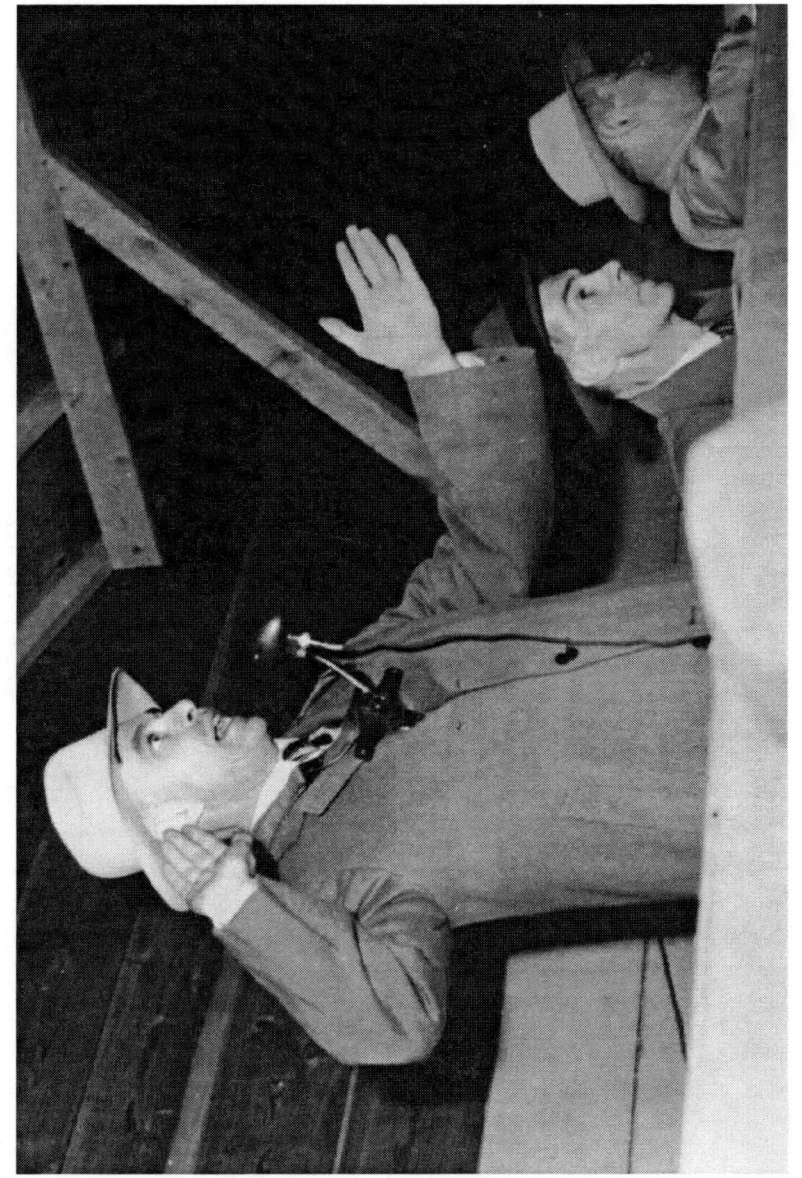

Mat. S. Hassen auctioneering at the Kamloops Bull Sale in the 1940s

Chapter Two

Musing with Ralph

Ralph Duncan Lockhart

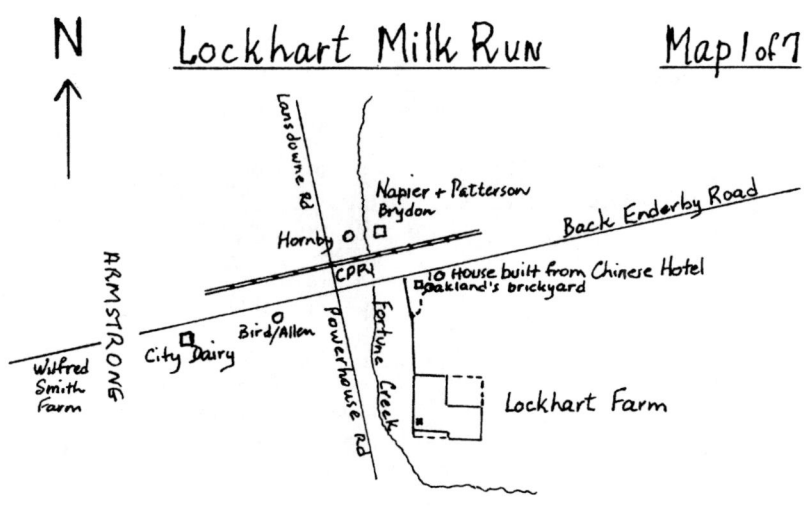
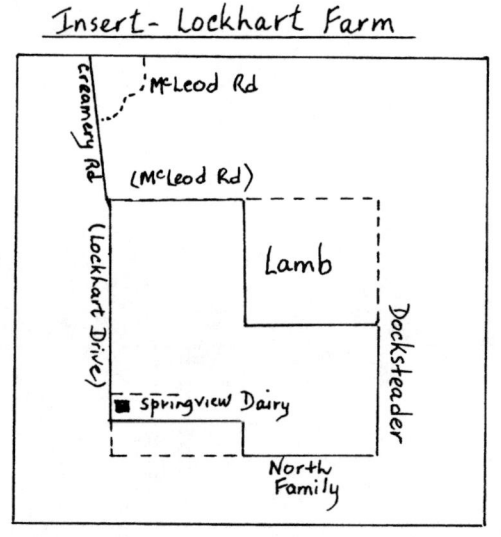

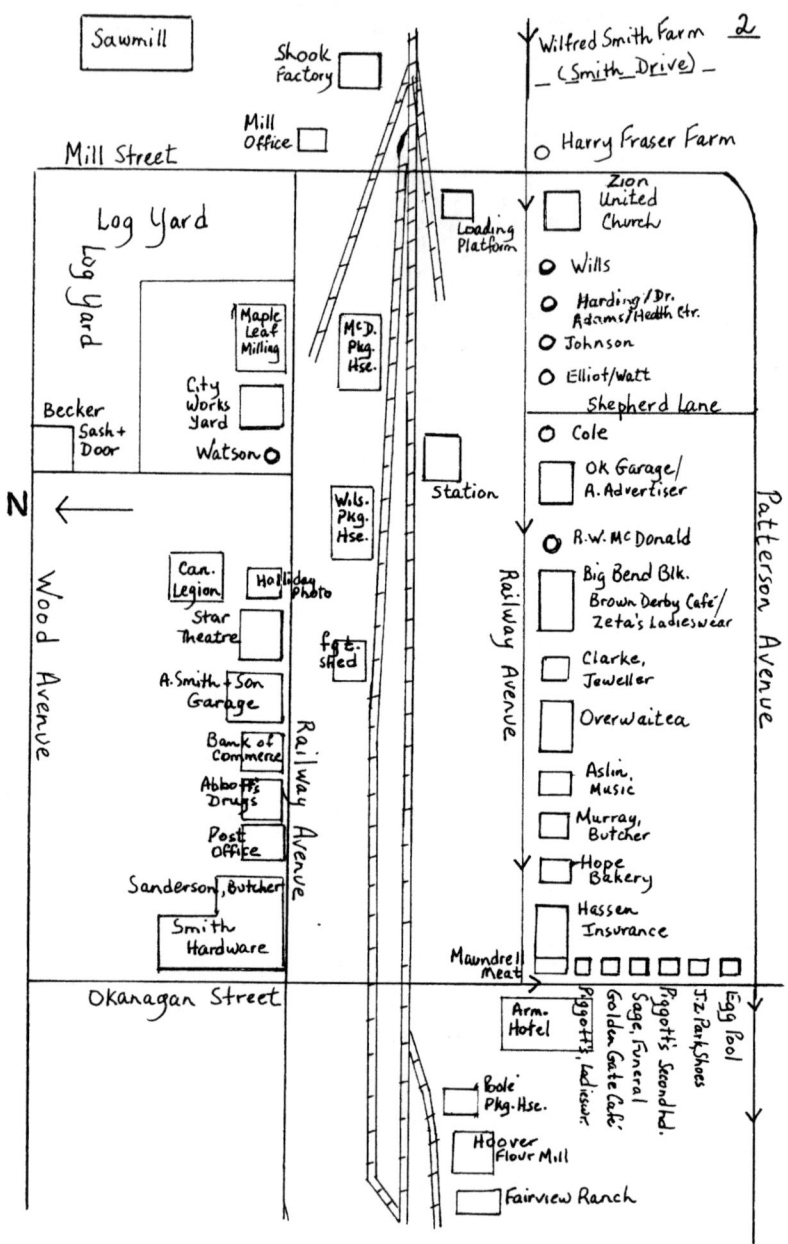

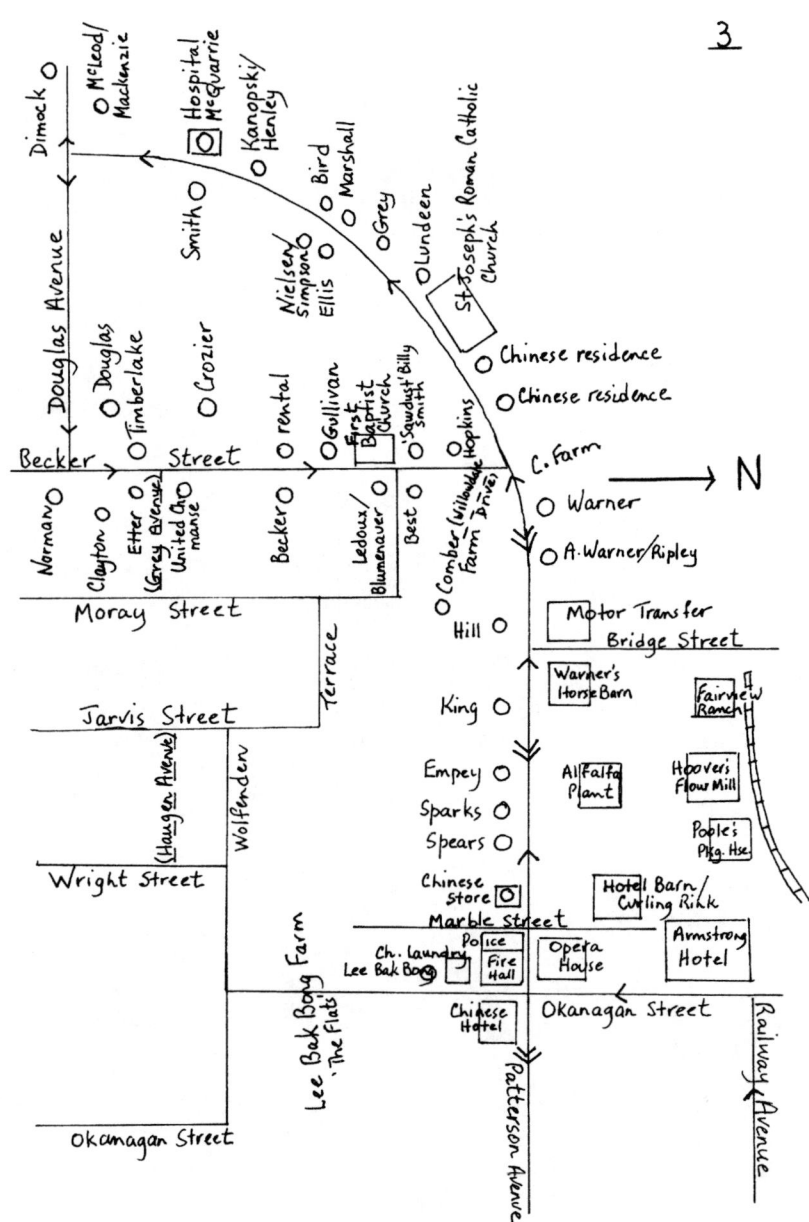

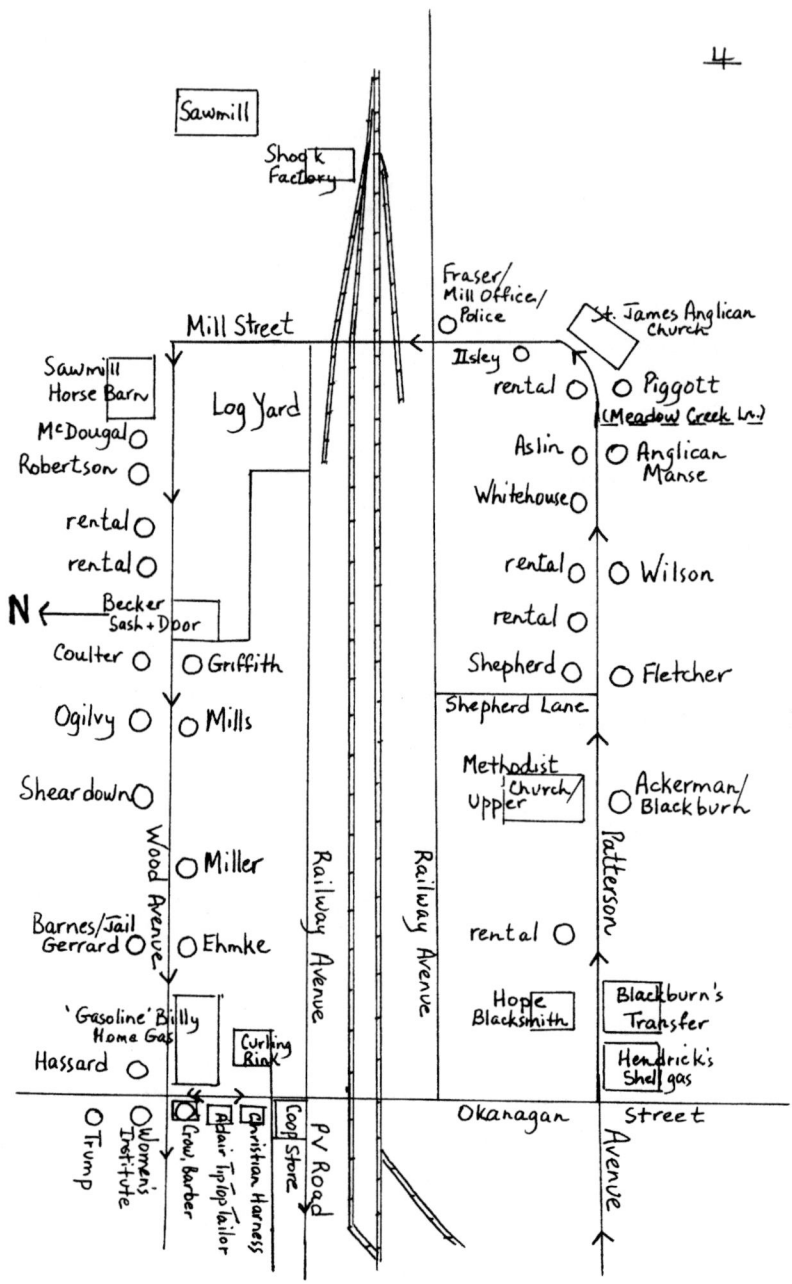

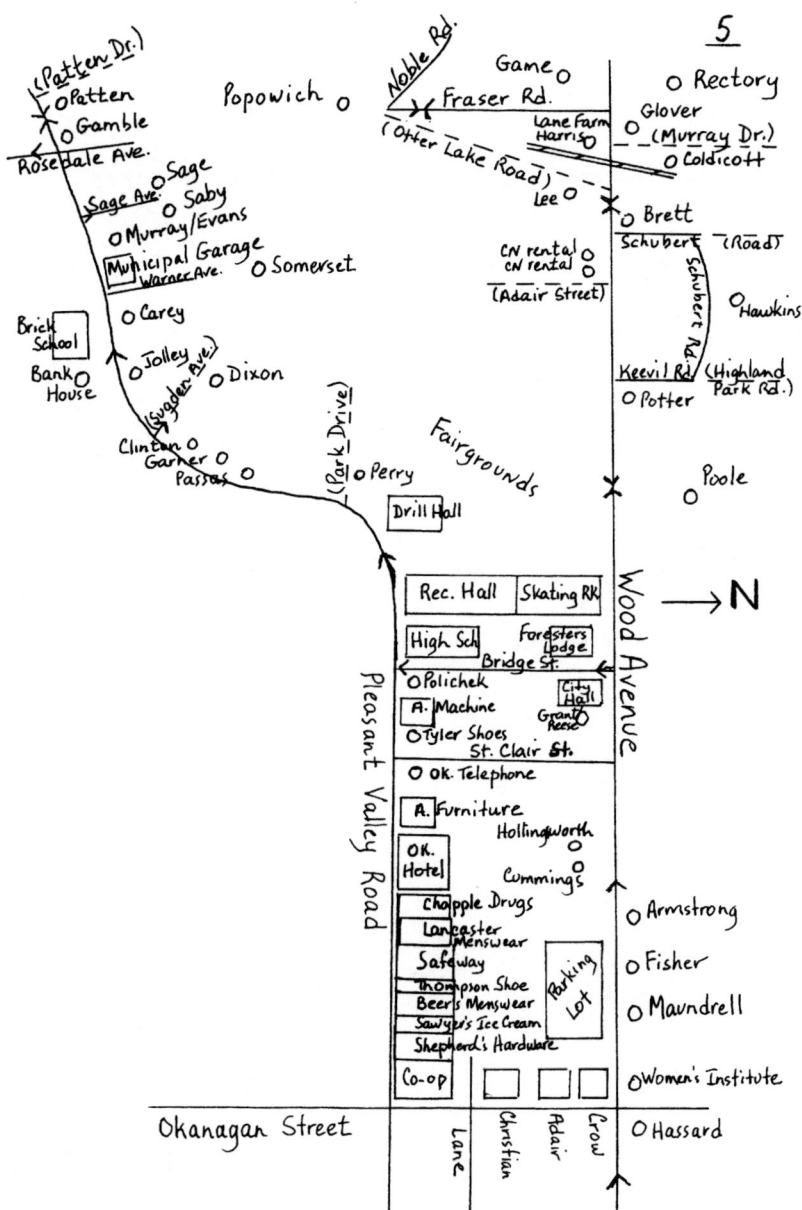

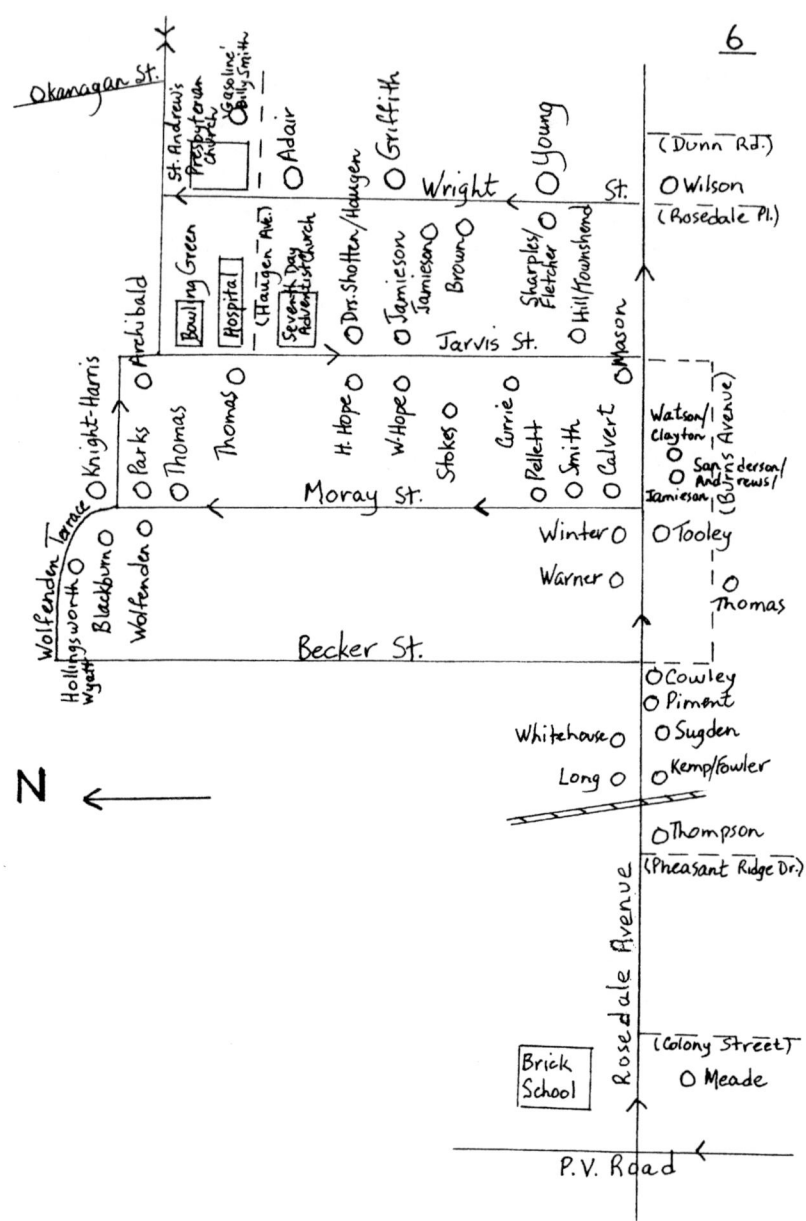

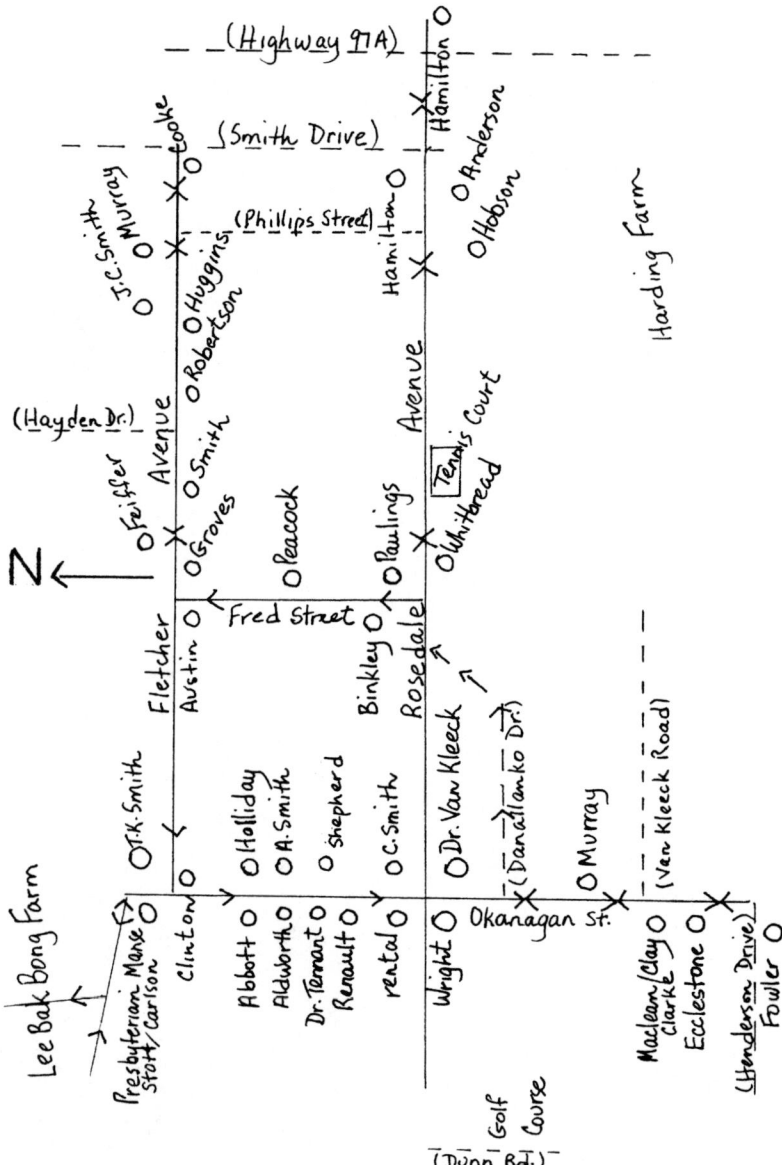

[The year is 1930. In this chapter seven hand-drawn sketch maps locate the homes and businesses on the Lockhart family milk run. The name of each family or business is found on the maps; the current house number is provided in the text. The letter *c.* preceding the number indicates an approximate location. Some of the buildings date from the period; others are newer but built on the same sites. Only in some cases is this distinction made. Present-day streets constructed at a later date are shown by dotted lines, the name bracketed. These maps are *interpretive* only, not drawn to scale, to allow room for names.]

The family was just ready to sit down to dinner when they turned up – their daughter Anne's two children from Manitoba. *They had flown to Kelowna and then rented a car. That was the biggest surprise – I had expected all the rest.* Twenty-five people in all – five of his six children – *Anne won't fly* – and his grandchildren had come to help him and Jean celebrate his 80th birthday, January 25, 2003.

By that date Ralph had become an Armstrong archivist specializing in the City's first half century – where people lived and located businesses, and which streets existed or slept under farmland. He gathered his information while driving a team of horses and delivering over three hundred quarts of milk – cream was extra – *every day, seven days a week. I used to know everybody.*

Ralph Duncan Lockhart was born at 3025 Jarvis Street in Armstrong *where the artist Frances Hatfield lives now. Spark Thomas lived there. He was the original manager of the Bank of Montreal. The Thomases lived in the Bank House – the Salter house – until the*

67

bank closed, then moved over to Jarvis. Spark used to keep bulldogs and goats. When I was a little kid, I went around the corner, and this bulldog came at me and scared the bejesus out of me. Spark came running: "He won't hurt you any." But I hadn't seen that dog before. I was delivering milk, you see. I started delivering milk when I was five years old.

Mrs. Thomas acted as a midwife, I don't know how many women she took nor the exact reason I was born there. Whether Mother went there so she'd be in town, or I just came along during a visit, I don't know. My parents were living on Creamery Road. The creamery sat on the eastern edge of that little park on Highway 97A, and Creamery Road went straight up the hill from there. McLeod Road didn't exist. Creamery Road is barricaded now at the top of the hill so you can't access the highway. The creamery burned down in 1927. McLeod subdivision is the location of our old farm.

It is a beautiful farm. Above the highway on a bench two miles east of town, one rich, flat field remains. The rest lies beneath a portion of the winding, treed roads that for easy reference local residents name 'McLeod subdivision.' [See Map 1.]

The corner of what is presently McLeod Road and Lockhart Drive was the beginning of our property. This field grew the feed for sixty head of cattle. Of course, we had irrigation and it was well farmed. In the field where those trees are, there's a spring that gave us the irrigation water. The spring just ran – a lot of water in it. We used ditch irrigation for the corn – we didn't have sprinklers at that time. We opened up the ditches every so far, and the water ran out and flood-irrigated.

The house, the barn and the dairy stood on what is now the corner of Lockhart Drive and Springview Place. Our dairy was called Springview Dairy. Some of the houses up here are built on what we used for pasture – it's gravel. Anybody that wanted to put in a lawn had to bring in topsoil. I guess if they had to build houses *somewhere, this was the ideal spot because it didn't grow anything – just grass.*

Down to the east of Lockhart Drive was all bush where we used to cut wood for the house – lots of good fuel – it kept us going. Lockhart Crescent is the southern boundary of the farm. At the time the North family property joined ours on the south, and Docksteader on the east. Now, it seems strange to me that they've got a Sidney Road and a Meggait Road here and those families never lived in this area, but the Docksteader name is not on anything. It's quite a settlement. They've kept the trees. They haven't grown very rapidly because there's not enough moisture up here. We haven't driven around this place for quite a while.

In addition to water from the spring, the Lockharts had water rights on Fortune Creek. *Fortune Creek, or Davis Creek, runs down from Aberdeen Mountain and along just west of the farm. We didn't use the creek very often, but our irrigation rights on that creek were eleven years older than Armstrong's water rights. Whoever owned our property at that time took out the rights and Spallumcheen Municipality didn't, since the City didn't incorporate until 1913.*

After the 1925 fire in the Fortune Creek drainage basin burnt off all the trees on Memorial Mountain, we called it Baldy! In the spring the snowpack would come down in about three or four days because there was nothing to hold it, and I tell you that creek used to run. It used to roll the rocks down off the mountain. You could hear those rocks banging – big rocks just rumbling. Even in the '40s it took out acres of land at the bottom. Everybody would be watching to see if they were going to lose the farm!

In 1933 during spring floods our hired man was coming back from town. Whoops! Got to stop! The bridge across the creek was gone. So they planked the railway bridge between Brydon's and Hornby's, and when you used it you had to watch there were no trains coming down the track. There would have been no contest. *In the summer the creek was dry from the bridge all the way up to the dam. Now it hardly runs at all.*

The farm and its accompanying milk business were a successful venture until 1945. However, Ralph's parents, Ross Gerald Lockhart and Ruth Eva Parmenter, had twice attempted other types of farming in the early years of their marriage.

Mother and Dad actually met in Summerland. Her folks came up there, and Dad was a foreman on the highway between Penticton and Summerland. As a child Mother had rheumatic fever that left her with a damaged heart. She and her mother went to Rochester, Minnesota, to the Mayo Clinic and Dad went with them. And Mother and Dad were married there. Then they came back and he tried fruit farming in Summerland for a year – a cherry orchard – and he got half a cent a pound for his cherries, and he didn't think that was good. Since Mother's parents had moved up to the Landon place on Schubert Road in Spallumcheen, they followed.

Dad rented a farm called Child's place on the highway on the way to Enderby – Pete Woronchak is now on it. The bottomland was very fertile – a swamp – and he talked about growing potatoes. Stepney rail siding was there and he could load them on boxcars. It was during the First World War, so he had Indians picking the potatoes and getting paid by the sack.

In addition to organizing his labour force, Ross had to sew up by hand the filled sacks of potatoes in preparation for shipping. *Dad used to tell this story on himself: "The sacks started getting smaller – less in them. So I said, 'You have to fill those sacks.' I came up to this one bran sack and it was full. They'd filled it all right – you can get 200 pounds of potatoes in a bran sack. I had a heck of a time sewing it, but I couldn't take a potato out of it. They watched to make sure I didn't. That was the only one they filled that way. They'd made their point."*

Selling potatoes was better than selling cherries but still not a paying proposition. Ross bought the farm that kept his growing family secure during the shaky twenties, the dirty thirties, and World War Two.

In 1920 Dad moved over to the farm along Creamery Road. There's a map at the Armstrong Museum dated 1922, and Dad's name is on the property. I really don't know who sold Dad the farm. It was a quarter section at one time – pre-empted in 1889 – and it was later owned by a man by the name of Fuenfgeld. You know Shirley Field? Fuenfgeld was her name before it was changed to Field. Shirley Field was the daughter of Lou Fuenfgeld and Dolly Connaty, who lived in Grandview Flats. In 1946 Lou changed the family name to Field. Shirley Field became a noted country and western singer and yodeller.

Our farm was 110 acres out of the original 160. It should have been bigger – a fellow who owned it had a man working for him and couldn't pay his wages, so he gave him ten acres off the back, and that's where Barry Seed is now. I don't know how come the Lambs got the forty acres off the front in two parcels, but that was very good bottomland – springs all over it.

And then Dad bought a milk business. People at the bottom of the hill on Creamery Road – Napier and Patterson – had a retail delivery in town that they wanted to sell. So for twenty-five years we delivered milk around town. We produced it from a herd of Jerseys – straight Jersey milk – the cream would be halfway down the bottle. At the last we were selling milk for nine quarts for the dollar. It had gone up in price because I could remember when it was a nickel a quart. Later it was sixteen quarts for the dollar, then twelve, and finally nine.

We had hand milking up until 1939 when we got the power on the farm. We were milking about thirty head. Occasionally we ran short of milk and had to buy from the neighbours to have enough to deliver to the customers. Quart bottles, pint bottles, half-pints and quarter-pints. Half-pints and quarter-pints were mostly cream. We had regular customers that would take one quarter-pint of cream every day. In those days they had it for breakfast.

Some people paid cash. Others would buy one or two dollars' worth of tickets. They'd stick the ticket in the empty milk bottle. If they didn't have a ticket and were regular customers, then they got a monthly bill. Dad did the paperwork. You'd have a name down and the number of quarts. Stick the bill under the bottle of milk and save on a stamp. Postage was only a penny, but even so. Next morning they'd come out and give you the money.

We would hit town anywhere from half past five to six o'clock in the morning. Everyone had their delivery before eight, and by eight when the stores opened we'd be downtown doing the commercial deliveries. Mrs. Mitchell had the café on Okanagan Street and she took a lot of milk and cream. I think in 1932 Con Passas bought the café from her and named it the Golden Gate Café. [They said] he made coffee fresh in two big urns on Monday mornings, and that coffee went to the next Monday morning. A little more water and a little more coffee! But Monday morning the coffee was good. Then we'd go 'round the corner to Murray's butcher shop. We dropped a lot of milk there in quarts and pints because fifteen or twenty trains a day stopped in Armstrong, and the trainmen bought milk at Murray's. We were always there before the CN passenger train came in at twenty after eight, as the conductors needed milk to go with their breakfast.

Despite this casual summary, the Lockhart milk run from their farm two miles east of town, as far west as Fraser Road off Wood Avenue, and then along the residential streets south of the commercial centre was a feat of timing, particularly as the mode of transportation for the times was a horse.

The team knew the route. If you delivered some milk and someone came out to talk to you, the team gave you so long and they were gone to the next stop!

In summer the deliveries were made in a democrat. A democrat was a heavy-duty buggy with wider (one and a half inch) wheels to carry more weight. Ross Lockhart had removed the seats to allow room for the crates of milk, and he and Ralph perched on a crate.

We started out around five-thirty in the morning and away we went. [See Map 1.] The team was fresh and they trotted right along. No road here, of course – just went out of our yard on a farm track. There's quite a drop over the bank there, and you look down on the farm below. Charlie Williamson lived there, followed by the Rahns. Carl Rahn delivered mail for years.

Creamery Road was just a gravelled wagon road. Creamery hill down to the highway was steeper than it is now. You'd have to hold the horses back going down and then give them the gears coming back. Lew Brydon lived at the bottom across the highway. Of course, it was Napier and Patterson when Dad bought the milk business from them.

The Lockhart team turned southwest on the highway. Present-day traffic from McLeod subdivision exits by McLeod Road northeast of Creamery Road. *The material used in the house on the northeast corner of McLeod and Highway 97A came out of the Chinese Hotel in town when it was torn down. It was a big, three-storey house on Patterson Avenue where the Credit Union is now. We always called it the Chinese Hotel because the Chinese were the only people that occupied it – just single men. For quite a number of years, there was a large Chinese population in Armstrong – over 400 at one time. They came originally to build the railway.*

On our left between McLeod and Creamery Road was Oakland's brickyard [Armstrong Brick Works]. A few houses around town were built of that brick, though the yard didn't produce many. They just had a little spot where they dug out the clay. Many years ago when Jean was working with ceramics, we made dishes from that clay and baked them, and they came out red.

The team passed the plantation southwest of Powerhouse Road. A family by the name of Bird lived here in the small, blue house beside the plantation. That house is over 100 years old. A family by the name of Allen also lived there. Some ten or fifteen years ago, the house was raised and a basement put under it.

City Dairy occupied the buildings on the south side of the highway a short distance from the present turn-off into town. You can still see their old barn back in from the road east of the former John Deere property. They were our competitor. The turn-off at that time was the highway, which went right through town and out Pleasant Valley Road. The bypass wasn't put in until the 1960s. A farm owned by Wilfred Smith sat where the power station is now. He had several cows. Consequently, Smith was not a customer.

The Canadian National/CanadianPacific rail line which runs through the present boulevard divided the highway into two parallel streets, both of which were locally designated Railway Avenue and allowed two-way traffic. [See Map 2.] Three spur lines on the east end of town and a fourth on the west end, sections of them still present, diverged from the main line to accommodate businesses on Railway Avenue and Pleasant Valley Road. On the south spur in front of the United Church sat a loading platform, which was mainly used by the sawmill. Farther west along the rail line was the train station, and on the second spur line, the freight shed. *In the '70s when the train station was no longer in use, it was vandalized by fire and then torn down, but Ron Brown bought the freight shed and moved it to Patterson Avenue to house his plumbing supplies.* East of the freight shed this spur line also gave easy access to two major packing houses, McDonald's and Wilson's. *The third spur line at this end of town was built for the sole use of Maple Leaf Milling,* located on the north side of Railway Avenue. Beyond the intersection with Okanagan Street, the fourth spur line moved south of the rail line to accommodate Poole's packing house, Hoover's Inland Flour mill and Fairview Ranch. *Fairview Ranch was a business for the dehydration of fruit and vegetables during the First World War.* The north side of Railway Avenue became Pleasant Valley Road, which continued as the single route out of Armstrong.

On both sides of Railway Avenue from Mill Street to Okanagan Street, houses and businesses were closely adjacent. The Lockhart milk run entered Armstrong along the south side of Railway Avenue.

A farm on the east side of Mill Street and extending behind the Anglican Church was owned by Harry Fraser. The police station is just about where Harry's house sat. We used to go straight in past the United Church.

In the first house [2345] we delivered milk were some people by the name of Wills. The next house [2365] belonged first to the Hardings, then to Dr. Adams, and when the house burned down, the old Health Centre was built on the site. Arvid Johnson lived in the new little yellow one [2115]. Where the cement block is presently sat a big house: George Elliot lived in it for some time, followed by Sam Watt. The space occupied by Cherry Lane Antiques/Sears was snugly filled: *A man by the name of Cole, a shoemaker, lived in a house on the corner of Shepherd Lane; next door the Armstrong Advertiser occupied a part of the premises of Okanagan Garage and Union Gas; and R.W. McDonald, who owned the packing house, lived just about where their parking lot is now.*

When Con Passas married Edna Docksteader, they moved their house back from the street and built in 1938 what Con called the Big Bend Block in front of it – you can barely make out the inscription. (At that time the highway followed the big bend in the Columbia River. It went away up north through Mica and then back again. Cutting out the big bend cut a day's travel time to Alberta.) Passas had his second coffee shop, The Brown Derby, in the Big Bend Block. When he closed the coffee shop, the space was taken over by Zeta's ladieswear. J.R. Clarke, jeweller, was beside him. Overwaitea was next door. The last four businesses on this side of the street were Wilmer Aslin's music shop (which later became a barbershop

– just room for a barber's chair and a mirror on the wall), Murray's butcher shop (which became Shepherd's hardware and is presently the real estate office), Hope bakery, (originally a house from the turn of the last century, since renovated and extended flush to the street), and Hassen insurance.

The north side of Railway Avenue was a busy mix of commercial enterprises that were not Lockhart customers.

The entire complex occupied by Shepherd's Home Hardware was the log yard for the sawmill. Where the Fitness Matters parking lot is now, Maple Leaf Milling sat. The City works yard occupied the site of the Pea Pod restaurant. A man called Watson lived in a little house on the east side of the alley; the west side was a vacant lot. Then came Holliday, the photographer. The Legion was set back from the street directly behind Holliday at the end of a short trail, and the Star movie theatre was beside him. The theatre was built before 1925. A. Smith and Son garage sat where CIBC [Canadian Imperial Bank of Commerce] and the parking lot are now, and CIBC was beside the garage in the old Bank of Montreal building. Abbott's Rexall drugs was next door. The last three buildings on the street were the post office, Sanderson's butcher shop, and Smith's hardware, where Margarieta's restaurant is located.

As the team turned south on Okanagan Street, they faced the east side of the Armstrong Hotel, which fronted on the main rail line and Pleasant Valley Road. The fourth spur line hemmed the hotel parking lot and served the manufacturing and commercial operations at this end of town. Given the large number of trains clanging daily in and out of town, hotel guests may have needed earplugs.

At the southeast corner of Pleasant Valley Boulevard and Okanagan Street, Maundrell's meat market occupied part of the site of the Hassen building [Valley First Insurance], followed by Piggott's ladieswear, which was managed by Mrs. Piggott, the Golden Gate Café, Sage's funeral parlour, Piggott's secondhand store, which he ran himself, J.Z. Park shoe store, and the Armstrong egg pool. Customers in this block received their milk at the conclusion of the milk run.

Large sections of the present residential area south of Pleasant Valley Road were either vacant lots or farmland, and many houses were rentals, as Armstrong had a significant transient population attracted by seasonal work on the farms or in the mills. To begin the bulk of the milk deliveries, the Lockhart milk wagon turned west on Patterson Avenue. [See Map 3.]

On the northwest corner of Patterson [Nelson's Glass] sat the Opera House, which burned down in 1925. Set back at the end of a lane beside it was a barn for stabling the horses of the Armstrong Hotel guests. When the barn was torn down, the curling rink, the second one, was built there in 1940. The name of the lane was Marble Street. It crossed Patterson Avenue and came to a dead end in the Flats. *Opposite the Opera House on the southwest corner, where Dumont and Reif is located [3395], was the fire hall. You can still see the large double doors facing Okanagan Street where the fire trucks exited. At the end of the fire hall on Patterson was the police station. Beside it [2675] is the Sun Country cablevision house that was recently donated to Kindale Developmental Association. It was originally a Chinese residence and store, and the ceilings are seven feet high. The Kindale office beside it [2725] was the home of Howard and Maudie Spears, who ran the egg pool. Bechtold Centre [2750] is a new building where Sparks, who owned the bakery at that time, used to live; Hope (a different family from the blacksmith) bought him out, and the name Hope Bakery has remained. Empeys lived next door in the pink house with the big tree [2775]. The sloped roof one [2845] was a rental house where a fellow by the name of King lived when he was manager of Overwaitea. There were only vacant lots until the big green house [2885], which was owned by Jack Hill. Beside him on the corner of Patterson and Becker streets, where Gates automotive sat, was part of Harry Comber's farm, which grew lettuce, celery, cabbage and other vegetables.*

The north side of Patterson Avenue to Becker Street held mainly commercial buildings.

Hoover's flour mill occupied the site of the present pellet plant just west of the hotel. When Buckerfield's bought Hoover out, they put up a building where they made alfalfa meal. Ab Warner's Transfer, renamed Motor Transfer when trucks replaced horses, occupied both sides of the lane, formerly a part of Bridge Street. *Just east of the lane, where Valley Automotive sits, Ab Warner's barn held his team of horses. Warner's Transfer was in the business of draying [hauling], ploughing, harvesting, and Chinese garden work. His office sat where the City's public works building is located. Ab Warner and his brother lived in two houses beside the office. After Ab died, Kate Ripley's parents bought his house.*

The Lockhart team continued west past the corner of Becker Street and made more milk deliveries along the north side of Patterson Avenue.

Comber's farm included the site of the present Park Glenn apartments. Between the farm and St. Joseph's Church were two adjacent houses [3395, 3385] owned by Chinese bachelors, who worked at various jobs in the vegetable gardens. The second house [3385] dates from the turn of the century. There used to be a driveway between this house and the church. When a survey was made, the driveway was found to be on church property and annexed. The present owners, Bob and Penny Taylor, were living there at the time. On the west end of the church parking lot, a fellow called Lundeen lived when he worked for the railway. His old house was eventually burned down by the local volunteer firemen as a practice exercise. Next door was Gordon Grey [3275], who lived there for many years with his mother. He owned the lot beside him and cut hay from it.

To this point there were no houses, only vacant lots, on the south side of Patterson Avenue. Then Ralph came to four houses fronting one another across the street. *This was Art Marshall's house [3205]. He worked at the Co-op store. And Pam Krazanows-*

ki's house across from him [3210] was a rental – a policeman by the name of Ellis lived there. Beside the Marshalls lived the Birds [3185] whose house faced another rental occupied many years ago by people called Nielsen [3190].

I remember the Nielsen kids got the measles, and there was a big red quarantine sign on their door with **MEASLES** in black letters. Mrs. Nielsen had to put out a bowl for milk, and after she had gone indoors, we could come and uncap some bottles and pour milk into the bowl so our bottles wouldn't become contaminated. At school when a kid got measles, his desk was marked with a big **X**, and the janitor would take all the books from the desk into the basement and burn sulphur to fumigate them.

After the Nielsens left, Fred and Betty Simpson lived there until recently. Then there were more vacant lots until the Kanopski family home [3075]. The Henley family occupied it in the '40s. Art Henley was steward at the Legion, and Mrs. Henley for many years kept the weather records. Like several others the house was cut down from a two-storey dwelling to a bungalow.

Mrs. Dougie Smith [3030] lived across the street from the first hospital in Armstrong [3025]. It's over 100 years old now – should be a heritage house – the front of it has never been changed. My earliest memory is that the McQuarries lived here and boarded teachers. There was a trail from the back of the property across the railway to the school. The top of Patterson Avenue was empty. Nothing in through here at all 'til you get to the old, corner house [2915 Douglas] on Patterson and Douglas. McLeod and later Jim Mackenzie lived here. McLeod had a daughter by the name of Elaine.

Douglas Avenue looks like a country lane and runs briefly to the west. *The only house back in on Douglas was Mrs. Dimock's [3135]. She was in charge of the primary school that was in the Memorial Park.* A short distance east, Douglas Avenue ends at Becker Street. *There's a big house [2915] in behind this corner house on Becker that was a rental, and a fellow called Douglas lived there.*

That was the main house on the property – the rest was all empty. Across Becker Street one milk delivery was dropped just south of the intersection – the Norman house – and another north of it – the Frank Clayton home. *You can't see it behind the trees.*

Farther north on Becker was the Etter home [2940]. *Mrs. Etter and her mother Mrs. Becker lived here. The property was all one big field then – Grey Avenue didn't exist – and the United Church manse was next door [3010]. It belonged to the Methodists, I think, before union in 1925. I remember when Jamiesons came here in 1927, they rented it.* When the new United Church minister and his wife, Reverend and Mrs. Runnalls, came to Armstrong in 1946, they and their family moved into this white-pillared manse and met their neighbour, Mrs. Etter.

There were a bunch of gunny sacks laying around. Jean's mother wanted to dry them out, and she hung them on the fence between the two properties. She came out in a little while and they were back on the ground on her side. So she draped them over the fence again, and I'll be darned if they weren't on the ground again. Mrs. Etter came over to the fence. "You're not hanging those on my *fence." So they didn't have too much to do with one another from that point. Mrs. Etter worked as a bookkeeper in the Armstrong sawmill for about twenty-five years.*

Across the street were more Lockhart customers. *Timberlake lived at 2925 Becker. Roddy Crozier lived back in behind 3025 – his house seems to be gone now. He was Works foreman for the City. The Crozier family came from Larkin X-Road.*

The Frank Becker house was 3070, and the one across the street [3075] was a rental. Gullivan, the station agent, lived in the big house [3125]. There were a lot of packing houses in Armstrong – McDonald's, Wilson's, Poole's – and everything they shipped went by express or freight. Gullivan received a commission on express items. Express items went out on the passenger trains and would be in Vancouver or Calgary the next morning. A large amount or a carload went by freight.

The Baptist Church was in its current location on the west side of Becker Street [3185], and the house across the street was a rental [2980]. Charlie Ledoux and his family lived there and later Charlie Blumenauer, who owned what used to be known as Abbott's drugstore on Railway Avenue. (Charlie's uncle bought the drugstore first and renamed it Blumenauer's, and then Charlie took over.) In a rental house [3220] across Wolfenden Terrace from the Ledoux house lived a family called Best.

On the west side of Becker Street beyond the Baptist Church was 'Sawdust' Billy Smith's house [3225]. T.K. Smith owned the sawmill, and his brother, 'Sawdust' Billy, was the manager. Another brother, George Smith, owned Smith hardware on Railway Avenue. After T.K. died, Billy got the sawmill. Presently, the Romaine family own 'Sawdust' Billy's home. Only two more houses were located along Becker Street. Jim Hopkins, an electrician, lived at 3375 Becker, and Harry Comber lived near his greenhouses on Willowdale Drive on the current site of Pioneer Square [2865]. Both families bought Lockhart milk and cream.

Returning east on Patterson Avenue and crossing Okanagan Street, the team passed several businesses and vacant lots, and stopped at a small number of houses. [See Map 4.]

When the Chinese Hotel on the southeast corner of Patterson and Okanagan [Valley First Credit Union] disappeared after World War Two, Wes Hendricks built a tire shop there and operated the Shell gas station [2575]. Next door at the present Wine and Brew [2545] was Josh Blackburn's Transfer. I worked for Motor Transfer; there were the two. Across the street where the parking lot is located was Harry Hope's blacksmith shop. The present dental office [2540] was a rental house; I don't recall the name. Where the chiropractor's office is now [2510], the Methodist Church was situated. After church union it was empty for quite a while. When Walter Upper moved here, he made a house out of it and built rental cabins in behind. In the little house across the street [2515], Herman Ackerman lived until 1933. He managed Beer's menswear up on Railway Avenue. Beer had another store in Salmon Arm, and after the Armstrong fire in 1933, they didn't rebuild here. At a later time Josh Blackburn lived in the Ackerman house, just down the street from his business.

Shepherd Lane runs north from Patterson to Pleasant Valley Boulevard. The Shepherds [2490] moved down here in 1940. The house on our right [2481] is the old Fletcher house. Bert and his brother Alfred were raised there – they had Fletcher's Garage [presently Cherry Lane Antiques/Sears] Those next two houses across the street were rentals [2480, 2470]. The one on our right [2375] including the property next door was where Jack Wilson lived. He owned the largest packing house and was mayor of Armstrong for a number of years. Up until 1934 Whitehouse lived at 2360 Patterson, and then he moved up to Rosedale. The house west of Meadow Creek Lane [2345] was the Anglican manse. The Aslins lived across the street [2340] just west of a rental [3405]; the name escapes me. Aslin was foreman on the section crew for the CPR and lived there from about the turn of the century. The Piggotts moved into their house [2335] beside the Anglican Church at about the same time. When they moved the Anglican Church from Lansdowne and set it there, it encroached on the Harry Fraser farm by about three feet. And it's still that way today.

The Church as its anchor, Mill Street curls away from the end of Patterson Avenue. *Ilsley's house was on Mill Street [3425] where the Ashtons live. Ilsley was an early vet here but he died fairly young. I told Jean that Wayne Ashton would like to know the history of the house. Wayne said, "I wondered, but I could never find anything out." The Ilsley house and Harry Fraser's farmhouse (where the police station is) were the only two residences on Mill Street.*

The east end of town – Mill Street and Wood Avenue East – was the scene of both heavy activity and dirt in season. The sawmill and log yard, the shook factory, and the mill office were all located on and around this small area. In addition, both Canadian National and Canadian Pacific trains and freights made daily stops at the train station or at the loading platforms associated with the three spur lines at this end of town. Traffic moving along Mill Street had to cross four pairs of train tracks laid within a few feet of each other. *You never went through this end of town years ago with a car because the mud was a foot deep. All transport at the sawmill was done by horses. Even horses had trouble because the ground was so wet.*

The mill didn't work in the winter because they couldn't saw the frozen logs, so in winter people just hauled logs into town and dumped them in the log yard between Wood Avenue East and the rail line [Home Hardware]. Sandy Grant worked with a team at the sawmill moving logs and lumber. He hauled the logs across to the sawmill, which was located east of Mill Street in the general area of Country West Supply. He hauled the lumber – fourteen- to sixteen-foot lengths – from the sawmill over to the loading ramp in front of the United Church where it was piled into boxcars. They'd run the mill from spring until October when it would start to freeze again.

When Crown Zellerbach Limited bought the sawmill from Laurence and John 'Jack' Smith, the company moved the mill office away from the muck of the mill yard to the present location of the police station on Mill Street. Judiciously placed on the third spur line in the vicinity of the sawmill, a second small mill, the shook factory, cut lumber for apple boxes to satisfy the Okanagan apple market.

About thirty women worked in the shook factory and only for about six weeks at a time. The wood came into the factory as three-quarter inch boards sixteen to eighteen feet long and twelve inches wide. That was when you had good timber. When the pine or other wood was cut, the knots stayed in the bush – you only brought pure material to the sawmill. The women sawed up the boards and made the bundles – the sides for apple boxes in one bundle and the ends, a different material, in a different bundle. Each bundle was perhaps thirty-five to forty pounds, so it was reasonably heavy work. It was repetitious but it was extra money – about fifteen or twenty cents an hour. There weren't a lot of trucks running around, so a [rail]car load of 'box shook' would be shipped to Kelowna, for example, when requested. The shook factory operated in the '20s and '30s and disappeared during the war.

So we had a very transient population here in Armstrong at that time. People would come in here and work for the summer, and in the fall they had to go somewhere else because there was no unemployment insurance. If they weren't thrifty, they had to find other work elsewhere. There were five rental houses along Wood Avenue alone.

As the area north of Wood Avenue from Mill Street to Schubert Road was a bog used mainly for Chinese gardens and cattle pasture, construction at some sites along Wood Avenue (present-day Emcon, for example) was precarious. *In later years when the sawmill used trucks instead of horses and operated in the winter, they used a forklift to lay down bundles of slabs six to eight feet deep and topped them with gravel in order to build a solid foundation. In fact, Wood Avenue was known as Slab Alley because it was built in this way.* In the twenties and thirties, however, Wood Avenue remained a rutted clay passage for the Lockhart milk wagon.

The horse barn for the sawmill [2320] sat on the corner of Wood Avenue, and Art Robertson lived next door [but one] [2340]. He was the caretaker at the post office. A fellow by the name of McDougal lived between Robertson and the barn, but his house is gone now. The log yard stretched right up to the alley where Frank Becker had his sash and door factory. This house [2480] and the next one [2490] were rentals; at one point three Coulter families lived along here – cousins – including the house at 2510. Opposite Coulter, Nels Griffith lived at 2505 and Mills next door [2525]. Ogilvies lived across the street [2520] and Harry Sheardown beside him [2524]. Harry's two brothers opened a store in Lumby. The last two houses on the south side of Wood belonged to Miller [2545] and Ehmke [2555]. The Norman house [2550] was both the home of a police constable named Barnes who was hired by the City and the city jail. Later Bob Gerrard lived there and took boarders. Doubtless the cell made a handy little room. *He also baked bread, and Dad would buy four to six loaves from him every week.*

The last house on Wood Avenue east of Okanagan Street is of special interest. *This big house [2590 Wood] across from the Co-op service station is old. It belonged to Jason Hassard; his property included the old Rainbow video site. Jason was no relation to other Hassards in town, a bachelor, and his sister Alta lived with him. In the early days he had the piece of property on Reservoir Road owned now by the Fish and Game Club.*

South Okanagan Street at Wood Avenue was a commercial area that continued around the corner along Pleasant Valley Road. The Lockhart milk delivery mainly ignored these businesses with the exception of one or two stops for customers who lived in quarters above the stores.

'Gasoline' Billy had his garage and Home Gas where the Co-op gas station sits [3550]. The Co-op is a real late investment here, as it came into existence only in 1922. And the curling rink, the first one, sat just south of it on an alley off Okanagan Street. (This alley used to run behind Smith hardware and across Okanagan Street behind the Co-op store; then everybody decided his piece belonged to him and it disappeared.) 3575 was Adair's Tip Top tailor and where True Value hardware stands [3545], a fellow by the name of Charlie Christian had a harness shop.

Stores hugged each other along Pleasant Valley Road. [See Map 5.] The Co-op store supplying groceries, clothes, and hardware occupied the northwest corner of Pleasant Valley Road and Okanagan Street. West of it was Shepherd's hardware. *There'd be a door here going into Shepherd's and beside it another door going into Sawyer's ice cream parlour – the same going up the street – a door here and another beside it – just narrow street space but fairly deep. Sawyer advertised a sundae that he called 'The Whole Damn Fam-*

ily.' After Sawyer in the following order came Beer's menswear, Thompson's shoe repair, Safeway, and Lancaster's menswear.

Lancaster had three fires in that block. His first fire took out Chapple drugstore next to him. Chapple didn't rebuild. Lancaster did and opened again. After his last fire in January, 1933, he was told that if he got another fire, he got no insurance. Lancaster lived above his store, and I can remember going through delivering milk after the fire, and their piano was covered with ice from the water.

Lancaster's uneasy neighbours included the Okanagan Hotel, which also burned in 1933 on the site of the present post office, Armstrong furniture, and the office of the Okanagan telephone company, *which was located in a house and operated by a woman called C.B. Wilson. Tyler's shoe shop was next door [The Brown Derby].* The lane east of Tyler's had a name then: St. Clair Street. The last business before Bridge Street was Armstrong machine shop [Armstrong Spallumcheen Museum and Art Gallery].

Following their few quick stops in this commercial section, Lockharts crossed Okanagan Street and continued west along Wood Avenue toward the farthest destination on the milk run.

The Women's Institute owned a house along here somewhere so that the women who came into town on the wagons would have somewhere to rest. That grey house on the northwest corner of Wood Avenue [2610] is the only one I think it could have been. An old fellow by the name of Trump lived in the brown shack at the back. In the house on the southwest corner [2625] Crow used to have his barbershop. It's another old house. If you see pictures of early Armstrong, Crow's house is there along with the Hassard place.

The parking lots on Wood Avenue behind Rose Valley Square and adjacent to the medical offices have been in use there from the earliest days. *People shopping at the Co-op store and people coming to town from all over the district tied their horses on two hitching* rails there. Later the chamber of commerce tried to develop the idea of the hitching rail to give the town an old-time look.

And this was Maundrell's home on the right [2750], Steele Fisher's was the green one [2760], and Armstrong's [2850], the last. Everything to the west of these houses on the north side was open farmland, swamp, and Chinese gardens. On the other side of the street west of the parking lot were Tom Cummings in the yellow house [2795] and Hollingsworth in the blue house [2825]. Two or three houses are gone. Sandy Grant, the sawmill teamster, and then the Reeses lived in one for years where the City Hall parking lot is on the corner of Bridge Street. The City Hall was built in 1907. The plans and construction cost are in the Museum, and, if my memory serves me correctly, the cost was $7600.

Ted Poole lived where the school board office [3130] was located east of Highland Park School. He owned one of the packing houses, and he had greenhouses to grow celery and lettuce for the Chinese until the Chinese decided they didn't want to pay the price and started growing their own in hotbeds beside their cabins. The fairgrounds, of course, were always here, but Meighan Creek (pronounced Mee-an) used to form a Y with Deep Creek in the centre of the property; in the '80s the decision was made to divert Deep Creek alongside Wood Avenue and take Meighan Creek underground through a culvert. Just about where that school sign is on Wood Avenue, a beaver has built his lodge and causes a bit of flooding.

The house on the northeast corner of Wood and Highland Park Road [3290] was where Potter lived. Highland Park Road used to be called Keevil Road. Ed Keevil lived back in there, and his property included the area where Colonial Farms chicken plant is built [3830 Okanagan]. Keevil was the vegetable inspector at the packing houses. He smoked a pipe and spent a lot of time keeping it going. He had no children. Keevil Road today is just a dead-end road off Highland Park.

The land between Highland Park Road and Schubert Road was

cattle pasture. *Immediately west of Adair Street were two houses that belonged to the CN Railway [3445, 3495], and a third one just past the rail tracks where Ernie Harris lived is gone now. These used to be two-storey houses; the custom in those days was to build a downstairs and an upstairs.* With the top storey gone, I find them harder to recognize.

Brett lived on the west corner of Schubert Road [3605]. He also had a farm on Brett's Road in Spallumcheen. Schubert Road in those days ran only to the bottom of the big hill above the railway tracks and then cut across beside Hawkins' place to meet Keevil Road (Highland Park Road). Otter Lake Road wasn't here then either. It went through in 1928. Harry Lee was the only one down on that bottom road that we delivered milk to – there was just a trail to his house. Harry always took milk [c.3545 Otter Lake Road].

Janet Coldicott lived at 3650 Wood Avenue. I remember when she and Bob were married and moved in there in 1940. Jean says Janet and Bob were 'Aunty Janet' and 'Uncle Bob' to all the children in the neighbourhood. *Mrs. Glover lived in that house on the northwest corner of Murray and Wood [3720]. One of the ministers lived in the big house up on the hill on the right [3890]. It was an Anglican rectory.* Ralph and Jean rented it. *It was a long way up a miserable hill.*

At this juncture, the milk wagon made the tricky left turn from Wood Avenue onto Fraser Road – *I hate this turn-off* – and headed for the last two deliveries in this part of town. *A fellow by the name of Game lived right above the road on the corner [c.3275] and he had a milk box for us at the bottom here. Fraser Road was all empty. Lane's farm was on the left [c.3865]. We turned down Fraser to the foot of Noble Road because one family lived there – the only one – the Popowiches – and they had a flock of geese. They never bothered me, but I teased them, so if my sister went on the milk run, they chased her! Then we turned around and went back Wood Avenue into town.*

By now the time was around seven-fifteen and the delivery, half completed. Empty milk bottles rattled in the democrat, money had been collected and milk tickets disbursed. The team turned off Wood onto Bridge Street. Pollichek had a house on the corner, now the Museum and Art Gallery parking lot [3415]. *He had the International equipment dealership.*

As the team headed west along Pleasant Valley Road, they passed the high school on the corner and beside it, the Recreation Hall. *The skating rink behind the hall stretched through to Wood Avenue.* The latter two buildings were part of the fairgrounds and used to house exhibits and an eating area. The Drill Hall was an adjacent landmark. *Centennial Hall was a BC Centennial project to renovate the old Drill Hall. During the First War these halls were built all over the country and used as a place to train the army.*

A big house owned by a lawyer named Perry sat where the Kinsmen RV Park is. The school for grades 1 and 2 was on the property occupied by Memorial Park. In order to enlarge the park, Con Passas bought the property at the southeast corner fronting Pleasant Valley Road and donated it to the City. The house that Eva Smith occupies [3265] was Bob Garner's – one of the teachers – and beside it was Clinton's [3245] – a relative of Phyllis Brett.

DairyWorld was just a deep gully that was filled in for construction purposes – nobody lived there. Dixons lived on Sugden Avenue [3270] and Somersets lived on Jackson Avenue [3635] but neither Sugden nor Jackson were named then. Off Pleasant Valley Road where it curves before it runs uphill stands the Bank House, a large heritage home built in 1911, ten years before the opening of its neighbour, the Brick School. *The Bank of Montreal house, where Salters live [3080], stood empty for a few years in the '20s – the bank wouldn't rent it. People by the name of Jolley lived on the corner opposite the Salter driveway [3035]. The green bungalow [3015] belonged to Stan Carey. He worked for the Municipality, and their garage was right across Warner Avenue from his house. First*

89

John Murray and then Mrs. Evans lived in the old house just west of the garage.

The area north and west of Pleasant Valley Road was mainly farmland and the houses were few. *We turned up Sage Avenue. There were only two houses here. Sage lived at 3625 and Mrs. Saby lived across the road from him [3630]. Sage Avenue only went this far, as the rest was a farm owned by a fellow called Fulton. We went back to Pleasant Valley Road and turned west. People by the name of Gamble owned this house on the southwest corner of Rosedale and Pleasant Valley Road [2795]. Then we headed for Charlie Patten's house on the corner of Patten Drive. There was no Len Wood School – it was open land owned by Charlie.*

After we turned around at Patten's and headed east on Rosedale Avenue, the closest one living over there was Homer Meade, and his house was away back in the centre of his farm. [See Map 6.] He was almost on Colony Street but that street didn't exist. You could go up the trail to his place with a team of horses, but you only went to the top of the hill. Meade had a milk box at the bottom on Rosedale for us.

Thompsons used to live where that pink one is on the corner of what is now Pheasant Ridge Drive [3245]. He was a shoemaker and had his shop on the block where the old Co-op store was. The elementary school skating rink was across Rosedale Avenue from his house. Art Kemp [3125] lived east of the railway track and Longs lived across from him [3110]. John Fowler lived where Art Kemp was for a time. In the '30s Whitehouse lived in the stone-fronted house [3010] and Frank Sugden lived at 3065. Whitehouse was Phillips and Whitehouse grocery store, and Sugden was the manager of the Co-op. Piments lived at 3015 Rosedale and Cowleys lived next door [2905].

The team crossed Becker Street. 'Deafy' Warner lived along here on the left [2940] – he was deaf. Tooleys lived at 2915 and Winters across from them at 2920 close to the corner of Moray

Street. Just east of Moray at 2875 Rosedale is a house that at one time or another has had three families in it: Sanderson, who owned a butcher shop in town; Tom Andrews, who lived in it years ago; and finally Jack Jamieson, who owns the Armstrong Advertiser. Just east of the Jamiesons was Bill Clayton [2825] who ran the machine shop that was transformed into the [local] museum and art gallery. Scotty Watson lived in that house before Bill Clayton went in.

At this point the Lockhart milk run began its zigzag course through the residential section of town north of Rosedale Avenue: north on Moray, south on Jarvis and north again on Wright Street. The number of homes was sparse and many beautiful ones remain. The tall trees along Moray Street are the same ones Ralph remembers.

Calvert, the dentist, lived right on the corner of Moray at 2880 Rosedale. Wellington Smith was a neighbour at 2860 Moray. He worked in the post office. And beside him at 2880 were the Pelletts. V.T.N. Pellett was the librarian, and the Armstrong Library was in his house. The rest of this street was vacant until we got down to the bottom near Wolfenden Terrace. Then we came to Dick Thomas at 3070 Moray. He had cows so didn't need milk from us. Beside him [3090] was J.Z. Parks, who owned the shoe store in town. Later Ella Davies, an elementary school teacher for many years, lived in that house. Across the street [3095] Wolfenden lived for a period. He was a catalyst in Armstrong's early political, economic, and cultural growth. *Across Wolfenden Terrace [3110] lived Knight-Harris. He kept the weather records for some time. On the opposite side of Wolfenden Terrace from him were two rental houses: Josh Blackburn of Blackburn's Transfer lived for a time at 3145 before he moved to Patterson Avenue, and Hollingsworth, the barber, at 3175. Ed Wyatt lived there after Hollingsworth did.*

It wasn't unusual for people in town to move from one house to another. *They were rental houses, and as somebody got a little more money, he moved up. Josh Blackburn, for example, lived on*

Moray, then moved to Fletcher, and then up to Patterson. He died in his car.

Jean picks up the story: *We were walking down to an old-time dance at the Rec. Hall and saw the car parked beside the road. We didn't see anybody in it. When we walked home from the dance, the car was still there, but it was a local car – we thought it had broken down and would be picked up the next morning – so we didn't report it. We found out the next day that he had climbed out of the front seat into the back seat and died there. We felt terrible.*

The team turned east on Wolfenden Terrace and prepared to move south on Jarvis Street.

This big house here [3095 Jarvis] belonged to a mechanic that worked for A. Smith – a fellow by the name of Ernie Archibald. Blue Horizon Gardens is recent – early '70s – that area was just the back end of Comber's farm. The bowling greens on the corner of Wolfenden and Jarvis Street have been here since the turn of the [last] century. The little clubhouse is in very bad repair. It was built in 1928, and the grounds were always wet because the septic tank from the hospital overflowed regularly. They had drains, of course, but they didn't work very well.

Just across from the Thomas house [3025 Jarvis], where I was born, I would run into the back of the hospital with milk, as this entrance was close to the kitchen. This house on the corner of Jarvis and Haugen Street [2980] replaced the Seventh Day Adventist Church that sat there. 2965 was an old rental, Harry Hope's house. Harry and William Hope were brothers and worked in the blacksmith shop together, but the business wasn't enough to support the two of them, so Harry stayed on alone. He was the older brother and deaf from the age of twelve, (probably a respite from the constant din of hammering iron into horseshoes and farm implements), *but he drove a car and did everything. William lived just up the street from Harry at 2945 Jarvis. William's son, Dave, went to live with Frank Poole, who had no children and needed someone to do the farm chores. He stayed there for the rest of his life and inherited the farm from him.*

2970 Jarvis was the doctor's house. Dr. Haugen lived in it for a long time, and Dr. Shotten before him. That house was built with bricks that were manufactured here by the Oakland clay works on the highway north of Armstrong. John Jamieson lived beside the doctor at 2950 Jarvis. The little one back there [2925] belonged to a schoolteacher by the name of Stokes. A family by the name of Currie lived in this green house [2865]. This house [2850] is an old one. Hill lived here first followed by Mary Townshend and her mother, who had moved down from Lansdowne. The little one on the corner [2810] was Bud Mason's. Mrs. Ernie Mason lived there.

Having reached Rosedale Avenue again, the team headed east toward Wright Street and their final deliveries before tackling Okanagan Street. Ralph recalled the farmland that lay south of Rosedale. *Tom Thomas lived on the south side of what is now Burns Avenue and he had four or five cows to supply his household.* No Lockhart milk sales there. *The big house just behind the corner house at the intersection of Rosedale and Wright [2730 Rosedale Place] belonged to the George Wilson farm. And from the turn of the century to about 1928, the land where Dunn Road sits was a 9-hole golf course. Then things got real tough in the Depression and nobody was playing golf.*

Although the houses on Wright Street were less numerous than at present, two important institutions, the hospital and the Presbyterian Church, buttressed the north end. The milk wagon headed towards them.

This house [2900] was built by Art Young. He was the engineer at Armstrong Elementary School when it opened – the furnace man and janitor. In the house across from him [2905], Sharples, the Anglican minister, lived for many years. He was the first minister that bought a house instead of living in the manse. Bert Fletcher followed him there. Harvey Brown, the plumber, lived at 2935 Wright, and John and Elda Jamieson lived beside him at 2945. In 1934 Nels Griffith moved up to 2950 from Wood Avenue. He hauled cream for NOCA [North Okanagan Creamery Association]. The big house on the corner here [2990] belonged to Adair, the Tip Top tailor. The Presbyterian Church next door [3020] was built in 1929 and '30. When the Methodists and Presbyterians formed the United Church in 1925, the Smiths and the McKechnies would have nothing to do with it. So T.K. Smith donated the lumber to build this church.

That's the old brick hospital on Haugen Avenue although Haugen Avenue then had no name. Dave Hope told me he was born in the big blue house [2620 Haugen] – 'Gasoline' Billy Smith's place – behind the Presbyterian Church. If that is the case, 3025 Patterson Avenue was the first hospital, number two was behind the Presbyterian Church, and number three was the Brick Hospital, which opened in 1921.

Okanagan Street south of Wolfenden Terrace boasted several substantial houses. [See Map 7.]

T.K. Smith lived in the present Reif home [3050] and the Smiths always took at least one half-pint of cream a day. In front of the house, T.K. had a double tennis court and a large fishpond. This house across the street [3065] was a Presbyterian manse. The first United Church minister after union lived there – a fellow by the name of Stott. Later the Carlsons were there, and a pair of twins, Meryl and Mervin, would be in the window every morning telling the team to "Giddap! Giddap!" At one time their dad had the butcher shop beside Smith hardware. We never sold Carlsons any milk because they got theirs from City Dairy, but Carlson didn't keep any milk at the butcher shop for sale like Murray's did.

Tom Clinton lived on the corner of Fletcher Avenue [2990]. Holliday, the photographer, lived at 2940. E.T. Abbott, the druggist, lived across the street [2945]. Abbott was permitted to sell whiskey for medicinal purposes. A. Smith of A. Smith and Son garage lived at 2920. Shepherds lived next door [2890] and sold in 1940 to the family that ran Hope bakery. A. Smith's neighbour across the street [2915] was Tom Aldworth, principal of the Brick School. Dr. Tennant lived at 2885 and, of course, he was no friend of Dad's. Renault lived at 2855; he had a dry goods store in town. 2810 used to be a big, two-storey house on the corner of Rosedale and Okanagan Street where Cyril Smith lived. He was A. Smith's son. Across from him was a rental with an extensive yard [2845 Rosedale].

Having crossed Rosedale Avenue, the Lockhart team faced a steep climb on Okanagan Street hill. Fortunately, by now the load was considerably lighter.

The big house set in on the southwest corner of Rosedale and Okanagan [2727] was Jim Wright's, and the golf course lay south of him along Okanagan Street and extended to Dunn Road. On the opposite corner of Rosedale, Dr. Van Kleeck owned an extensive property running north to Danallanko Drive, which was then the driveway to his house. He had a swimming pool – not heated, but still a swimming pool. He and his wife had five children and were one of our best customers. Dr. Van Kleeck used to buy a book of tickets – probably 150 quarts in a book. They took four, five, six quarts of milk a day. Dr. Van Kleeck believed in using milk.

George Murray, the butcher, built a house [2560] on a large property that ran almost to Van Kleeck Road. At various times Maclean lived at 2485, as did Clay, the teacher, and Clarke, the jeweller. Ecclestone, the manager of the Bank of Commerce, lived at 2451. Bush covered the hill south of Van Kleeck Road. Van Kleeck Road itself was a trail that went back into Harding's farm at the southern extremity of the present City limits. Harding's farm now includes the Royal York golf course and Meighan Creek subdivision. John Fowler used to live on the corner of Henderson Drive and Okanagan [2505 Henderson], and we delivered his milk. Okanagan Street at this distance from Rosedale was just a grass-grown track, and the street went no farther. We used to turn around, go through Van Kleeck's property on what is now called Danallanko, and back out to Rosedale, moving east.

Beyond Okanagan Street the east end of Rosedale was mainly farmland. Neither Smith Drive nor Highway 97A had been constructed.

Van Kleeck's property included quite a strip here on Rosedale Avenue. In 1935 Miles Whitbread moved to 2355. Before that time he was the gardener for T.K. Smith and had a room above the garage where he batched. Where Dorothy Powell now lives [2325], there was a tennis court, the second one; the first court sat where the swimming pool building stands in Memorial Park. It was on the grounds of the school that was situated there. The current tennis court is on the corner of the same property.

There were no other buildings on Rosedale until Hobson's [2185]. He was a vet who lived on the hill behind and to the west of the Armstrong Bible Chapel. Bob Anderson spent the winter in Armstrong at his place east of Hobson's, but he also had a farm up on the mountain east of town. (Elaine Jones, the artist, is now on it.) The Andersons went back to the farm in summer, where they grew raspberries, strawberries and fruit for a living.

On Rosedale Avenue [1986] just east of Highway 97A on the hill was a house belonging to J.D. Hamilton. Hamilton's farm was east of and included the present highway. His barn was down here on the flat, and his house, up on the hill. So it was pretty tough to keep walking back and forth. When he got too old to hobble down to the barn, he built a house beside his barn on the corner of Rosedale and the highway [2110] and moved in. Neil and Ruth Bosomworth lived in the old Hamilton house on the hilltop when they came to town in the '40s. And the Heals moved there later. They all took milk from us.

Ralph Lockhart has watched Armstrong grow.

I've sure seen some changes. When we were delivering milk along Rosedale Avenue, these streets weren't here – Phillips Street, Fowler Street, and Wilson Avenue – it was a farm. Fred Street, though, was on our route, and we retraced our steps along Rosedale to reach these customers. Paulings lived here on the corner of Fred and Rosedale [2380]. He had a butcher shop in town. Binkley lived in the old one [2835]. He was a teacher at the elementary school. Then there were no more houses until you got to the end of the street. Peacock lived in that one [2930]. He was a baker from the Coast. Groves lived at the corner of Fred and Fletcher [2375] where the de la Salles are now. Across the street where Bob Nitchie lives [2415 Fletcher], was the Austin house, I believe.

The team moved east along Fletcher Avenue. Ralph was hurrying to complete the residential deliveries before his final stops in the town centre.

This house – 2360 Fletcher – has been here for a long time. It belonged to the City clerk, a fellow by the name of Feiffer. These were all old houses here. Smith lived in that one [2325] in the '40s – he was no relation to the other Smiths in town. People by the name of Robertson lived in that yellow house [2285], the Hugginses lived at 2255, and J.C. 'Juicy' Smith lived there at 2260. Juicy's initials and his manner of chewing tobacco earned him the nickname. Juicy and his son Wilfred farmed this whole area north of Fletcher. Hayden Drive wasn't there – seems strange, but true. Fred Murray lived at 2230. There was just one more customer along here – a fellow by the name of Cooke [2175]. He worked in Ted Poole's warehouse and had planted crabapple trees all along his property where Phillips Street is now. After dropping his milk off, we turned around, retraced our steps along Fletcher to Okanagan Street and went back to town.

Coming across the Flats, Ralph noted that this area too was once farmland. *The Flats was all Lee Bak Bong's farm. He shipped a lot of lettuce and other vegetables. Lee Bak Bong's was the only Chinese family in town; the rest were single men. The brick building on the west side of Okanagan Street nearest the Flats was their home. He married twice and had quite a large family. I was in school with Ming, Wing, and Kwong. Ben Lee was one of the younger family.*

Between the Lee house and the old fire hall was the Chinese laundry. [See Map 3.]

Ralph quickly dispensed the last of his milk and cream.

We delivered a lot of milk to the Golden Gate Café (where Country Café is now). Then we'd go upstairs and deliver milk in the Brick Block – the apartments above the stores on the southeast side of Okanagan Street. Although obscured by paint, the bricks made in the Enderby brickyard are still visible – *Oaklands didn't make enough bricks. The Armstrong Hotel bought milk on alternate months from us and from City Dairy. That way they kept everybody happy. Then we'd turn east on Pleasant Valley Road and make our last delivery at Murray's in time for the trainmen who came in on the passenger train at 8:20 a.m. Then it was time to go all the way home, wash bottles and start the farm work.*

Springview Dairy delivered milk to the majority of homes mentioned during the milk run. The Lockharts' competitor in town was called City Dairy.

Our milk tickets were dark red and the cream tickets were yellow. The other dairy used green for milk and blue for cream. We saw quite a few different owners of that business over the years. One chap I recall was a fellow by the name of McQuaid. And he sold out to Merriott Brothers. (Les Merriott looked after the Memorial Park for a number of years.) And they sold the business to people called Perley, and they sold to Ralph McKinley and then McKinley sold to Myers Fransden. By that time people wanted pasteurized milk. Fransden was prepared to go into pasteurization and Dad said, "To heck with it" and sold out to him in 1945. Then Myers Fransden sold to the Cheese Factory in 1947. If you notice in last week's Armstrong Advertiser [February, 2003], Jack Jamieson had an article that a visitor was buying a paper for his mother on the prairie and said the family had owned City Dairy from 1943 to 1952, but the name didn't ring a bell with me at all. However, it could have been Fransden's daughter.

The fellow from a second-hand store was here a while ago and he'd never seen a quarter-pint milk bottle, so I took him down in the basement and showed him one. "Oh," he says, "didn't you have your name on the bottle?" I said, "At that time you didn't have your name on bottles." I remember one woman in town, she'd take milk from us for a couple of months and then she'd buy from City Dairy. Occasionally, she'd miss putting an empty bottle out, so in a few months she had a washtub full of our own bottles to sell back to us!

The bottles as I recall weren't that expensive, about $1.50 a dozen. They came from DeLaval, and Country Freight Lines, I think, delivered them. We'd order about fifteen or twenty dozen at a time to make it worthwhile. I believe the headquarters were out of Vancouver at that time. They were a big company – DeLaval separators and other equipment. NOCA in Vernon handled the DeLaval milking machines – there were quite a few different makes around.

Ralph was the second youngest of five surviving siblings. Irma was the oldest, then came George, Evelyn, Eric, Ralph, and Hazel. *Eric died at the age of seven. He was vaccinated [most likely, smallpox] on Friday and died on Sunday. They said it was pneumonia, but I never believed it nor did Dad. Evelyn almost died too – her arm blew up to three times its normal size. Consequently, I was never vaccinated, nor was Hazel.*

From the age of five, Ralph accompanied his father on the daily milk route. He was handy for running up and down the driveways to set out the milk and collect the empty bottles. He was fast on his feet. When he married and had children, none of them could outrun him.

Do you see this chip out of my front tooth? I was sitting on the milk wagon one morning and Dad reached over and pinched me to see how fast I could move. I ducked but I had my arms full of bottles and one of them broke my tooth off. I went to the Cow Testing picnic the same day and ate three cones of ice cream, so I guess the accident didn't bother me much.

Reaching Murray's in time to meet the CN passenger train at 8:20 a.m. served a double purpose, as Ralph had just a short distance to get to school.

I didn't start school until I was nearly seven because my birthday was in January. That September it took them three days to get me to class. The grade one and two school was in the park where the swimming pool is now. We had no car at that time. Dad drove me up in the democrat and said, "There you are, kid, go" and dropped me off on the sidewalk. Hey, I'd never been around any place like that! I was home darn near as soon as he was! So the next day he says, "Don't you dare come home. You'll have to go back." Well, I was a little smarter the second day because I ate my lunch on the way home, so he didn't take me back – no lunch. On the third day he took me inside. Mrs. Dimock was the principal and Bertha Fowler was the other teacher – Terry Fowler's aunt. Mrs. Dimock says to me, "We're not going to hurt you."

The older kids went to the consolidated school – the Brick School – up to grade eight, and the high school was downtown on the empty corner on PV Road across from the Museum. Originally the school downtown on the corner was the primary school and the one in the park was the high school. Then they reversed them and, two to three years afterwards, built a second storey on what would become first the high school and then the old junior high.

Having attended the Brick School in its early days, Ralph recounts some details about it.

Manual training and home economics were on opposite ends of the Brick School. Home economics was in a room in the basement on the east end, and manual training was in the basement on the west end. Then across from each one of these was a play area, one for the boys and one for the girls. No gym or anything. It took a long time to get a gym on that school – now they want to close it. Presently a possibility is to use the building as an elementary or a middle school. *And it's hot water heat, the most economical. At least it* was hot water heat. There were two boilers side by side. They could spell 'em off – use one one year and the other one the next year. And the pipes and machinery were all interlocked.

They originally bought cordwood, and that was the length that went in the furnace – four-foot chunks of wood – so the 'hold' in the furnace was big. And they contracted out the work. The wood was piled along the fence between the school and Salters' in a long strip, and then they alternated between the two transfer [outfits] to bring the team up and move the wood into the furnace room. One would do it one month and the other, the next month. Blackburn's Transfer had four or five teams of horses; Warner's had two. That was before tractors came in. It was a good way of heating the school, I think. Of course, nowadays people use gas. They are fussing about the pollution from burning wood.

The school had a solid slate roof, and in winter you had to be careful the snow didn't slide off it and bury you. Sometimes the slates came too.

When I was at school, I had two friends that I chummed with all the time – Harry Winters and Frank Jolley. Harry had several careers. He started out in the Mounties. I don't know what happened there, but I think he got married and they kicked him out. Frank Jolley went to work for the railway in Revelstoke. I saw Harry two or three times after we left school but I never saw Frank again. Now they're both dead. When I was growing up on the farm, I knew the neighbour boys – there were Walter and Bob Docksteader, and the Meneices, Ken and Alvin. Alvin was more of a friend than the others. Bob Docksteader is still living – he went through the war and had his shoulder blown all to pieces in Italy. Walter is dead and I'm not sure about Alvin Meneice – he was somewhere out in northern Alberta and I haven't seen or heard of him in years. Then there were Ronny and Joe Lamb. Both Ronny and Joe are gone. I'm fortunate to be still here.

The Lockhart farm was really two businesses: raising and feeding cattle, and bottling and delivering milk. Chores were lengthy. *You got every third Sunday off. I never had a lot of free time – I had lots of work to do. Cows were brushed and cleaned every day. Udders were washed before milking. Always a bunch of calves to feed, and the young stock in a separate barn. The barn was cleaned; we used shavings for bedding. Everything was a lot of work.*

We grew mangels – all pitted – the little Globe mangel like a large turnip, but mostly the Giant Whites that weigh up to sixty pounds apiece – huge things. We had a root pulper to smash them up, but some of the cows liked them whole and they'd just scoop those mangels out with their bottom jaw. Two and a half feet long, ten inches through – chewing that was a lot of work! We always grew between an acre and an acre and a half of potatoes. One year we'd make money on them; then everybody would grow potatoes the next year and the price would drop. Then we'd feed the potatoes to the cattle.

We grew our own hay and alfalfa. We had two wooden silos made from vertical 1-inch by 6-inch shiplap which was girdled horizontally with 2-inch by 6-inch bands set two feet apart all the way up to the top. The original silo was octagonal in shape, 16 feet wide and 40 feet high, and a later one built in the early '30s was 12 feet by 30 feet. A wooden platform at ground level caught the silage when it was thrown out of the silo for feed. One silo was filled in the summer with pea and oat silage, and the other in the fall with corn. So we pretty well had year-round silage to feed the cows.

In winter we'd put the hay through the silo filler to chop it up – absolutely no waste – because if the hay was a bit coarse, the cows would eat it anyway, and they generally had molasses on it too – kept them in good shape. The silo filler was driven by a motor – we had a car motor – that turned over very fast, and it had three sharp knives on it. A belt carrying the hay came in towards the wheel, and then rollers would press it down and hold it while the knives cut it off as it fed in. We went around to the neighbours with the silo filler too.

Having the silo filler come to your farm for the day was serious business.

Outside the silo was a team of horses with, say, a load of corn on it. You fed the corn into the silo filler, and the corn silage was blown up a pipe on the outside of the silo and came down from the hood of the machine, which was lined up on the centre of the open roof. Inside the silo you had somebody tramping it down. Our silo was forty feet high, so if you were the one inside the silo, you wore a sack over your head – because when those chunks of corncob hit you, they stung!

A silo that was twelve feet across gave you quite a big area of silage to spread. As it got higher underneath you, you put the 'doors' in to make a continuous wall. These doors were built to fit spaces one above the other between the horizontal bands, and they were stored underneath a ladder that held them against the side of the silo. We never used the ladder to get into the silo or to position the pipe from the silo filler into the hole at the top of the silo – we just went up hand over hand on the bands. Jean climbed up once when we were going together. She was in a skirt. "You stay away!!" If you were inside the silo, there was no danger of fumes, as it was wide open at the top and the doors were out. The cut corn had a pleasant smell.

We always put the corn in before it froze and we got a sweeter silage, but some of the neighbours liked the corn to freeze first. They talked about the loss of moisture otherwise, but we always thought it was about the same. Ours never bled much. I asked Lew Brydon about it one time. We'd filled his silo for him, and four or five days later he gets up in the morning and his pigs are laying around in the yard. "What the heck??" He kicks one – "Ugh!" – and it doesn't move. They had been drinking the liquid draining between the boards of the silo – it had pooled and fermented – and they were all drunk! When your silo is forty feet high, there's a lot of pressure on the stuff at the bottom. Lew was curing his hams before he butchered.

Ralph did not begrudge the long hours spent keeping the farm and dairy in the black. *I think we were better off than some others because we had a little money changing hands. Dad always had a hired man and paid the highest wages of anybody around. The man got his room and board and Mother did his laundry. One fellow was there for eight years. He was lame in one leg but you couldn't ask for a better worker. He got mad if anybody was up in the morning before him.*

We were different from the other kids we knew because we had an indoor toilet and hot and cold running water. The stove heated the hot water tank in the kitchen, and when you got the stove going, that tank would get so hot it was just dancing! Bang! Boom! You'd turn on the tap and it would be straight steam! Jean was scared to be in the kitchen in case it exploded.

Some people, though, were downright lazy – wouldn't even have a garden – they were on relief – fifteen dollars a month. We always had our own chickens and a big garden. A few cents for seeds and you could grow a lot. Mom and the girls worked in the garden, they helped her can, we had cherries and prunes and apples. We always put an animal down for meat.

In the early '20s at five cents a quart for 300 quarts of milk, plus cream, Ross Lockhart took in from fifteen to twenty dollars a day before expenses. A week's take would gross around $125. In the depressed thirties, this small but steady income represented security. Others were not so fortunate. Some resorted to pilfering.

We had neighbours who had nothing to eat. Dad always killed a couple of hogs for meat and sugar-cured the hams – he had a special recipe. After they were cured, he wrapped the hams in burlap, dipped them in lime to seal them, and hung them in the basement. The basement had an outside entrance, but nobody locked a door in those days.

One time they sent me down to get one. I put my hand up to untie the burlap and it was empty. I tried another one. Two or three were empty. [The thief] would undo the package, take the ham out and do it back up so you didn't notice. One night my brother happened to look out, and here's this old fellow just gone down over the hill behind the house carrying another of these hams. George opened up with a .45-70 and he dropped the ham and ran. I think he got wet because there was a fairly broad spring right there that he'd have to cut through. We didn't lose any more hams though.

I remember Lew Brydon hired the fellow one time and put him in the haymow to spread the hay when it dropped from the fork. The hay would go up. "Trip!"… "Trip!"… Every time a forkful of hay came up, he yelled, "Trip!" So around ten o'clock in the morning, Lew went to have a look, and the mow was built right up under the fork and this guy was sitting up on a beam – he hadn't moved any hay back. It's a real mess when you do that – nothing pushed back – everything plugged up – you can't get the hay out to pitch it into the stable. Lew sent him home. But that old son of a gun, you know, he could sit down at a piano and play anything!

Ross Lockhart made little use of his fruit trees. Time was too short to play about.

When Dad went on the place, there was about two acres of orchard. As I grew up, there wasn't much left because there was no money in it. Dad always told the story that there were apricot trees there, and the apricots were just about ready to pick. He went out in the morning – no apricots. Bears, maybe? *Bears with two feet! The next year when they were just about ripe, Dad turned the irrigation water in there. And when he went out to check, he found the tracks of a man and a woman six inches deep in the mud. After that he took out the apricots, and we only had five apples: a Snow and a Yellow Transparent, a Duchess, a McIntosh, and a Gravenstein. The Gravenstein is one of the nicest summer apples, but you can't get it any more – a beautiful apple – not quite yellow with a small blush on it. We had a walnut tree there too, but we never used the walnuts because Dad said it was a Black Walnut and poisonous, so they just dropped on the ground. If you husked one and broke it open, your hands would be as yellow as iodine.*

Milking, bottling and delivering milk was a laborious daily task. Everyone in the family participated. *The hired man, Mother and George would do the milking in the morning while Dad and I took off to deliver the milk. The girls helped out in the dairy. The morning's milk and that night's milk were bottled, then went out the next morning.*

Equipment included an aerated cooler and a bottler.

Cold water went in the bottom of the aerated cooler and out the top, and the milk ran down the outside of the cooler and was cold by the time it got to the bottom. Then it ran into milk cans. The milk cans were placed in ice water in a tank about a yard high. We'd get ice out of Otter Lake before it was polluted as it is today. When you'd get a good winter, you could skate all over Otter Lake. I remember one time going out there – that's quite a ways from our farm – and Joe Glaicar came with a truck, and he tied a rope on the back and dragged us around the lake. You'd get ice up to three feet thick.

The lake supplied about 200 tons of ice in winter, and we took thirty tons for our own use, as we had no electricity until 1939. The warehouses needed to 'ice the boxcars' when they shipped produce. Each car had a hole in the top, and the ice would be placed in there over a false ceiling. Then Vernon got an ice plant, so the boxcars were iced there first and then brought back to Armstrong to be loaded.

Bottling the iced milk was the next step in the process.

We poured a can of milk into the top of the bottler. It bottled four quarts on one end and five pints on the other end. We put a milk crate on each end of the bottler and lined it up. A crate held twelve quarts or twenty pints. We pulled the handle down; the crate went up, pushed against rubber washers with a spring above them so they made a seal, and the milk ran into the bottles. We didn't have a capper. They were all capped by hand – the only time we touched the milk – cardboard caps with a pull tab. We'd put the crates back in the tank, bottles all underwater, of course, and we'd set the ice into the water on top. It was cold on the hands when you dipped in to pull the crates out in the morning. I was never a keeper of anything so we haven't got any of the milk tickets or the caps.

Milk producers had to meet acceptable standards of hygiene. Ross Lockhart carried on a running feud with one health officer over Springview Dairy's methods of production, which Ross maintained were sanitary.

The empty bottles went into one tank. We had a steam turbine with a brush on it, and every bottle went onto this brush, was cleaned, put into the rinse water and then into the crate upside down, and from there went into the steam room. A steam boiler heated water into steam and sent it into the steam room. Two rows of half-inch galvanized pipes with holes in them ran all around the inside of this room, which had ten-inch walls stuffed with sawdust and lined with galvanized sheet metal on the inside. The door was two inches thick. When we finished washing all the bottles and cans and milking machines, everything went into this room, and about sixty pounds of steam turned on. We never opened that room until we were ready to go milking in the evening. You couldn't touch the bottles, they were still that hot.

The district health inspector, Dr. Tennant, come out one day. Dad and he didn't get along – my father wasn't the easiest person to get along with – and Tennant says, "You get that stuff outside on a rack in the sunshine!" Dad says, "I don't think so, Tennant." Tennant says, "If you don't, I'll close you down!" Dad didn't do it. The next week the provincial area inspector come along and Dad told him the story. I guess Dr. Tennant got a talking-to.

Another time Tennant came out because he wanted to see us washing the equipment, but we had finished by the time he got there, and the steam had been turned into the steam room. Dad got Tennant right beside the door and then pulled it open. Never heard any more from him in that regard.

Dr. Tennant used to send samples of milk to Vancouver for testing the bacteria count. If it was under 10,000, you could put it on the market as whole milk without pasteurization. He was supposed to come to the dairy and draw three samples – one stayed with us, one stayed with him, and one went to Vancouver. [Instead] he always used to just grab a pint off the milk run in town. The last time he and Dad tangled, Tennant got a sample, and Dad says, "You keep that to yourself. I don't want to know what it is!" A couple of weeks later, Dad was walking along the street and met Tennant. "Tennant, what did that milk test?" "I didn't think you wanted to know!"

Delivering milk in summer was pleasant. In winter it was an ordeal. The Lockharts exchanged the democrat for a bobsleigh. *The runners on the front of the sleigh could rotate left and right and the runners on the back were rigid. A lot of cold days going to deliver milk in an open sleigh – we don't get the cold like we used to.* One day we came around the corner at Hassen's – they used to have a thermometer hanging on the wall there – and it registered minus 54 degrees Fahrenheit. At the firehall Vern McFarland had set a thermometer and it read minus 44. We went along to Harry Comber's – he was the official weather keeper at that time – and his thermometer said minus 38. Well, it was just the variance in the level of the land, the dampness, and it showed how quick the temperature could change.

A few years later I told one fellow how cold it was that day. "Oh," he says, "you're crazy. I've got Mrs. Henley's records." "Well," I says, "this was a good twenty years before Mrs. Henley started keeping records." Prior to Comber, Knight-Harris kept the records. Now where Comber's records went or Knight-Harris' records went, I don't know – but in those days we had cold weather!

Keeping warm and dry in cold weather was not easy.

The jean pants today are very expensive, and they are worn for graduation ceremonies and everything else. Back in those days jeans were the workingman's garb. They had two weights: an eight-ounce and a ten-ounce. The eight-ounce was ninety cents at the Co-op and the ten-ounce was a dollar. Now you'd think the ten-ounce would wear better, but they would get a crease in them, and it didn't matter if you ironed that crease or not, it stayed there, and the pants would gradually break along the crease. Besides that, as you tramped through the snow and slush, the bottoms would get wet, and you'd be walking with frozen stovepipes around your legs.

As the winters passed, Ross and Ralph devised ways to make the trip more comfortable. Customers always had to be quick in getting their milk off the doorstep.

We'd take the cab off the democrat and put it on the bobsleigh for cover. That was a lot warmer. Next we bought a little Coleman heater – a single burner – that we'd take inside with us to keep warm. But after it was set out, the milk would soon freeze if people didn't take it indoors. It would knock the cap off the bottle and you'd have this column of frozen Jersey cream. Vern McFarland lived over the old fire hall where he was the caretaker and he had a dog. And I remember delivering his milk – we went on Patterson, down Becker and along Patterson again – and by the time we got back to his place, the milk was frozen out of the bottle and his dog was licking it.

In the 1930s the Co-op always put a dance on for their patrons around the first part of November. This particular November the temperature nose-dived a seventy degree change in one day. It happened to be the day of the dance. Of course, in those times you didn't have antifreeze, and our old Model T Ford, along with half a dozen others, met their fate that night – froze up – broke the blocks – so from the remains of it we made a 'Bennett buggy.' A horse pulled it and it rode lower than a buggy because the wheels were smaller, but it was a lot easier to ride on and easier to pull because it had better springs and rubber tires.

But overall we had a good life. In the winter every Friday night there was a dance on one farm or another. I remember one New Year's Eve there were 101 in our house – that was common – not a big house – move the furniture out and away they went – a piano, or somebody on the fiddle and the accordion. We had a skating rink too for three or four years. Dad opened the irrigation ditches and let the water through into a piece of a back field that had a slope in it. It made a dandy rink. Then he realized that we were doing the work and the neighbours were doing the skating! "That's enough of that!" said Dad.

In the summer our farm always seemed to be the meeting place. We played ball in the back field so the neighbour kids would come and probably stay for supper – Mother always had a crew on Sunday night. Ourselves and the hired man made eight, and our friends besides. I don't know how she ever did it. But we always had lots of milk, and cream that was hard to pour out of the bottle. Bread and milk at night before you went to bed was a common thing in the early days – bread crumbled up with brown sugar and lots of cream – it was good. Jean calls it BABS, for short.

Farm life in Spallumcheen included participating in the Armstrong Fair. With their herd of purebred Jerseys, the Lockharts were a significant support.

Dad was instrumental in getting registered cattle into the area. There is a clipping in the museum from the Armstrong Advertiser about a carload of twenty-five registered Jersey calves that came in from the Coast. It listed all the sellers from the Coast but not the buyers here – Charlie Williamson, James McCallan, Frank Poole, Ross Lockhart…. I don't know why they weren't mentioned. The calves were unloaded at the ramp in front of the United Church and tied up to the hitching rail beside it and to trees in the church parking lot. They would become the foundation of our dairy herd. Dad always had good cattle and he was very active in the fair.

In fact, at one point in its early history, the Dairy Division had two chairmen: Lew Brydon in charge of the Ayrshires and Ross Lockhart, the Jerseys, as Ross had forceful opinions about how the division should be run.

He was Barn boss at the fair for quite a few years. And he'd tell you one story. The year before Dad was Barn boss, some exhibitors on horseback used to drive the beef cattle from the range and run them into the Show Barn – cattle that had never had a halter on or never been touched. They were nice-looking animals and in good shape, but wild! Once inside, the riders would chase them around and rope them – like a rodeo.

The following year Dad saw Mr. Hales coming with his beef, and he closed every door in the cattle barn. "No, you're not coming in here with all these registered animals." But the doors to the horse barn were still open, and the men drove them in there amongst all the stallions and mares and foals. I'm amazed that some of them didn't get damaged because not all the cattle were polled animals at that time. That was the last year that any beef came into the fair that wasn't on a halter. The final year we showed, I think we entered twenty-eight head. A sizeable number indeed.

On the last day of the fair there used to be a Livestock Parade. The exhibitors lined up with their animals and walked them around the oval in front of the grandstand and back to the barns. To amuse the spectators, the fair manager, Mat. Hassen senior, always made some pointed comments over the microphone about the owners and stock passing in front of him. This particular year we had six or seven female teachers including Jean – friends of my sisters – helping to lead our animals. Mat. says, "Ross Lockhart herd." Dead silence. The gals left him speechless.

There was a Jersey breeder in Vernon by the name of Chambers. He had been in India and been bitten by an insect or something and had sleeping sickness. He smoked a pipe. He'd be standing there in the Livestock Parade and go to sleep. He always led a Jersey bull – they can be mean! – and that bull would just stand there with him. We often wondered why he was never killed when it happened to him. He'd be standing there and his eyes would close for half a minute – never dropped his pipe.

Of course, Ralph participated in the fair too. *It wasn't 4H when I was growing up – it was Boys and Girls' Club work. I had the honour one year of winning the Oke Swenson Trophy. It was a nice trophy – on an oak frame, a beautiful plaque in the centre – something to win! And you got a keeper cup with your name on it. That year I had chickens, a great registered Jersey calf, and potatoes. So I came out with the highest points.*

The fair then was the last week in September. You'd go into the barns in the morning and there'd be hoarfrost hanging a foot or so from the ceiling. It was just like a rainstorm in there when that started to melt.

As the 1930s progressed, Ralph acquired more responsibility. He was a big, strong boy and enjoyed farm work. He was also the only son on the place. *When George got to be eighteen, he and Dad disagreed and he left. He went to the Coast and found a job down there for a fellow by the name of Jake Grauer. He had a big herd of Holsteins just off the airport in Vancouver – George worked there for a number of years.*

I'm not that tall – six feet – or used to be – and my brother George was six feet two. Dad was not a big man. He was about five foot seven and had a very slight build. Mother was taller than Dad by a couple of inches. When I was fourteen, I weighed 184 pounds, so I had no trouble at school. I was never a bully – take me as I am, but if you get in trouble with me, that's too bad.

The last two years I was in school, I didn't get back to class every morning until recess. I missed the first two periods because I delivered the milk by myself, took the rig home and then had to come back to school by bicycle. I'd hoof it back in the wintertime. Only two miles – it wasn't long – twenty to twenty-five minutes. Then I would ride the school bus home and do my chores. There were three buses. I wanted to ride Irwin Trudel's – I could have gone through the dip – 500 yards and I'd be home. Instead I had to ride Charlie Patten's bus. He'd let me off where the fruit stand is on Powerhouse Road – he wouldn't let me off at Creamery Road – so I had to walk back.

When Ralph was small, Creamery Road no longer boasted a creamery. In the late 1920s when livestock prices were very low, its absence enticed Ross Lockhart to add another aspect to his milk business.

After the Armstrong Creamery burned down in 1927, NOCA agreed to collect cream from the local farmers and haul it to Vernon to be processed. Pat Burns, a livestock buyer with packing plants in Alberta, had some connection with NOCA. Dad said, "No way is Pat Burns handling my cream." For one thing, Pat Burns didn't pay much for beef and pigs. I remember my father taking three 250-pound hogs to sell, and he was offered $1.25 for each one. "I'll take them back home first and knock them on the head!" And that's just what he did.

So Dad bought a truck and started a route, gathering up cream from local farmers who didn't want to ship through Burns and hauling it to Salmon Arm instead. He kept it up for a couple of years and then sold the business to A. Smith and Son, and an employee by the name of Archibald drove the truck for them for quite a long time.

In many ways 1939-40 was a watershed period for the Lockharts. Ralph applied for his driver's license, Ross agreed to install electricity on the farm – no more hand milking – and, after a short stay at home, George followed Evelyn's example and enlisted in the Second World War.

The government had brought in the driver's exam – it was just after the new post office opened in 1939. The exam was in three parts: a written test, a timing test, and a driving test. The whole exam took about twenty minutes to half an hour. About once a month the examiner came to town, rented a room in the old post office on Railway Avenue, and set up the replica of a car about three feet wide with pedals in it and flashing lights in front of the seat to record the time between taking your foot off the gas and shoving on the brake. You weren't allowed much time to react.

At the time we had an old '27 Pontiac. Claytons had gone into the automotive business in the building that is now the [Armstrong Spallumcheen] Museum and Art Gallery, and they sold Shell gas. They had brought in a mechanic by the name of Cecil Clark from the Coast, and he owed Dad sixty bucks or so. About that time milk was sixteen quarts to the dollar – almost 1000 quarts. Clark said, "Well, take the car."

I'd just turned 16. I was driving before that, of course, but I'd never driven Dad's 1935 Ford. It was off limits to us. My brother and I drove the Pontiac. Of course, Dad pulled a trick on me – he drove me in the Ford to take my driver's license.

A provincial man gave the test and he was a surly one, but I got along fine with him. It was a short test route. We came along in front of the museum and turned up the hill over the tracks [formerly the extension of Bridge Street] and you had to stop, and you weren't supposed to roll back more than a foot. Well, the cars weren't automatics and you weren't allowed to use the emergency brake, so you had to be real quick with the gears. Then we went on down to Patterson Avenue, past the United Church and back up on the other side of Railway Avenue and that was it. One thing I didn't do – the only mark he didn't put down – was that if a car was parked on the side of the road at the time you went by, you were supposed to blow your horn. I forgot. Apparently the hill on Bridge Street was supposed to weed out the novices while blasting the horn was a courtesy to pedestrians. After that I used to take the Pontiac to school, and two or three times a week I'd go to Hoover's on the way home for four or five sacks of grain to feed the milk cows.

Ralph had passed his driver's exam; installing electricity on the farm, however, became a test of wills between Ross and the West Canadian Hydroelectric Company at Shuswap Falls.

You see, the powerhouse was above our farm, and the power line to town came straight through the ravine to Rosedale Avenue. Because there was no road, nobody lived between Powerhouse Road and Rosedale, and that section of line was unprofitable. Instead, the company wanted the line to come up Creamery Road, where there were a lot of people, and then onto Powerhouse Road. That way they were getting some return for their investment.

Ideally, a person whose property was the farthest out was willing and able to pay for the power line to his place, and then intervening property owners could hook up to it without an expensive personal outlay. This practice caused some ill will.

Harry Grant, a neighbour, was in charge of making the sales for the company's power lines. He came to see Dad one day and says, "How about the power!" "How much?" "$700." "No way!" says Dad. "Well," Grant says, "your neighbours are going to be awful mad at you!" "Let the neighbours be mad if they want. When you bring the power up here and hook it to the house, you can go through and that's fine, but no $700." A couple of weeks later, Grant comes back. "We're going to put the power in." So the line went through and that was when we got electricity – 1939.

Just about the time the war started, George came home again determined to make money selling Serge milking machines. Well, I think the only one he sold was to Dad! Instead of a bucket attached to a long hose, a Serge milker hung on a strap around the cow's back – the cows didn't object to it while they were milking – and the teat cups and attachments were on the lid of the bucket. We had two units so we could milk two cows at once. It was a one hundred percent improvement.

Not everyone was enraptured with the advent of electricity,

particularly because rather than the normal, discontinuous 6-volt charge – *the wire that goes tick... tick... tick* – Ross Lockhart's electric fences carried a continuous charge which could be increased to suit the occasion.

Our electric fencer was controlled by a light bulb inside a little transformer we took from a radio. If you put a 25-watt bulb in, you got 2500 watts of dry voltage. (No amperage – it's the amperage that will kill you.) Put a 60-watt bulb in and you got 6000 watts. Generally we used a 60-watt bulb. You'd get a charge!

We had one young heifer that persisted in going out of the yard underneath the electric wire – she'd cringe – but she'd keep going. And by the time you got to the box to turn up the wattage, she'd have run back inside. One day she got out and I went around behind the machine shed so she wouldn't see me, and I put in a 100-watt bulb. Then I stepped into view. She came charging back into the yard and she hit that wire and it knocked her flat. She never went out again!

I remember one time Dick Rahn came up: "I forgot about that damn fence!" It was summer and he'd shot a deer and was bringing it home, and he'd walked into the wire. "I dropped that god-damned deer!" He probably fried it on the spot – had the meat all cooked before he got it home.

We had a neighbour, Alec Lamb, and he was almost blind, but he knew we had this fence. One time his son Joe came over and he was mad! "You get rid of that fencer. The old man almost killed himself!" Apparently, Alec had got down on his hands and knees to reach through and touch the wire to see if the current was on. It had rained and the ground was all wet, and when he touched the wire, he couldn't let go.

One of the stock, however, unwittingly made her life a series of nasty shocks. *One cow called Flo was a big animal and made me laugh. We had a hot wire along the irrigation ditch to protect the crop. Flo would walk along the fence swinging her big rump from side to side, and she'd swing into the hot wire. "BAARRH!!!" And the old fool would keep on walking along the fence and hitting it with every step – "BAARRH!!!" ... "BAARRH!!!" .... She never got the hang of it.*

Ralph never got the hang of his father's management style. Full of nervous energy, Ross interfered in his son's work and undermined his authority.

We were on ROP – Record of Production. In the barn we kept a big sheet with the days of the month down one side and each cow's name along the top. Every morning and night we recorded the weight of milk for each animal, so we had quite a bit of bookkeeping. About every six weeks the ROP inspector came to the farm to check our results. He'd draw a sample from each cow morning and night, put it in a little bottle, and the following morning spin it to separate the butterfat. He used a Babcock tester that could analyze the milk of four cows at a time. Then he sent our sheet off to Ottawa. You had to take him along afterwards to the next farm he was visiting.

Ottawa would keep track of production and award ROP. When you owned a cow that really produced, you received a certificate that made her worth a lot more. My job was feeding the cows, and Dad would come into the barn. "Oh, you haven't given that one enough." I had one cow really going for a record – he overfed her and she got sick – so that was the end of my record. He would interfere that way.

And he always felt he was short of time. If you had to make a repair out in the field, there was never time to take the tools back to the shop. You dropped them and went. Well, to me that wasn't right. The first set of wrenches I bought myself, I still have. But four hours of sleep a night was all he required. He'd work until ten o'clock at night, come in, maybe have something to eat, go to bed; he was up by four o'clock or earlier next morning.

There was no question that Ross worked himself hard and was an equally hard taskmaster. Sometimes his neighbours strained his patience.

We were in a water district, in today's terms, and we were the top ones, the last in line on the water distribution system. Dad went down to one woman below the hill and said, "We're out of water. Would you mind shutting your sprinkler off?" "Oh, okay." Still no water. He went back – she'd shut the sprinkler off but had the hose running!

The water right on our property was older than the City's water right, and when the City dammed the Devil's Pot, as the hole in the stream was named, we didn't have any water coming down the creek. So Dad went to complain. The response was "Oh, the hell with you, we've got the water." Dad said, "We'll see about that!" and visited the Water Commissioner in Kelowna. Shortly afterwards, the City ran a pipe from their water line across to ours and fed us water.

The Whitaker family also had some irrigation right on the creek. *The Whitaker boys, John and Foster, were good friends of mine and worked very hard. They used to be sent out at night to monitor flood-irrigation on their farm. They'd open up a hole in the ditch and then sleep on a coil of hay at the limit of an area with their bare feet on the ground. When the water hit their feet, they dammed up that part of the ditch and opened another hole farther along.* In summer they didn't get much rest.

Foster was a great runner. Once he was working in Oyama and wanted to come home, but the bus schedule didn't suit. So he ran all the way to Armstrong in a couple of hours – probably got here about the same time as the bus would have. He became reeve of Spallumcheen.

In 1945 consumers demanded pasteurized milk. Ross had been delivering raw milk since 1920. He decided to sell his milk delivery business to City Dairy, which was willing to undertake the new process. For the first time in twenty-five years, the Lockhart milk wagon vanished from Armstrong streets. Ralph was twenty-two. He enjoyed farming and thought that the market for their milk could be the Armstrong Cheese Factory, which had opened in 1938 and used raw milk to make cheese.

I worked in the cheese factory for a short time. One day the district inspector phoned from Kamloops and said he'd be there by five o'clock. He came, and he checked a pound of butter and there was water in it. It just happened to be a poor churning. "I'll be back tomorrow at eight o'clock and go through the rest." I got to work at seven the next morning and Joe Mullen was already there. He had re-churned the whole batch of butter so the inspector wouldn't find any water in it.

When we were in the milk delivery business, though, there was no warning – the inspector would just appear on your doorstep – so everything always *had to be clean. But you should have seen the go-round at the cheese factory that time the inspector said he was coming back! Oh, the brooms came out, the floors were polished, and it's the same now – they warn when they are coming. They should just drop in.*

Ralph found another interest – Jean Runnalls. Jean was a teacher who worked at the school in Ashton Creek. Her father was the United Church minister. *We went to the United Church, but I actually met Jean through my sister Hazel, who was very active in the church's young people's. There was a young people's camp down at Hurlbert on Okanagan Lake, and Hazel said, "Oh, my brother will take you down." By that time I had my own car – I was on my second one by that time – a '32 Ford Coupe – a snazzy little car, I thought, and I drove her down to the camp, which ran for ten days. Of course, I went back home – work to do. Jean tells me: "When I saw you, I thought you were the biggest man I'd ever seen!" I had a yellow shirt on and she couldn't believe it!*

In 1947 they eloped. Jean felt her family couldn't afford the fuss of a wedding, and Ralph thought anything Jean wanted was fine with him. *We went to Salmon Arm and got married by the United Church minister at the manse. It was a Sunday. A friend of mine stood up for me as best man. Jean was by herself. Then we went down to the Hudson Café and had dinner. Nobody knew.* Jean's parents were predictably horrified. Her father said, *"No muss, no fuss, no wedding presents!"* Her mother said, *"You've made your bed, now lie in it, and don't come crying to me!"* However, with the passage of a little time, Mrs. Runnalls admitted, *"You always said you were going to elope."*

The couple moved into the Lockhart house and Ralph continued working the farm with his father. However, Ross Lockhart was capable of surprises too.

He took the notion to sell the herd and he never said a word to me. He sold it in 1948 to Bill Savage from Ladner. He was a Jersey breeder and Dad knew all of them. Bill came up to me at the Armstrong fair and asked me about it. It was the first news I'd heard. "Oh," he says, "I guess I spoke out of turn."

I would have kept the herd to ship milk to the cheese factory and to NOCA. Dad wanted to sell half the herd regardless of what I'd say. We farmed by a team of horses, and he figured he'd maybe get a tractor with the money. Dad says to me, "You've got lots of time to see what you want to do – as long as you let me know by tomorrow morning whether we sell the milking half or the heifers or the whole works." Well, he made me so angry I said, "Sell the whole works."

The farm had a herd of registered cattle, and he didn't get what he should have. At that time if you had a cow that was very good, you could get it classified. It cost a bit for classification but once you did, if that animal dropped a bull calf, at birth he was worth 1500 bucks. This one particular cow had a bull calf with her. So when Bill Savage took the herd to the Coast, the first thing he did was have her classified. So she's $3000, the calf's $1500, and that's almost what he paid for the whole herd.

Once the herd had gone, Ross saw no reason to keep the farm. On this issue Ruth sided with her husband, and Ralph found himself the odd man out. *I wanted the farm but Dad wouldn't let me have it. Otherwise, I'd probably still be there. He wanted the money out of it. Mom didn't want me to have anything to do with the farm either. She thought Dad would interfere too much – never give up control. But I was kind of allergic to the hay dust anyway – when I was moving hay, my eyes would get so sore.*

Right after the herd was gone he sold the farm to a fellow by the name of Earl Robinson, who farmed down on the Coast and had married a girl called Betty Downs. The Downs had been a neighbour – lived here for years. Ted Downs' farm was right where the fruit stand is on Powerhouse Road. Since Ted Downs only had a small acreage, he grew a few potatoes. One year he thought he'd really make money. He planted about four or five acres of rhubarb. He thought he could sell it to the packing houses in town. No, they didn't want it – didn't have a market for it – everybody had rhubarb in the garden. It was a disaster.

Married for just over a year, Ralph and Jean began cobbling together a life that didn't involve the Lockhart farm. They knew the change would not be easy. Jean says, *We promised each other we would never say, "If only we'd done differently." Decisions are made and you live with them. You can't go back and change them. Why get yourself all worked up?* Whenever they began to dwell on the past, Jean reminded, *We're not talking "If only...."* They had already started a family, which eventually grew to six. Lynne had been born while they were still living on the farm.

Jean remembers: *It was a hot, hot summer, and on this particular Sunday the whole family had decided to go for a picnic at Shuswap Falls. We went and had lunch and I wasn't feeling very perky – my back was a bit sore – but I really didn't know what having babies was like – I'd only read about it. About three o'clock in the afternoon I said to Ralph, "I think you'd better take me home." We stopped at the hospital on the way, and the doctor said, "You'd* better stay." So Ralph said, "I'll go home to do chores and come back." By the time he did, we had a baby! For the first one, that was exciting – and she was about three weeks early! Maybe the back pain was worse than I had thought!

After Lynne was born, Ralph and Jean began a series of moves as Ralph undertook a series of jobs. His strength and stamina, and Jean's independence and fortitude were put to use.

We rented a cabin in Green Meadow Auto Court down where the John Deere building is on the highway. That's where the City Dairy farm was. Myers Fransden built the auto court and about 1950 moved it to Salmon Arm. You could rent by the month, so we lived there first. Then, of course, Jean and I tried farming for a year on a little property at the end of McLeod Road [Chickadee Ridge Miniatures]. We put in about two acres of potatoes and thought we were going to make money on them.

That summer was a hot one similar to this [2003], and I got a job on the highway on a blacktop gang. Another chap and I were on the mixer. We were fourteen feet off the ground. The mixer was below us and the hot gravel and sand were above us. It came out of the dryer into these tanks and we mixed it by weight – a hot mix. He put in the coarse gravel, I put in the sand, then he put in the asphalt, and we'd watch until it was mixed and dump it into the truck below. It was a 'batch mix' plant at that time. About five batches made a truckload. Every once in a while the batch would catch fire and when it did, we'd just dump it into the truck and away he went and unloaded it burning on the road.

That's how hot the stuff was. Once a rock came down on me and hit me in the neck, and before I got it out of my clothes, I was burned all down my chest. Hot, dusty and dirty – oh, man! Jean's washtubs were black with grime and tar. *Today the stuff goes in one end of a big mixer and comes out the other end and nobody touches it.*

We worked at Enderby, Vernon, Westbank. The plant was on

wheels and they hauled it to the job. I got ninety cents an hour and Allen Messer got ninety-five because he was the head man on the mixer and had the extra lever to pull. We worked a twelve-hour day at least, sometimes longer, to get a job done. When we worked in Enderby, I could come home every day. When we were in Westbank, we stayed in a packing house on the second floor. They put up cots and fed us in the café. We paid so much off our cheque, of course.

The foreman came along one day and said, "Let's see how much tonnage we can get out of these guys." We wanted a raise, so that day we produced a record 1208 tons of mix. He never said thanks or bought us a beer or anything. So after that we couldn't seem to get over 600 tons. I quit, and the gang went over to Sorrento, but they couldn't get over 500 tons a day.

That fall the potato crop looked promising. *They were doing great!! Just before they were ready to dig, we went out one morning and overnight they had all gone black. The blight had hit them and wiped out the crop.*

As Jean recalls, she and Ralph had better luck with babies.

The next one was Ross and he was born in February. We were living out on the little place at McLeod Road – it was also a Sunday, and it was 40 below zero. Ralph couldn't get the old truck to start. He worked all morning and I said, "I think you'd better do something because this is getting closer." So he said, "I'll go out and try one more time, and if it won't start, I'll go over to Dave Hope's and get a tractor and pull it." Fortunately, the truck started, but it had snowed about fifteen inches that night, and being Sunday there wasn't a road plowed. We bucked the drifts all the way to town and Ralph kept saying, "If you don't have to go, I'll sure be mad at you!" (which he has listened to now for fifty-seven years or so!).

Anyway, we made it to my parents' place on Becker Street where my mother was supposed to look after Lynne. But when I dropped her off, I discovered that Mom was in the hospital having some mi-

nor surgery done, as this baby was not due for another couple of weeks. We got stuck for a while backing out of the driveway, and then we went around by Wolfenden Terrace but couldn't make it up that little hill to the hospital – no tracks anywhere – so we went over to Okanagan Street and onto Rosedale, where a vehicle was stuck right in the middle of the road! The fellow said, "Just give me a push and I'll be out of here." "I don't have time!!" said Ralph. And we backed up to Okanagan and came at the hill from the other direction where there was a better run at it. Twenty minutes after I got to the hospital there was a baby!

Still believing that farming was his best suit, Ralph decided to work for Dave Hope. In addition, however, he took jobs hauling for local transfer outfits and was often away from home.

We moved in October over to the little cabin that Dave and Marion Hope had on their farm and worked for a year with his herd of Jerseys. Dave's health was never strong, and I had worked for him as well when we were on the little farm. Dave's furnace ran on cordwood heat, so I cut fourteen cords of wood for him in the bush. That winter it was cold. The house we were in, if you left a bucket of water on the counter at night, it was frozen solid in the morning. Six weeks at 20 below. You couldn't see out the windows for frost on the panes, and the ceiling was covered with frost. Dave and Marion knew what that was like. They had lived in the house themselves when the Pooles were alive. *Beautiful sunshiny weather though.*

Jean remembers a comparable winter in Prince George before she was married: *If you dropped water on the floor, it froze instantly.* In these days most houses had no central heating. To combat the cold both outdoors and within, the lucky ones tended to eat heavy meals larded generously with butter and cream and lavishly endowed with sugar for body warmth and energy. *I'd bake a two-layer cake just covered with gooey icing, and the two of us would eat half of it at a sitting.*

That same winter their third baby arrived, again on a Sunday. Again Jean was the centre of the action:

Anne was born in January. Ralph had come home for the weekend, and we had driven out to see Marion and Dave Hope. On the way home we had a flat tire at the top of the hill on Mountain View Road and had to stop and change it. By this time the birth was imminent. *He dropped me off at the hospital and said, "You'd better stay here." He was supposed to be going back to work the next day but instead he had to stay home and look after the other two.*

Trucking became a major part of Ralph's life. His jobs for Motor Transfer and later for Valley Auction in some ways replayed on a larger scale his years on the milk run: he roamed about and knew the ground intimately. *I used to travel pretty well all over the area. One day I had to go away over beyond Nakusp for a load of cattle. That was the farthest.*

Doug Murray owned Motor Transfer then. It sat on Patterson where the City works yard is today. Doug got hold of me. "Could you come for a day?" "Sure." Six weeks later I was still working there. Doug was under the weather quite a bit. When he'd been butchering, he'd stuck a knife in his leg, gangrene set in and they had to cut his leg off. So he just had a stump – he was in a lot of pain because he always had boils and sores at the end of it. Sometimes I wouldn't see him at the office for three or four days. Sometimes he'd come in but he wouldn't be much help. So I more or less ran the place for a long time – had to open the safe and conduct business.

There was plenty of work for trucks back then – lots of people hired trucks: Chinese garden transfer was all so much per hour; grocery delivery from the Co-op and from Phillips and Whitehouse, so much – you could phone in your order and have groceries delivered to the house; rail express, so much per month. In one job during that six weeks, Shug Wardrop and I loaded twenty-eight rail cars of hay and straw for Buckerfield's to ship. (Mostly they were loaded right in town above the bridgehead – roughly across from the bank.) We went around to the different farms and trucked in the hay and straw. They were all pressed bales and averaged 125 pounds. I guess the heaviest bale I ran into was 273 pounds. There's a knack for handling them. These wimpy bales they have now – you stick a hay hook into one and it falls apart! Shug ended up as manager of the Credit Union for quite a few years.

Then Len Wood bought Motor Transfer. He also bought the building uptown that had been the tire shop at the Shell station [Valley First Credit Union] and operated out of there. I worked for him for quite a while – did all the contract work he had bid on.

One trip for Motor Transfer proved unforgettable.

Motor Transfer had a truck. Oh, that son of a gun would let you down, you never knew where. Once I was going to Grand Forks to deliver a load of cattle – Jean came with me that time – we took off about six o'clock in the evening. We got down to Kelowna. The truck quit. Got it going again. Got to Greenwood at four o'clock in the morning – the old truck just about out of gas – so I woke a fellow up at the gas station. He wouldn't take the credit card I had, so I was left with only a little bit of cash for food.

At Eholt, a railway stop five or six miles east of Greenwood, the truck quit again. A Greyhound bus come along and stopped: "What's the problem?" Said he'd get a mechanic to come out from Grand Forks. We didn't get up the road a mile until it quit again. So this is getting on to ten o'clock in the morning. We were sitting there, and a woman came out of the bush and took Jean off to her house for a cup of coffee. No coffee for me because I had to wait for the mechanic. After sixteen hours on the road, the cattle weren't feeling so good either.

Anyway we kept chugging along. Old truck would go and quit … go and quit…. We got down to the bottom of the hill going into Grand Forks, and there's this elderly Doukhobor walking along. We passed him…. He passed us…. We passed him again…. He passed us. He said, "I think, better you walk!" Of course, that didn't help matters at all!

In Grand Forks they took the gas tank out of the truck, drained it, checked everything – it ran pretty good then. I had to deliver these cattle, then pick up another load to bring back. The district agriculturalist over there was supposed to have the cattle all ready for me in one spot to pick up. He hadn't done that. So I had to run around picking up some cattle here and some cattle there. I finished loading about eleven o'clock at night.

By now Ralph and Jean had been thirty hours without sleep. We drove the truck to a hotel, parked it and went to bed. After an hour the manager woke us up. "You've got to move those cattle – they're disturbing everybody." So we took off again and got up to the flat above Grand Forks, and I said, "Jean, I can't go any farther. I've got to stop." So I lay down and put my head in her lap, but in about five minutes I was wide awake and we were moving again.

We had the worst experience, though, on the bridge that used be at Skaha Lake. A gasoline truck came up fast behind us, and I guess he was running for the ferry at Kelowna. Gasoline trucks had to take a special ferry – it only ran twice a day – and he passed me on the bridge. My side mirror scraped along the entire length of his tank – it could have exploded – and the side of our cattle rack gouged a slice about four feet long out of the bridge. If he'd forced us over another inch or two, we'd have been over the edge with the load of cattle. I don't know how he didn't kill us. We were pretty shaken up. Sometime later we heard a news report of a fatal accident on the Hope-Princeton highway, and we wondered if it was him.

I was supposed to stop in Kelowna on the way back and pick up a bunch of pigs, which were going to run around inside the truck underneath the cattle. Fortunately, the pigs weren't ready when I got there. That truck ran perfectly all the way back. Then Ernie Hallam took it on the next trip and it did the same thing to him. He was a mechanic and he couldn't figure it out. Luckily, not all Ralph's trucking jobs were so tangled in frustration and peril. Perhaps as in the naval superstition, a woman on board a motor transfer brought bad luck. On the other hand, on that trip Jean may have been Ralph's angel.

Several years had passed since Ross Lockhart had sold the farm and left Armstrong. In Haney in the Fraser Valley, Ross sold Fuller brushes for two or three years. Then he worked in Spence's Bridge as cook at a café owned by his daughter Irma and her husband. *Dad was a good cook although I never remember him in the kitchen for that purpose at home.* After Ruth suffered a severe heart attack, they moved back to Armstrong where their friends were, and Ross decided to go into the business of contracting on the highways. He worked for a contractor for a short time putting up guardrail and fence, saw how it was done, and then got a contract himself. He asked Ralph to join him in R.G. Lockhart & Son Contracting Ltd.

When I told Len Wood I was going to work for Dad, he said, "Well, you might as well. I'm losing money on everything you do anyway." But it was all contract work – Len could only make what he had bid. We worked all day, drove all night, worked all day. We handled a lot of coal at that time, and when I wasn't working with Dad in the winter, I was the first one he'd call to shovel coal. That was a dirty job! If we could afford it, when we'd order a [rail]car of coal, we'd have it oiled to keep the dust down. That would cost another dollar a ton. A carload of lump coal came in at forty tons in a car, and you delivered that around – a ton here and half a ton there – all by hand – shovelled it with a big scoop shovel out of the boxcar into the truck, and then shovelled it out of the truck into the coal bin wherever you delivered it.

Highway fencing required both heavy labour, which Ralph could provide, and exact measurement. Because early guardrails included pre-drilled iron beams and curved plates, the accurate placement of posts was essential.

Dad and I put in guardrail all over a good portion of BC from Burnaby to north of Prince George and points in between. It was *all post-and-beam construction. You'd dig a hole by hand four feet deep to set in an eight-inch square post in a frame that was sixteen feet long. The post would go in the centre of the frame and had to be accurate within 1/1000th of an inch. If the hole was four feet wide, I was spread-eagled over it because the post had to be plumb and the iron beams level and not angling up and down along the guardrail. Brackets to hold the beams fit on the post and were spring steel so that when vehicles hit, there would be some 'give' to it. Most guardrails now are concrete. The last ones we put in disappeared this past spring [2003] along Wood Lake.*

The easiest fencing was for the PGE railway (Pacific Great Eastern, also known as Please Go Easy, or PG Eventually, or Pig, Goat and Elephant) north of Prince George because you didn't use a tape – you just paced out twenty or twenty-five feet and put in a post – whereas for the government the posts had to be exactly sixteen and a half feet apart, or a rod, and you had to trim the posts off on an angle with a chainsaw. Railway fence was Class A fence – straight Page wire – little squares like chicken wire. Highway fencing was Class B fence because it was Page wire with one strand of barbed wire above it. In both cases you just stapled the wire to the posts along each 300 yards and then tightened it with a tractor.

When rock prevented the drilling of a post-hole, Ross and Ralph were required to build an A-frame, set the post in the centre with a support on each side, and secure the base with rock. They encountered some opposition when they began to fence along the L&A Ranch south of Armstrong.

The government plan called for a twelve-foot two by six to brace each side of the post and a load of rock. The manager of the L&A Ranch said, "You're not putting in those stupid things that way. Only four-foot supports – that's all that's going in." He wanted shorter braces because of the cattle ranging there. The government specs also called for six-foot jogs in hilly areas, and L&A Ranch was hilly in places. "You're not going through my property unless you eliminate the jogs." So we made the jogs three feet wide. We had a little engineer with us and he didn't like it, but he had to go along with it to get the fence built. Dad and I worked on fencing for quite a number of years.

During this time their family was growing, and Ralph and Jean needed more room. Jean remembers that the drama associated with getting her to the hospital on time never ceased:

We had moved to the old house on the hill above Wood Avenue. Kay was born on a Saturday morning and Ralph happened to be home because it was a weekend. At seven a.m. I said, "I think I need to go to the hospital." My sister Joyce was supposed to come and look after the kids, but she was working at Marion Hope's for the month because Margaret had been born three weeks before. I phoned Joyce anyway and asked her to come right over. She did. Ralph and I only got as far as Park Drive when the car ran out of gas. His folks lived across where the Kin RV Park is now, so he scooted over there, got his Dad's car and got me to the hospital with not much time to spare.

When Garth came, we were still in that house. Ralph was away working and my mother had come up from the Coast to help out. She had left my dad and my sisters, who were going to university, living on their own, and she kept saying to me, "You hurry up. I've got to go home. Your dad's there alone with no one to look after him." Since Garth was a few days early, all the people we had lined up to take me to the hospital were not available, and my mother was phoning around desperately trying to find somebody. At that point she had the other four to look after as well. Jean was too busy holding her stomach. *Finally she got Ken Bell. We flew out of there and bounced over the railroad tracks, and I said, "Ken, you can slow down; it's not quite that desperate." I can still hear him: "You're not having that baby in my car." By this time I had a reputation!*

When it was Tannis' turn, we were living in a small house down the hill behind the cheese factory, and Mother said, "I'm not coming up until that baby is almost there." So she arrived the day before.

Of course, I had somebody staying with me at night because again Ralph was away. When I woke up that morning, I said to Mom, "I don't feel too well." And she said, "You're off to the hospital!" She'd never driven our big, old car, so on the way I'm giving her driving lessons! She left me there and nothing happened, and I kept saying, "I want to go home!" "No, you've got the last bed and if you leave, somebody else will come in and take it." Tannis arrived about seven that night. She completed the family.

Meanwhile, Ralph's next adventure was logging, and there he had the opportunity to use both his strength and his ingenuity.

After 1961 there wasn't much road construction – it just dried up. So in 1962 we bought our first new long-logger – a 1962 Hayes – and we hauled out of Christian Valley into Greenwood. We hauled a lot to Penticton too because it was the same mill, and some to Rock Creek mill. At that time everything was done with tongs – one log at a time. I worked for Walter Palm and Eric Cox. Cox had a heel boom for loading logs. He could grab one or two logs at a time so that the balance would send one end of the log under the tongs and he could swing the boom where he wanted it.

The Hayes was a very popular truck – the plant was in Vancouver. In 1976 they quit making them, but quite a few of them are still around. The bunks were eight foot six inches long. The bunk sat on a pivot plate with a pin to it so it could turn as the truck went around a corner. Then the trailer was set the same way. Two bunks were needed to carry a load of forty-foot logs: one attached to the truck and one to the trailer – and a 'reach' attached the two together [Truck, bunk, reach, trailer, bunk]. Stakes up the side held the logs.

The logs were loose – you'd 'trip' the front stake and then go to the back and 'trip' the back stake, and the logs would roll off the truck. Then you would have to try to remove the logs from the stakes so you could drive off for another load. That was a lot of work. Besides that, the stakes weighed a couple of hundred pounds or more, and you had to swing them up by hand and hook them on a cable.

Then I heard about spring-loaded stakes that popped back up, and I found out how it was done. I was working in Princeton, and when I came home one weekend, I had the machine shop spring-load the stakes on my truck. On Monday the guys couldn't believe it. When I went back the following week, half of them had spring-loaded their stakes. Then they came up with a 'gut wrapper' – one 5/8-inch cable around a load with a trip chain on it.

After that I went down to Kelowna, and up to Barriere and hauled logs there. The logs were cut either from Crown grants or timber berths. Timber berths were forestland given to the railway. For example, we hauled from a timber berth up the mountain at Silver Creek, and in five miles there were twelve switchbacks – it was steep! Now, where's the railway? Salmon Arm was the closest one. At that time I was hauling for Smith sawmill when they were right in town here.

Fernie Vandenborre was the road foreman for Smith sawmill, and if Fernie could get the bulldozer down the mountain and make a turn, that was a switchback. And I'd be coming down these switchbacks with a big load of logs. I had to back up on most of them. I was coming down one day and I didn't make the corner, and I backed up and broke two axles. And there I sat – nobody could get down or up. Of course, no radios then.

When Crown Zellerbach bought Smith out, I hauled for them quite a long time. By 1975 I had traded in my Hayes truck and got three others. Once the boys got out of school, Ross drove one, Garth drove one, and a son-in-law drove the third. The name was Lockhart Contracting. It was a good life. I always enjoyed it.

Deals were still made on a person's word or a handshake.

I ordered a 1970 Hayes truck in Kamloops, and when I went to pick it up, I asked the shop foreman to install the 'self loader' I had asked for. It was a pin placed underneath the cable at the centre of the 'reach' so that the cable would pull at an angle instead of on *the level – less stress on the equipment. He said he'd have to ask his boss. "No," I says, "I want it done. If you don't do it, I can walk away. I signed no order, signed nothing." "Well," he says, "you're the first man I know that's ordered a truck in here and didn't have a contract." The dealer had brought the truck in with the specs I needed and never asked for a contract. That truck cost $29,060.60, but now the same set-up would be about $180,000. The old tractor I use was around $2900 in 1952. Buy the same horsepower today and it's about $70,000 to $80,000.*

With the boys handling the logging, Ralph went to work for Valley Auction, just south of Armstrong. *I worked there until 1987.* In one respect he had come full circle. He was once again handling livestock.

I'd go out on Wednesday and collect a load and bring it in. People would haul cattle from Vanderhoof to Armstrong instead of to Kamloops because they got two or three cents a pound more here. It was a better market, and the cattle could be sold in small lots – one or two instead of fifteen to a pen, for example – and would, therefore, bring a better price. One fellow would go to the Kamloops sale on Tuesday, buy cattle, and then sell them here on Thursday and still make money.

We had five-foot sticks for cattle prods, and if you took care, there was never any problem. The only time I got in difficulty I was moving cattle in the ring. This old cow got upset and came at me. I had the stick pointing to the ground, and she got her head against it and started shoving. One of the buyers, Frank Dangel, slapped his hat against the ring and she jumped back, and I ran in behind the iron partition. Open the door and let her go! You never know exactly what they are going to do.

On certain occasions Jean may have expressed similar sentiments about the children:

Ralph wasn't home very much – he could be gone for two or

three weeks at a time – and I pretty well had to raise the kids. There were two things I promised myself. When they got into a little trouble, I never said, "Wait 'til your father gets home!" I dealt with it myself because I didn't think it was fair that when he did come home, he should hear all these problems. And the other thing we had to clamp down on was bringing presents with him because it got to the point where it wasn't "Hi, Dad," but "What did you bring me, Dad?" So he'd bring them something once in a while as a surprise.

I did use the strap occasionally. When you're dealing with six children, things can get out of hand. I was raised that when you did something bad, there were consequences. Ross would not come home from school on time. I had the rule that you be home from school by four o'clock, report in, tell me what you were going to do, and then you could go ahead. Everyday he was late and I'd give him a lecture. One day when I had the window open, Bobby Vliet and Ross were coming home, and Bobby says, "You're late, Ross, you're going to catch it!" And Ross says, "My mother never does anything – she just talks." Well, I was so mad at myself! This kid by now is pretty near six feet tall – he's looking down on me – and I remember taking the strap off the top of the fridge and giving him a whump across the bum. And he stood there with this silly grin on his face and patted me on the head and said, "It's okay, Mom." And you know, he was never late again! That was a good lesson for me.

We as a family had a good time and the kids are all very close to each other. They never really fought. They support each other when the need arises. The youngest one was the hardest to raise because she was spoiled by the older kids. They'd soothe her if we gave her the dickens for something. The day that Tannis started school, I went back to teaching – this time at Kindale. I said, "Well, Tannis, I won't be able to take you to school, you know." "Oh, that's okay, I know where to go." She was very independent and always has been.

When Ralph and Jean were living on Wood Avenue, their landlord owned fifty acres between Highland Park Road and Schubert Road. Jean asked him if he'd sell us an acre. "Oh, I guess I'll sell it at the side of the field." So we bought the acre – five bucks here and five bucks there. That's the way we paid for it. And what we paid was all done by the shake of a hand. If he'd died before it was paid for, we'd have been out! But he lived, and then we built up here.

They moved into their unfinished house at 3810 Schubert Road in 1958. The house wanders within tall evergreens. Added to as the need or fancy arose, it feels tranquil. Ralph's beautifully finished antique furniture and Jean's handmade quilts meld the past with the present.

We didn't cut down a tree that we didn't have to. We had a back porch off the kitchen that used to rub on a nice one. Lots of people said, "Why don't you take the tree down?" Why would we want to take it down? So we moved the back door and took down the porch!

On Tuesday mornings Ralph and Jean work with other archivists at the Armstrong Spallumcheen Museum on Pleasant Valley Road. Their object is the preservation of the history and culture of the area. Ralph's memory is on constant call.

The other day a lady came into the museum asking for information about the Municipality. Someone had told her that Harding Road "was and always had been" the boundary between the City and the Municipality. That was totally wrong. Ralph is holding a map of Armstrong. *The first fellow that pre-empted that farm had the name of Hunter, and then there were various people on it afterwards, and now it's all houses except for the southeast corner. Here at this jog at Maundrell Avenue was George Elliot's lot, and the municipal boundary went right through it. His lot and chicken house were in the Municipality, and his house was in the City.*

At that time the municipal yards were in town on Warner Avenue right across from the elementary school. Now the City and the Municipality used to work together on snow plowing, etc. The City would plow south of the jog (in the Municipality), and the Munici-

pality would plow Schubert Road (part of which was in the City) on their way out of town. So they traded work, and from Maundrell Avenue south as far as Harding Road became City property.

City council cannot successfully bury its errors because Ralph can resurrect them.

It was real wet here many years ago. When the railway came through in 1891-92, they built a trestle across the bog from where the pellet plant is on Patterson Avenue up as far as Centennial Hall. Bridge Street commemorates this history. Then when Deep Creek was dredged, the land drained, and the trestle was no longer needed. At that point, before the railway filled it in, city council was asked if it wanted an underpass built there, so people could drive through with a wagon. "Oh, we'll never need an underpass." All of the woodwork, all those piles and everything, is still there underneath the ground, and the fire hall has always been on one side or the other of the tracks! They had the opportunity but didn't take it.

Armstrong, though still a small town, is different in one way from Ralph's boyhood memories of it:

I used to know everybody. Now I don't know anybody.

Ralph Lockhart at age sixteen

Chapter Three

A Tribute to Ellie

Janet Marion (Hilliard) Coldicott

Hilliard Family's Neighbours in Deep Creek

N ↑

It was a hard time for women. The man was 'boss of all I survey.' Nowadays they say, "Oh, we had a fight!" But there was no fighting in those days. The mother just went around it – whatever was happening. Mother used to say, "The less said, the sooner mended." And the women worked.

From her father Janet has inherited her height – *he was an inch under six feet* – her striking good looks, and her pride; from her mother, her warmth and grace, and her artist's eye and skill. In the living room a still life glows – *it's the only one I have left* – and on the table a dozen lace-edged, hand-sewn, white lawn handkerchiefs lie in stages of completion – *I like a handkerchief in my pocket.*

Janet was a middle child. Yet the lengthy spacing between her sibling groups gave her both a taste of being the baby and a longer apprenticeship in being responsible for others.

I was the middle of thirteen years. Ruth and Ethel were about seven years older than I was, and my two little brothers about seven years younger. I was born in Vernon on September 8, 1914, in a house just about where the Village Square is, near the tracks. My parents had come from the Kitchener-Waterloo area in Ontario. I think Mother worked in a shirt factory, making collars and such. She was Ada Ruthella Graybill but they called her Ellie. She was the second youngest in a family of five girls, and her mother died when she was seven. There was a little brother too, but he died early of 'water on the brain' – I don't think they knew in those days – it was just something to say. Mother's father, Levi Graybill, was mayor of Waterloo. I went back once for Aunt Claribel's funeral, and Cousin Catherine, who lived nearby, showed me from her window where

Grandpa had lived. She told me, "In all my lifetime I have never heard anything but goodness of your Grandfather Graybill."

Levi Graybill did not remarry until his children were adults, but he had strong family support in raising his children. His deceased wife's parents, the Wegenasts, lived next door, and George and Hattie Wegenast, his brother- and sister-in-law, were in the neighbourhood.

George had some authority in the family. He had arranged to have his niece Florence's crossed eye fixed. *He had it stitched in place to look straight ahead. The eye was blind, of course, but she was taught to turn her head, not her eyes, when she was spoken to, so both her eyes would be looking at you.*

Great-uncle George Wegenast was the managing director of Mutual Life Insurance in Waterloo, and he and Great-aunt Hattie had no children – that *was beneath him. Uncle George didn't like Dad at all.*

Brock Hilliard was a lineotype operator by trade and worked for the *Waterloo Chronicle*. The Wegenasts were professional people – two of Ellie's sisters, Florence and Claribel, were nurses, Ethel was a stenographer, and their father, the mayor. George himself lived in a substantial house and had impressive business credentials. Brock, he felt, didn't measure up.

Grandpa Graybill never interfered with Mother's choice. He was courting a German lady – a widow who didn't speak any English – and he came home one night and Dad and Mother were hugging in the stairwell. Without a glance at them, he hung up his cane and went on up to bed. The next day he said casually, "Oh, where's Brock? I haven't seen him around for a while."

Dad came out to work in the prairie to earn enough to get married and when he got to Calgary, somebody rolled him and took all his money, so he couldn't go back home. Uncle George wouldn't have been surprised. *He found a job on a newspaper in the Kootenays near Greenwood, in what used to be called Phoenix – a mining place that's now all covered with trees – saved his money, moved to Vernon, and worked on the Vernon News. Then he sent the money for Mother to come out. She stuffed it into her sock and told no one what she was up to.*

Uncle George arranged for Mother to go to Boston to get her nursing certificate. The family saw her off, but instead of going to Boston she headed for British Columbia. She came by train as far as Revelstoke, and Dad came up from Vernon to meet her, but when her train got in at two o'clock in the morning, he wasn't at the depot. The conductor walked her over to the hotel. "Yes," said the clerk, "his name is right here." They were married the same day.

After the ceremony Mother wired Grandpa to say where she was. He was especially fond of her, and Aunty Florence said he had been walking the floor ever since the Boston hospital had sent a telegram to say she hadn't arrived. Being young, she hadn't realized the hospital might contact her father or how worried he would be.

Ellie remembered her first sight of the Rockies. *She had never seen a mountain before. Of course the train had a steam engine, and the whistle resounded so strangely in those mountains that she wondered where she was coming to.*

They came back to Vernon to a little house that was once on 7th but is now 32nd Street. Ruth was born there. Then a wonderful job opportunity arose to print the day's proceedings for the state government of Oregon – night work, as they had to be in print by the following morning – and the family moved to Salem, Oregon, where Ethel was born.

Unfortunately, Ellie's weak lungs could not withstand the damp climate of the Pacific west coast. *It rained and it rained and it rained.* Brock resigned his job with regret and moved Ellie and his daughters back to the drier climate in Vernon.

They settled into a two-storey house below the cemetery. That was the place I first remember. Aunt Claribel came out to be with my mother for the delivery, but I was in a hurry and just about landed on the floor. She, of course, had brought all her nurse's uniform and she ended up doing the job in her dressing gown! I guess I was the last baby she delivered.

Ellie had wanted to name her little daughter Mary Jane after Brock's mother, but her sister tactfully suggested Janet Marion, which alluded to but reversed the two names, and also permitted a tribute to Claribel's best friend, Janet. *I was glad she did. I didn't like Mary Jane.*

The family enjoyed Vernon. They made friends. Ellie bought a *Mason and Risch* piano, and Ruth and Ethel took piano lessons from Mr. Temple. Ruth became proficient. Ethel was found to be too young and was allowed to give it up.

Mother believed that every child should have an 'accomplishment.' Ruth's was the piano, Ethel's was singing, and mine was elocution. A coloured photograph shows twenty-year-old Janet in recitation on stage at the United Church young people's in Kamloops: a tall, dark beauty in a slender gown, one bare arm sweeping dramatically above her head, the other gesturing afar. When the boys were born, Douglas would *play the piano 'somewhat' while Donald accompanied him on a small violin, a lady's violin, that my Dad held on to. I saw that violin hanging on the wall in Douglas' son's house, Brock Hilliard, Dad's namesake.*

My mother was a very, very energetic person. She worked hard and was ambitious. Over the years in Vernon she acquired three cows, Nellie and Spotty were two of them, and on their way to school my sisters would deliver in lard buckets fresh milk straight from the cow to her customers. My dad purchased two light horses, Lucy and Brownie, and a McLaughlin buggy in which they used to drive to the Methodist Church. I can remember Ruth telling me how nice Mother looked when she went to church. I was christened by Reverend Vance.

Mother also had some chickens. One day I was playing out in the barnyard and I got some chicken wire stuck in my hand. Of course, the girls put it under the tap in the yard because that's all the running water we had, but I can remember my mother sitting me up on the kitchen table and rolling cotton batting around my hand. I don't remember how we got to the doctor, but I do remember sitting on Dr. Morris' knee while he took off the bandage and attended to me. And he said, "I don't know why you're crying now – it's all finished." And he was right. I had been so interested in watching what he did that my nerves let go afterwards.

Next door to us was a couple by the name of Smith whose grandson named Guy Rowsen lived with them. I was only three or four and he was a little older. He'd come over and we'd sit in the front yard watching for those heavy draft horses that used to come down past our house with loads of apples from the BX area of Silver Star. The driver used to sit on top of the boxes of apples behind his great team and throw us each an apple. Guy would catch the first one for me and the second one for himself. We always knew when that wagon was coming along and we always got our apples. I asked my mother once if she had any idea where Guy had gone, and she said, "Yes, I think he's managing a Hudson's Bay store somewhere."

The neighbours on the other side were Mr. and Mrs. Lewington. When I was in my teens she invited me back for a visit. She told me that one day when I was two years old, I had crawled through the dog hole in her gate and tearfully told her my troubles. I had lisped, "I pried and I pried and I pried."

Another memory I have from that house is about two young couples that years ago went up skating on Goose Lake – that's the Bluejay subdivison up that way and I guess it's a sort of reservoir. They fell through the ice and drowned. I watched up above at the back of our place the entourage coming towards the cemetery – the *wagons and sleighs barely crawling along, as they did then. We had a tiny black cocker spaniel, Benny, and the whole time he just howled. I couldn't understand why and Mother told me the reason. Years and years later after she had passed away and was buried in that cemetery, I went back and found the graves of those young people – it was tragic.*

Vernon's Armistice Day celebration on November 11, 1918, was an explosion of excitement after a long and ruinous war. The Vernon volunteer firemen, of whom Brock was a member, decided to make the climax memorable. Janet was newly four.

I remember quite distinctly. Where the cenotaph is now was a great big hole. At one time a building must have burnt down – they didn't tear things down in those days – and left this big hole. I remember as a child walking along the sidewalk and looking down into it – they didn't bother fencing it off. The hole was just next to the old post office, which was on the corner of 30th Street and 30th Avenue. The post office was a lovely, old, three-storey cement building with a cupola on top, and stairs to enter it from the street, and people lived on the top storey. (I remember my sister saying she climbed to the third storey to visit a little friend who lived there.) Beside the hole on the other side was the Presbyterian Church, now the bus depot. Across 30th Street from the post office was, I believe, the city hall, and on a big chunk of land across the street from the hole was the fire hall. Perhaps this proximity made the scope of the celebration possible. Joe Harwood, however, supplied the momentum.

Joe Harwood owned Harwood Transfer. He was a short, 'big tummy' man and he had these big, heavy horses – you saw them clopping along – and he was a noted person and a favourite citizen. He had come out from the Dr. Bernardo Home – an orphanage – in London, England, years before and really made something of himself. He believed that children should have an education – maybe because he didn't get one himself – and he was on the school board. He had married a short, little lady and they had a great big family, and everyone brought a friend home for dinner. They had a fully extended table – six leaves in it – and she never knew how many she was going to have. She was one of those wonderful women. When he came home, he'd go all over the house looking for her, and when he found her he'd give her a little love tap on the cheek and grin, and then he knew everything was all right and he could go and sit down.

Joe Harwood told everybody to bring all the junk they could find and dump it into that hole – boards and trash – and they built it up into a heap two storeys high. On the top they put an old trunk containing gunpowder. Then they lit the bonfire. The whole town was in the street watching. My mother and two sisters and I were upstairs in the fire hall looking out the windows – the fire was on a level with us – it was a wonder it didn't burn Vernon down. My mother told me, "They're burning the Kaiser!"

I remember when the gunpowder exploded. It blew out all the windows in the Presbyterian Church. A lady standing on the corner fainted. But the greatest thrill for me that day was my trip down the 'slippery pole' in the fire hall. It was metal, and if the firemen were upstairs playing cards or something, and a call came in, they could slide down. Dad put his left arm around me and we slid down the slippery pole.

Despite joy and relief, however, the end of the war brought unforeseen changes to the Hilliard family.

My father had bought a 'quick print' shop and printed invoices and receipts and other small items. However, after the First War people were losing their jobs, and things were bad. I don't know whether he got worried about his business or what, but in 1919 he decided to apply for a homestead. You went to the courthouse and put a little money down and promised to work on improving the land for a certain number of years. He bought it sight unseen, and it was away up in Deep Creek north of Spallumcheen Municipality. He had a bicycle that he had used for years and years, and he bicycled up to see what he had signed for.

He found the area had been burnt over by a forest fire, and hot ash holes still smoldered in the peat soil. His neighbours were pioneers, Mr. and Mrs. Henry Hill, and they had situated their farm along Cedar Creek – they've changed the name now to Henry Creek – and that creek used to roar down through their property the whole summer – now it's dry as a bone. They had a nice cottage amidst flower beds on a lawn, and two great big hay barns joined together so you could drive underneath, and a dairy, and a little shed that sat over the creek and looked like a two-hole outhouse inside, but they dropped their milk cans, butter and cream down there right in the water – refrigeration all year round! And they had a huge horse trough full of water all the time. The creek supplied the house with indoor water and fed an indoor toilet. Oh, my!!

Not only was there a stark contrast between the Hill farm and the homestead, but also the Hill farm was located in such a way along the creek that it cut off access to the homestead.

No matter what way you looked at it, it was just hopeless. The homestead was up on a hill – no flat land, as Henry Hill had settled all the flat land at the bottom. There were no fences, and the Hills' cattle pastured on the homestead too. So Dad took a look at the burnt piece that cornered on it. It had a four-room log house with a lean-to and a cottage roof [a four-sided roof sloping from a central peak] and a barn still standing. It had red ash pits all over it, but still it was 160 acres, thirty acres wide, and eighty acres cleared. And there was still a lot of timber on it. He found out from the courthouse that it belonged to Mr. O. Klemmer in Kamloops and they decided to rent it.

So they loaded the piano and the bedding and the rest of their possessions on the wagon and tied the cows on behind, and drove the horses and walked the cows the whole way from Vernon to Deep Creek. Of course, the cows got tired and lay down, and they had all kinds of trouble with them, especially when they got to the big dip outside Armstrong on Pleasant Valley Road – just south of Mountain View Nursery – where we spent the night. That was a dip in those days – you went right down into the gully and up the other side. We were also carrying a yellow cat called Canary in the wood stove oven, and Ethel fed it bits of bacon rind through the door, which had been left open just a titch so she wouldn't get out. I don't know what happened to the chickens, as they didn't come with us. It took them several days to move everything up – they went back and forth to Vernon several times and did everything themselves – and it was dirt and gravel road. When my first child was born, they were just beginning to lay the hard surface to Vernon.

Brock and Ellie made a brave beginning on the Klemmer place. Janet was four and a half, Ethel and Ruth around eleven and twelve.

On the main floor there were just two bedrooms, so I slept on a couch in the living room. Mother and Dad had the front bedroom and my two sisters shared the second, which had two beds in it. I can see Mother yet knocking an iron bedstead together the first night so we could sleep.

When we started up, we drank the water from Deep Creek, but everybody's cattle pastured around there, and we got sick. Mrs. Hill said, "Oh, you mustn't drink from the creek." So water had to be carried in buckets from a spring on the Beadle property a quarter mile away. Mother scrubbed and scoured the old log house and then laid down her best rugs on the wood floors. She put the Axminster rug in the living room. It had a geometric design on it – Persian. The rug in the kitchen I liked the best – it had big pink roses on it.

We had no chimney at that time – our house just had a tin pipe running from the stove up through the attic and out the roof. One day something dropped to the floor from near the pipe. Dad picked it up and saw it was a hot nail. I remember watching him climb up through the trapdoor into the attic with water to put out the fire. And so they got Mr. Mitchell to come and build a bracket chimney. Being 'burned out' was a fearful prospect in bush country. I remember Mr. Hayhurst coming around to collect things for someone who had been burned out the night before. Dad gave him a sack of rolled oats that he had just bought. Mother and Dad were good that way. Dad used to tell us stories of fires he had fought in Vernon.

Having arrived in the spring, the Hilliards faced some hard labour before winter set in. Full-time farming became a process of trial and error. The community spirit, however, which they found in Deep Creek sustained the newcomers. Donald and Mary Lindsay, who lived south of them, were a godsend.

Dad was a better printer than a farmer. Of course, he had no equipment, but he had good neighbours. He borrowed a plough and one share, which had to be sharpened by Donald Lindsay, a tall, fine-looking Scot with black curly hair, a blacksmith, an excellent farmer who became a good friend. Dad ploughed as best he could, and then he had to borrow a disc, and next construct a 'float,' which flattened the soil for seeding. A float consisted of boards nailed across a couple of logs that were dragged by the horse over the ground. Since you sat on the float to drive the horse, all the dust and dirt flew back in your face until you turned black.

Dad put Ruth on the float. She hated *it, she just* hated *it. She had loved living in Vernon and going to all those little handkerchief showers and Sunday school picnics. She loved all the niceties of life. She got it from Mother's side of the family. I remember her coming to the house after she got off that float and getting a bucket and walking all the way back up to the spring for water to take a bath.*

That first spring Brock hand-seeded his fields, broadcasting fistfuls of seed from a fifty-pound bag slung over his shoulder. He tried oats first and borrowed a fanning mill from Henry Hill so that he could remove the husks from the crop.

A fanning mill was quite a size, as I recall, with a great handle on the side that it was my job to turn. You poured the oats in, the chaff and dirt would blow away, and it gave a sort of finish to the seed. Then he found that oats wasn't good for the cattle because they ate their heads off and used the rest for bedding, so a lot was wasted. Next he tried alsike clover and timothy. This seeder hung around his neck too, but he turned a handle to broadcast the seed a certain distance. And he worked his way back and forth across the field [like a zamboni]. The cattle liked this hay, and it was good for the horses. Later on, when alfalfa was grown here, he seeded a piece of sloping land with alfalfa, but we had problems with bloat in the cattle and sheep.

Ellie meanwhile quickly tried to resurrect her milk business.

Mother had a lovely Guernsey cow when we first came from Vernon – she was a wonderful milker – she filled the bucket right to the brim. Unfortunately, she had a great udder that hung down low, and she would come home from pasture in the bush with her udder and teats torn so badly that she couldn't be milked. Mother had to buy something that looked like a darning needle to insert into the teat so that the milk just ran out without the discomfort of milking. We had a lot of trouble of that nature because the back eighty acres of woods and bush hadn't been cleared yet and was full of fallen dead trees and snags.

Mother had a number of white enamel milk pans, each about fourteen inches across and three inches deep, that were placed all in a row. The fresh milk was poured into them so that the cream would rise to the surface. The cream skimmer was made of tin. It was no larger or deeper than the width and depth of my hand and had a handle just big enough to be held between your thumb and finger. The skimmer had tiny holes in the bottom so that the milk would go through and the cream would be caught – the cream was thick like clabbered cream and took two days to rise to the top to be skimmed off for making butter. The skimmed milk was fed to the pigs. The pans at the end of the row were then washed and scalded and rotated to the beginning of the row. For cleanliness you put a kindling stick across each pan and laid a nice fresh tea towel over the top.

I saw a cream skimmer in a shop in Enderby, and I stood and giggled because it wasn't labelled correctly.

I said, "Do you mind me telling you that's a cream skimmer?"

"Oh, somebody told me it was a flour sifter. Well, we'll mark it as a cream skimmer or *a flour sifter."*

Dad dug a well up by the spring. The soil was moist and soft, and ferns grew there. You could hang the butter and the cream can inside the well and the cream would keep for a week. But we still had to tote the water.

Mother made butter in a barrel churn in the kitchen. It had a lid that clipped on and in the lid was a piece of blue glass. I used to love to watch that blue glass because when it was clear and not cloudy with cream, you had butter. And the butter was always covered in buttermilk. She wrapped the one-pound blocks in butter papers which Dad had printed for her: 'Fresh Dairy Butter, Beaver Meadow Farm.' *On Saturday she would take me with her in the buggy to Enderby to sell her butter and purchase a few groceries. In those days we drove on the old road to enter the town, and the entire street was lined with piled lumber. It was like driving through a high-walled canyon. Enderby was closer to us than Armstrong. The only hitch was the long, steep Canyon Hill climb for the horse on the way back.*

Since Ellie hadn't brought their chickens from Vernon, Mary Lindsay gave her a black Minorca hen with a clutch of baby chicks to start a flock. *They're black with a floppy red comb and a little heavier than a Leghorn. They were good both as layers and meat birds. I never hear of them anymore.*

That September Ruth and Ethel walked the three and a half miles to attend Hullcar School across the municipal border in Spallumcheen. Janet had just turned five and still had a year of freedom. She tailed along behind her dad as he collected wood for fuel and fences.

You had to have fences everywhere for the cattle. Albert Hayhurst lived up beyond us and he used an A-fence. It sits across a ditch like an A, but the cross-rails are laid along one side only. It was grand – you could sit on the rails and brace your feet. A snake fence, though, was my favourite. It snaked across the field like a series of long Zs lying on their sides, and in each corner of the Z was a wild orange blossom bush, a syringa bush, a hawthorn, or wild columbine because, of course, the plough couldn't get into these corners. So all around the edge of the field these little places were left in their natural state. And this is where the robins nested. I thought it was beautiful. A snake fence was economical because each long side of the Z required only one upright stake, but it wasted a lot of land. Dad did a very good job of eventually fencing the entire property including a long lane from the barn all the way back to the woods. Whatever he decided to do, he did well.

Most people cut their firewood in winter, but we had arrived in the spring. So that first year when we needed firewood, we went into the woods and cut down a dead tree because it was dry. Those trees were big, so in later years we had a bee – the neighbours coming along to help saw up the logs. The drag saw is the first one I recall. It went back and forth on an engine and resembled the crosscut saw that my father used and taught me to use – "Don't do that, *you have to do* this *so it won't bend."*

Winter in Deep Creek took the family by surprise. The temperature could reach 60 degrees below zero Fahrenheit.

That winter was bitter cold. My father had butchered a cow and a pig. The halves of beef hung from the rafters of the lean-to attached to the kitchen and stayed frozen there while we consumed it bit by bit. The hams and bacon were cured in brine in a barrel, then wrapped and hung up on great spikes in the kitchen. With potatoes and many beans we somehow survived.

We had a big wash boiler on the back of the cook stove that we replenished with snow every morning. Doing the laundry was an entire day's job. The wash was hung outdoors and froze stiff and hard enough to stand alone. Each day a few articles were brought indoors to dry overnight on a rack over the stove so that by Saturday all was in order.

Saturday night the rinse tub was brought in before the cook stove and the oven door opened down flat to hold our clean garments. Then the baths began, the youngest first. (Was I the dirtiest?) A kettle of hot water was added as each person took her turn. Toenails and fingernails were trimmed, ears and elbows thoroughly cleaned. We were allowed to wear our clean underwear under our night attire. Then we were off to bed where we stretched our feet down to the warm brick wrapped in newspaper and an old sock. Woe betide the one who forgot to return the brick to the oven next morning!

Winter also meant Brock had to clean the pipes in order to keep the wood residue from accumulating inside them and catching fire. Fire roaring in the pipes was a frightening predicament. However, working with tin pipes in winter was cold and exasperating work.

We were all sent to bed to keep warm while the strings of pipes that ran from the stove through the rooms were all taken down and carried outside to be cleaned. Then Dad had to put them all back together again, and sometimes he couldn't get them to fit. That's the only time I heard my father really swear. He had to squeeze the end of one piece inside the end of another piece until he got them back together. Then he could light the fire and we could get up.

Spring did come again and Deep Creek flowed over its banks into the fields. Mrs. Donald Lindsay drove my sisters and whoever else was taking domestic science to Armstrong with a team and democrat once or twice a month to attend class. That June Ruth passed her entrance exams for high school.

A student could attend high school in Armstrong if one lived close enough to the school to walk, could get to Hullcar School in time to catch the school bus, or had a relative in town with whom to board. The Hilliard children had none of these advantages. Winter conditions were terrible, and there was no money to spend on board. When they finished grade eight at age thirteen or fourteen, therefore, they had little further formal education and had to look about for work. The options were few. For girls housework was the common choice.

Ruth was determined she was not going out to do housework. That summer the family received a tantalizing invitation. *There was one cousin, that's all, in the east, an only child. Aunt Olive and Uncle Arthur said, "Why don't you let Ruth come and stay with us and go to school with Catherine?" Mother would have let her go but Dad said no. Maybe he was right. It would have broken up the family all right – because in those days you didn't ever have the money to bring her back for the summer. She'd be gone. But it would have been wonderful for her. It was just her type of society. She'd have been in her element. In the end she went to work for Dr. Van Kleeck – his office was up that long stairs beside Hassen's office – and she boarded at Mr. and Mrs. Tom Cummings in the old house which still stands beside the medical offices on Wood Avenue.*

That fall Janet turned six and walked the long miles to Hullcar School with Ethel, who was in grade eight.

Miss Taylor was my teacher. She boarded at Dan Martin's and walked one and a half miles to and from school. I used to play with Amy Pyott. I went until the end of October. When I got back home at the end of the day, I'd lay down on the lounge to wait for supper and fall asleep. One day Mother came to me and said, "Would you mind if you didn't go to school for a while? I think Daddy will get busy and make a new school." So I stayed home the rest of the year. By that time there were other children in the area who had come from England and Scotland and Ireland, and so my father and theirs got together and built a one-room school. Henry Hill sold them an acre of land for one dollar, and Mother suggested the name Hillcrest School. It was only half a mile away and took me twenty minutes.

The district formed by the new school was under Enderby supervision and extended from Spallumcheen municipal boundary on the south (one mile north of Hullcar Hall) to the boundary of Murray and Parker property in the north. Thus Deep Creek Valley was divided into two school districts: North Deep Creek and Hillcrest. The first school board consisted of Jim Duncan, Albert Hayhurst, and my father.

Hillcrest School was a one-room affair with two cloakrooms and a huge box heater. Outdoors was a flagpole, two three-hole privies and a woodshed annexe for a two-day supply of firewood. In the winter we each in turn brought a syrup pail of milk to make the cocoa that we all shared. If the weather was very cold, we were allowed to pull our desks about the stove for warmth, and the closeness gave a cosy feeling.

To begin with, there were nineteen students, some of whom had transferred from Hullcar School. In winter we played Fox and Goose, and used our hand sleighs in turn on the sloping ground. In summer we played Anti-I-Over over the school roof, Prisoner's Base, Pom Pom Pull Away, football or baseball. Once a week we had a period of physical exercise. The last year Hillcrest was open there were seven students, as the teacher had bought little Georgie Smith a pair of shoes so he could attend to make the necessary seventh pupil to keep the school open.

At school at Christmas time we entertained the parents with a concert and star drills. We marched in formation holding up two-foot kindling sticks with a silver star pasted to the top of each stick. (The heater took two-foot logs and we had lots of kindling.)

On the last day of school in June, the parents attended while Honour Rolls were presented. I still have a couple. Janet fishes out a report card. *See? One October I was bad and didn't get my Thanksgiving turkey sticker, but I did get a flag for June-July. The stickers were for special achievement.*

The school picnic, however, was the highlight of the final day. It started out at our place and at a later date moved to Donald Lindsay's. We had a huge yard and it was just like a park – trees growing naturally everywhere – poplar, balm of gilead – in those days we didn't crowd ourselves into small spaces – no lawn cutting, of course – we turned the sheep into it once in a while.

The school picnic was the one and only time many of us had an ice cream cone. Mr. Duncan by this time owned a Ford car, and he brought a large container of ice cream from Mr. Sawyer's in Armstrong. We were lined up twice for a cone, and what was left over we all ate from a dish. We had a great day, and many earned ten cents winning foot races or sack races. Then everyone stood together for the snapshot that concluded the event. School picnics were a dressy occasion. Group photographs show the girls in pretty frocks and the boys in shirts, ties and short pants. Janet names them all. She remembers her teachers too.

My teachers from grades one through eight were Miss Earla McDonald (1921-22), Miss Florence Weeks (1922-24), Miss Verna Ford (1924-27) and Miss Rachel McKay (1927-29). As I recall, their salary was $100 per month minus thirty dollars for room and board.

Janet locates the families who lived along Deep Creek and whose children attended Hillcrest with her. She begins at the northern boundary of the Hillcrest school district – the Murray and Parker land – and proceeds south to the Spallumcheen municipal boundary. [See the accompanying map.]

Murray – *One family that arrived to spend several years on this property were the **Ludwigs**. Elsie was the eldest to attend school with her sisters, Margaret and Mary, and a brother, George. There were older boys at home as well as a small girl named Rosa. They were well brought up and worked hard. I distinctly recall the ten-pound lard bucket of lunch they brought to school. Elsie would gather them all around her and distribute the lovely big slices of* homemade bread spread with butter. Some years later a family named **Horton** took over the farm and a little roly-poly boy called Tommy attended school. He brought soft-boiled eggs in his lunch and loved them, much to our chagrin.

Gillick – South of the Murray farm lived Jack Gillick and his wife Edith (nee Mills) with their children Pat, Ivy, and Jackie. My mother stayed with Mrs. Gillick briefly after Jackie was born. I spent the night periodically with Ivy and marvelled at how much she did to help her mother.

Hayhurst – The Hayhurst family had the next farm. Millie, Eva, Norah, and Lena attended Hillcrest School with us. Vera was a little 'afterthought.' Eva was in my class. Millie when she first came to school always dropped her h's in pure Yorkshire fashion.

Grant – The 160 acres adjoining the Hayhurst farm was the home for many families. First and foremost were Harry and Mrs. Grant and their daughter Genevieve. Sandy Grant lived with them but homesteaded across the creek and was quite a character. He used to sniff and then say, "Yep, yep, upon my word." It was Sandy and Harry that helped my parents unload their goods on arriving at the Klemmer property. Mrs. Grant and Mother became good friends. A little boy was born later to the Grants – I think his name was Douglas. They moved to Armstrong and lived on the old Whitaker place. Mother and I visited them once with a horse and buggy.

On the east property, the Grants were followed by the **Schaffers**. One or two of the boys (Emil) attended our school. They did not stay long. Mr. and Mrs. Tom **Demaid**, a Welsh family, came next to farm the Sandy Grant place. Elizabeth, Celia, Gwen, Bill, and Gladys Mae were their children, but only the latter three were pupils at Hillcrest. The teacher had quite a time with Gladys Mae at first – she would run off home every chance she got. Bill was a marvellous football player.

McCahon – Across the road from the Grant place lived Jim and

Mrs. McCahon. They had one little girl named Bessie. When they first moved to Deep Creek, they lived in a two-room log cabin. One day Bessie wandered out to play and was later found in convulsions. She passed away shortly thereafter. It was thought she might have eaten wild parsnip or some poisonous weed. The McCahons then moved to the Harry Grant place nearby [the west property] which they purchased as their home for the rest of their lives. They had no more children.

Duncan and Lawson – *They were south of the Sandy Grant/Demaid place. Dave Lawson, a returned soldier from World War One, was married to Jim Duncan's sister Nell. They all were Scots. The two families each had a house on the property. Jim and Mrs. Duncan had two boys, Jimmy and Johnny. Jimmy was in my class and we always had a race as to who would rank first. The teacher at Hillcrest School always boarded at the Duncans', as Hillcrest School was only minutes away.*

Duncan and Lawson were considered somewhat prosperous farmers. They had a Holstein cattle herd and a pump house, where the cream was kept sweet with water and ice. This ice was hauled on several occasions by my father from Otter Lake or Parkinson Lake in Spallumcheen. In summer Jimmy and I used to dig through the sawdust in the ice house and smash off a piece to suck on.

Dave and Mrs. Lawson had a wee baby girl, Helen, who died at birth. How well I remember my mother crying in sympathy for them. Dave tended to be accident-prone. He had an old-time baler with a team that walked round and round to operate a plunger that forced the hay into the bale. Most men used a fork to feed the hopper with hay, but Dave used his foot. One day he wasn't quick enough and the descending plunger crushed his leg. He did not lose his leg, but he suffered all his life from the wound that never seemed to heal.

Barney – *Across from the school was a long lane that reached back [east of Duncan and Lawson] into the woods. George Barney and his parents lived up in this locality. His father was a carpenter and*

161

a day labourer. George had the most wonderful collection of home-made blocks.

Wolfgang – Up this lane also lived Lola Wolfgang, who rode a horse to school each day and boarded it at Duncan and Lawson's. She was a student in her final year when I came.

Dodds – Another homestead about two and a half miles up in these woods was run by Mrs. Dodds and her children, Emily and Vincent. It would have been closer for them to attend North Deep Creek School, but as they were in the Enderby district, they came to Hillcrest. My father, being on the school board, blazed a trail through the bush for them. Their attendance was irregular because they would stop to play in the woods and pick flowers. They were students for about three years, and then Mrs. Dodds returned to Vancouver to be with her husband. Emily still lives in Burnaby and sent me a Christmas card in 1991. The front of the card carries a picture of the wooden shanty in Deep Creek in which the Dodds family lived.

Hill – Mr. and Mrs. Henry Hill's family had all grown and gone out in the world except for one son, Roland, who lived at home. 'Rollie' was about the age of my sisters and later married Sarah Malpass from Lansdowne. They lived in a two-room house that he built on his parents' farm. During that time they had a baby son who died. My mother helped Grandma Hill prepare him for the burial. Mr. Henry Hill was the brother of Mrs. Thomas Hayes and we often met the Hayeses there. She and Mr. Hill were of very small stature.

Klemmer – Originally homesteaded by **Stroulger** from England, Lawson Stroulger of Enderby is the only remaining member of the family in the area. The farm worked by Brock and Ellie **Hilliard** was located here.

Beadle – Bill Beadle and his wife came from Ontario and had no family. They homesteaded across from our place in a two-room log cabin. He used to make fence posts – years ago all our properties were fenced and cross-fenced, none of it open. I think he had a bit of army pension as well.

A big stream came down in front of his cabin, and he had dug a hole in it – the stream ran into and out of the hole – and they dipped out a bucket of water for the house whenever needed. It was dandy! And in the winter he could just chop a hole in the ice and the water was there underneath. It was running water at its best.

Mrs. Beadle was a little bitty thing, and she had the most brilliant eyes – like little beads. She used to make quilts, and where she got the men's silk ties from for her quilts, I couldn't tell you. Men only wore ties to weddings and funerals. But she made lovely silk covers. He used to go to town once in a while and get on what the men called a bender, but he worked hard. I think Terry Nitchie is on his place now.

Lindsay – *Our good neighbours to the southwest were Mr. and Mrs. Donald Lindsay, a true Scottish pair. He was everyone's blacksmith as well as a farmer. He wore his cap backwards and said, "Dang," when things went wrong. Donald Lindsay on occasion stuck a roast of beef under the seat of our cutter to help us out. Their family had grown and left.*

However, in the interval Mrs. Lindsay's sister-in-law died in Medicine Hat, Alberta, leaving a family of three boys and one girl: Wilbert, Harold, John, and Mary. Wilbert stayed with his father for a year before he came west, but the younger three came to live with Aunt Mary. If ever a boy appreciated what his uncle and aunt had done for them, it was Harold. From the outset he became the Lindsays' right-hand man. Little Mary was handicapped in some way – she might have had polio – as she stumbled a lot and seemed to have trouble with her legs. Here again, my mother came to the fore and made her several dresses until such time as Aunt Mary could get her feet under her. These children attended Hillcrest School and Wilbert was in my class for a time.

Some Sundays when there was no church at Hullcar Hall, Harold would hitch up the Lindsays' beautiful team of Clydesdales to a big sleigh and take as many young folk along as it would hold, often sitting on a fresh bed of hay, to attend church at Knob Hill. I don't remember the minister or the service but the jolly comradeship was indeed memorable.

On that same Lindsay property was a one-room log cabin. Here Mr. and Mrs. Lindsay's niece, Mrs. McKinnon (nee Gates), lived after her husband died. Her three children were Hector, Murray, and Nora. Donald Lindsay added an additional room for a bedroom. Mrs. McKinnon had a widow's pension of thirty dollars a month, and her eggs and milk supplied by the Lindsays. She worked out during the apple harvest to clothe her children in winter. She was a wonderful person and spent her money six times mentally before she actually disbursed it. I remember so well how Nora was always remembered on her birthday – once Hector saved up his earned pennies to buy her a little broom, and once Grandpa McQueen gave her a lovely doll.

Mr. and Mrs. McQueen were Mrs. Lindsay's parents, whom they had brought with them to Deep Creek. I remember them both. Mrs. McQueen had canaries, and I was there on one occasion when she brushed out her long silver hair in the morning sunshine – a joy in itself. On another occasion Mrs. McQueen expressed the wish that my sister Ruth play 'The Bluebells of Scotland' on the piano. When my sisters had walked the remainder of the way to our house, my mother received a phone call to say that within a few hours of hearing her favourite song, Grandma McQueen had passed away. Grandpa McQueen went on alone for many years.

Hedman – South of the Lindsay property was a farm owned by Hedmans. To this house came another printer from the Vernon News, Bert **Campbell**. He brought his wife and quite a family: Roy, Muriel, Dora, Ted, Leslie (or Lal, as he was called), Ida, and Ruth. These children all attended Armstrong Consolidated School, as the Hullcar School had been closed. The Campbells stayed only a year and then moved to Kamloops where Mr. Campbell worked for the Kamloops Sentinel.

They were replaced by Mr. and Mrs. Theophalus (Offie) **Jones**, relations of the Hedmans, who stayed for many years. Mr. Jones worked in the woods away from home and his wife, Laura, ran the establishment. Bill and Gordon walked to school with me on many a morning. I learned all about the wonderful Uncle Georgie in Enderby. A little sister, Eleanor, was born much later. Bill Jones' ashes are spread on Hullcar Mountain behind the Hedman farm.

Barber – Mr. and Mrs. Barber lived at the back of a long lane to the east of the Hedman place. It was originally the **Calley** place. Calley's Lake lay to the back of it. It froze over every winter and my sisters and their friends would often walk the three miles to skate with companions there. The Barbers had two teenaged sons, Eddie and Leslie.

Pyott – Behind the Barbers' away up on the hill lived Amy Pyott and her two sisters, Jessie and Jean. Her mother at that time was a widow. Amy and I used to go on little ventures. We'd take a piece of bacon, make a tiny fire and fry it. We'd wander up the creeks, and that would be in early July and there'd still be snow in the bush. All those creeks used to roar down there in springtime. When you clearcut, every creek is as dry as a bone.

Yesterday afternoon my daughter Alice and I went away up Pyott Road where there's a slough. It was full of bulrushes with little water paths through them. Four or five wild ducks were there, and (with *my* eyes) I thought I saw an island. Alice said, "That's not an island, Mom. Those are little baby ducks." They'd got beyond the yellow colour and turned brown, and they were all in a cluster in the centre of this bit of water. We saw a yellow-headed blackbird – although I thought Vernon was the only place they could be seen – and red-winged blackbirds, and two wild geese with babies along the edge.

I was trying to show Alice where the Pyott house had stood – all that is left is the old lilac – and how far they had to pack water in a bucket, and where the backhouse was. They used to have a bit of an orchard and blackcurrant bushes, and Mrs. Pyott would borrow the neighbour's horse and hold the cultivator while Amy drove the horse. People today have no idea how hard they used to work. Well, the work was there and someone had to do it or you didn't have anything to eat! That's all there was to it!

Beddington – *Neighbours to the north of the Pyotts', the Beddington children, Laurie, Audrey, and Marion, walked with Amy Pyott the three and a half to four miles to and from Hillcrest School each day. I recall one morning when Amy brought Audrey into our house on the way to school. The child's feet were nearly frozen. There was a great depth of snow and the thermometer often dropped to minus 40 or 50 degrees. Laurie was in my class for several years and then was advanced to a higher grade.*

Mr. Bill Beddington drew an army pension, so Mrs. Beddington was able to manage. He also worked at Okanagan Landing during apple season, as there was as yet no railroad to Kelowna.

Kenny – *South of the Hedmans', Mr. and Mrs. Seth (Harry) Kenny lived on the last place bordering the boundary of Spallumcheen Municipality. They had four children: Allan, Evelyn, Beulah, and Jack. The three eldest went to high school in Armstrong, but Jack had to take his grade eight at Hillcrest. By the time I came along, they were all gone from home. Allan married one of my teachers, Miss Weeks; Evelyn was a teacher and married when she was about sixty-five and retired in Victoria; Beulah married a Mr. Jeffrey (Geoffrey) Veale from Salmon River Valley; and Jack became a minister and was in India for a long time, but I believe he eventually married, and the last address I had for him was somewhere in the United States.*

Mr. Kenny was many years older than his wife, so he went to bed quite early. Mrs. Kenny, though, loved having young people about her. She always made doughnuts on Saturday, and that night she would invite all the young folk in. We played darts and crokinole; sometimes she would play the organ and we'd sing. Later she served cocoa and doughnuts.

The old gentleman had a big moustache and always drank from a moustache cup. It had a proper little china piece across the middle so his moustache wouldn't fall into his tea. With our big group there were never enough cups to go around, so some man would have to have the moustache cup. You can imagine the fun that caused! We giggled so hard, half the time we had the cocoa coming out our noses!

She'd put on some wonderful Hallowe'en nights. She'd maybe bake bread, and we'd have to sit there in the dark and pass it all around from one to the other, and this bread was supposed to be the lungs of a corpse, of course, and something else was the brains – ohhh!! She had all kinds of ideas to keep us amused. Mrs. Kenny was a lady to be remembered.

Living in Spallumcheen just south of the Kenny place, Harry Smith also became part of Mrs. Kenny's circle of friends and had a place in Janet's memories.

Harry Smith had a beautiful voice and he would sing while Mrs. Kenny played the organ. She arranged to have the three of us perform at the radio station in Kelowna. Harry sang 'Rose of Tralee' – I think he and Mrs. Kenny also sang a duet – Mrs. Kenny played the piano, and I recited 'Somebody's Mother.' All the folks at home had their radios on!

Janet can still recite that poem and does so by request:

Somebody's Mother

The woman was old and ragged and grey
And bent with the chill of the winter's day.
She stood at the crossing and waited long
Alone, uncared for amid the throng

Of human beings who passed her by
Nor heeded a glance of her anxious eye.

Down the street with laughter and shout
Glad of the feeling of school all out
Came the boys like a flock of sheep
Hailing the snow piled white and deep,
Passed the old woman so aged and grey
Hastened the children on their way
Nor offered a helping hand to her
So meek, so timid, afraid to stir
Lest the carriage wheels or the horses' feet
Should crowd her down on the slippery street.

At last came one of the merry troop,
The gayest laddie of all the group,
He paused beside her and whispered low,
"I'll help you across if you wish to go."
Her aged hand on his strong young arm
She placed; and so without hurt or harm
He guided the trembling feet along
Proud that his own were firm and strong.

Then back again to his friends he went,
His young heart happy and well content.
"She's somebody's mother, boys, you know,
For all she's aged and poor and slow,
And I hope some fellow will lend a hand
To help my mother, you understand,
If ever she's old and poor and grey
And her own dear boy is far away."

And somebody's mother bowed her head
In her home that night, and the prayer she said
Was, "God be kind to that noble boy
Who is somebody's son and pride and joy."

                                    Author unknown

The Hilliards settled into life in Deep Creek. Janet remembers their first couple of years as *pretty good. Mother was in good health and Dad took an interest in things.* The family participated in community activities and got to know their neighbours. As the youngest, Janet enjoyed herself.

When I was little, Dad used to take me with him to North Deep Creek Hall – an old two-storey house that doubled as a church – when he went to play whist with the other men. Mr. Hayhurst took Lena, and Lena and I became friends. We used to crawl underneath all the coats that were piled on the sway-backed bed upstairs while the games went on downstairs.

One thing about Dad – he always made me a swing. And to this day I like to swing. If I get a chance, I go down to the school when the kids aren't there, and I swing. I don't know what it was, but it was good for me.

She and her father played Santa Claus in their sleigh on Christmas Eve. *Dad would phone the neighbours on Christmas Eve and say, "I'm going down to Enderby for the mail. Is there anything you'd like me to pick up for you?" Quite often Mr. Hayhurst would send to Eaton's for Christmas presents for the girls, and if they didn't come around with the mail lady, they'd be stuck in the post office in Enderby over Christmas. So we always went for them. We had a pair of light horses and a nice little cutter, and we'd pick up the parcels and deliver them. A swift ride home with sleigh bells ringing and snowflakes falling brought joy to my heart.*

Farming in Deep Creek, however, was a difficult proposition, particularly for novices. The Hilliards couldn't rely on a garden because there might be a killing frost any month of the year. Deep Creek rose in Mount Ida and ran south through a long, narrow valley; the cold air drained down from Mount Ida and from Hullcar Mountain on the west side of the creek and killed the vegetables and grain. Even the mainstay, potatoes, was off limits. If potatoes got frostbitten early enough, they might re-grow, but a second frost would finish them.

We had to buy our potatoes from Mr. Ken Smith in Knob Hill [Spallumcheen], and if Mother wanted a bit of jam for winter, I remember quite well she used to go to Mrs. Bill Pringle. Like the Nobles, the Pringles grew fields of blackcurrants, and my mother used to go there to get them. One year she made jam from some sour cherries somebody had given us. Oh, my goodness, was that ever a treat! Most of the time we were given prunes [plums], and to this day I am not fond of them.

When Janet was about seven, Brock and Ellie had the first of two little boys, born within a year of each other, and so alike they seemed twins.

Mother had wanted a little boy very badly, and I think Douglas was expected, but Donald was more of an accident. But they were good company for each other. (Edward) Douglas was the first boy born in the Armstrong Hospital, now called Haugen Centre, on the corner of Wright Street and Haugen Avenue. In my eighth year after Christmas I was sent to Mrs. Lawson's to stay. I never knew why, but I knew I had to go home on Saturdays to visit my mother. One Saturday Mother immediately sent me back to Mrs. Lawson's with the message she was not feeling well. (It was probably a ruse to get me out of the way, as she could have used the telephone.) Later that day I was told I had another brother. It was the 28th of January, 1923.

Donald Lindsay had hitched up his team of Clydesdales and driven to Hullcar Hall to meet Dr. Van Kleeck, whose car could negotiate the snowdrifts no farther, and brought him to the Hilliards' for the home birth. Thus the new baby was named Donald Brock. Ellie's way of thanking Donald was to slip a teaspoon of brandy into his coffee when he came to saw logs each year. *He thought that was pretty nice. Mary wasn't too fond of drinking, and I think he kept a bottle in the barn to have a nip.*

As Hullcar Hall was also used as a church, my two little brothers were christened there together. Mrs. Kenny played the organ. Donny was held by Mrs. Tom Garrett of Vernon because she attended my mother after the birth. Douglas was held by my father, and the minister was Reverend Dow from the United Church. The minister before him was Reverend King. I think the minister came out to Hullcar three Sundays a month and the fourth he went to North Deep Creek Hall. I used to walk up there for church too.

My sisters were both gone now. Ethel had left to work for Mrs. Dan Martin, who had moved from Spallumcheen to Ladner in the Fraser Valley. I slept in a bed in the boys' room. I had one bed and they slept together. This went on for all my life there, more or less.

As the 1920s wore on, the Hilliards experienced considerable financial strain. Brock never farmed the homestead and continued to pay rent on the Klemmer property. He had no money for farm equipment and was forced to rely on the support of his neighbours. The only girl left at home, Janet watched the decline of her parents' fortunes.

I think after the boys came, things became more difficult. The rugs wore out, and Mother started scrubbing the bare boards. We always had porridge for breakfast and sometimes it wasn't too much. We didn't go hungry – let's put it that way. My school lunches were not very interesting – two slices of bread with prune jam in between, and that was about it. When I came home from school in the wintertime, Mother maybe had cornmeal porridge for supper or cream of wheat – we always had something different from breakfast. Or we might have a great big baked potato.

The only time I ever saw an orange was at Christmas. Mr. and Mrs. Tom Garrett would motor up from Vernon and bring those great big oranges that were absolutely marvellous. And Dad would buy a box of Japanese oranges and they'd be put under the bed and not touched until Christmas Day. Mother's sisters in the east always sent a parcel, and we had to put that under the bed too. One sister would send a box of satin candies – all different – and Aunt Olive used to send a book, or something that we never usually got, and that made our Christmas.

Mother made the most of what we had – she did the best she could. The summertime was the worst because we had no place to keep anything – no deep freeze like today! The telephone came to Deep Creek in 1922 – I remember the big reel of cable unrolling behind the truck as it went up our road – but we didn't have electricity. We had a cellar that Dad made out of logs – a kind of hole underneath the house. We put milk and things in the small-screened 'safe' that had a shelf in it and a door on it, and we kept it in the cellar. If we'd had electricity, we'd have lived in absolute luxury!!

We had guinea fowl for a while and I got quite good at cleaning a couple for supper. Sometimes in the summer Mother used to wonder what in the dickens to cook, and she'd ask Dad to go and get a grouse. There were a lot of lovely grouse up in the springs where we got our water, and I used to regularly see them there. They were out of season in summer, of course, but he'd take a .22 and shoot a couple. He didn't do it often, but when he came back, she'd just take the breasts and burn the feathers to get rid of the evidence.

We always had lots of eggs in the summer – we had our flock of hens and we had brought geese with us from Vernon – but you get so sick of eggs after a while. Mother made scalloped potatoes and baked potatoes because we had lots of milk. She made bread all the time.

But some of the women in that valley were better off in a way than my mother. They worked hard too, but I remember Mrs. Hayhurst used to have lemons to make a lemon pie. Well, Mother never saw a lemon from one month to the next. Mrs. Lawson made a lot of scones – they were Scottish – and Mrs. Duncan had the teacher's board money and that helped. She made milk puddings. Once in a blue moon, maybe, Mother would have the big round tapioca for puddings. We had custard because it was milk and eggs. When you *sold eggs, you got six cents a dozen. When Mother couldn't sell her eggs in Enderby, she gave them to Mrs. Walker. Mr. Walker produced the Enderby Commoner and Walker's Weekly.*

Everybody had rhubarb in those days and we didn't have any. Eventually I think Mrs. Kenny gave her a root. And she told her, "Now put lots of manure on it." Well, we had that! So then we had rhubarb in the spring. So we had rhubarb in everything, of course, from that day on.

In some ways feeding the family was easier for Ellie in winter. *Once the weather got cold, we could keep the food out in the lean-to kitchen. Everybody had one in those days. The kitchen door opened into the lean-to, and its outside door was the back door of the house. And the lean-to was cold!! If you butchered, you had to find someone to buy a share of the carcass. It was the only way to make a bit of money. Otherwise, you ate the same thing day in and day out until you couldn't look it in the face!*

One nice thing I remember happened when the men got together and sent to Winnipeg for horse harness – the martingale or some other piece of harness would wear out. So they'd send an order together, as the express would be cheaper. And while they were at it, to make the amount worthwhile, they got a box of finnan haddie apiece [smoked haddock]. Ohhhhh, to have that nice finnan haddie after having beef and beef and beef and beef or pork and pork and pork. It was just wonderful! I can see that wooden box yet with all that delicious finnan haddie in it.

The sewing skills that Ellie had gained in the shirt factory before her marriage were turned regularly to good use. The photographs of Janet and her siblings show the ingenuity and artistry with which she dressed the children.

Aunt Claribel, the nurse, was a spinster, and she used to send out her used clothing. (There were no things like thrift shops – oh! if there had been thrift shops!!) Sometimes in those days the clothes were sweaty under the arms. Well, Mother cut them down for us. I don't know how she ever did it. She never got a magazine to tell her the patterns for children, but she always seemed to know.

A cowl neckline was 'the thing' – rolled – and I remember Mother going to town and buying a kind of mauvy dress material, and a small piece of sand material to make a little cowl neckline, and she tied the dress at the back to make it young looking. Another time she had some navy material and made a collar, and at the ends of the collar two long tails, made from a cotton belt, hung down the front. She used some red yarn to make a Grecian key design all the way down both sides. I remember Mrs. Kenny saying, "Oh, your mother is a marvel in what she does, you know."

Well, she **was** a marvel. I remember my mother going out in the field one day and coming home with an old coat from a scarecrow. I said, "I wonder what she's going to use that for." She took the coat apart and turned it inside out because it wasn't sun-faded on the inside, and she put patch pockets over the inverted pockets and sewed up the slits and made a coat for Douglas.

My sister brought home a cast-off coat and I used it for two years, and then Mother cut it down and made a smaller coat for Donny. She always turned clothes inside out – the material was always good on the inside – and pressed it. To cover us up in bed, she made crazy quilts out of pieces, and feather-stitched all around each piece – until we got sheep; then we'd pull [card] the wool and fill sugar sacks. Sugar sacks then were thin material, and you could sew them together to make a light covering for the stuffing material.

Mattresses needed sturdier treatment. The mattress lasted in our parents' room, but ours wore out. Mother made cases by sewing wheat sacks together, and each summer the boys and I filled them with fresh hay, red clover and sweet-smelling plants. Once you got a hole for your backside and another for your shoulder, sleeping on them was quite refreshing. The following summer we'd dump the old stuffing in the pigpen and refill the cases.

Once we persuaded our parents to let us sleep overnight in the hayloft. It looked so soft and comfortable. They came with us because they wouldn't leave us out there alone. I don't think anybody slept because we were scratching all night, but it was wonderful all the same. We had climbed the ladder and slept in the hayloft!

The children found their fun where they could, but the lives of the adults grew more sombre. Ellie faced the daily grind of meals on the table and clothes on the back. Trained as a compositor, not as a farmer, Brock didn't keep abreast of the farm work and grew dictatorial and quick to take offense.

He dropped off the school board because he had to have things his way. And if he didn't get his way, he didn't want any part of it. It was poor sportsmanship, really. He wasn't open-minded. When some people don't get their own way, they sulk, and he did!

Dad didn't bother shovelling the deep snow off the roof in winter, particularly on the north side where their bedroom was, and when it melted in spring, the water ran underneath the shingles and down the inside walls. The bedroom was papered with building paper – two feet wide – and laths covered the joins. So the paper was always wet and covered with black stains. Mother didn't complain but she didn't like it.

We went years without a well near the house. Instead Dad made a special rack with two holes in it on a sleigh. We'd set two milk cans in the holes and drag the sleigh to the spring and fill the cans to do the week's washing. Then one of us would haul it back home while the other person steadied the cans. When Douglas was about six or seven, Dad finally dug the second well. He was down in the hole shovelling dirt into a bucket, and Douglas was up on top pulling up the bucket and emptying it out. Being a kid, Douglas didn't lower the bucket – he just dropped it down the hole – whammo! – and hit Dad on the head. Then he came into the house and told everybody that Dad was lying in the bottom of the well!

Broken windows were patched, when possible, by an ingenious method: another piece of cracked glass and two large, coat buttons. When the windows broke, I'd help my dad mend them with other bits of cracked window he had around. I'd be on the inside of the window and he'd be on the outside. I'd put a large coat button over a crack in the replacement glass, and thread a needle through the button and through the cracks in the two pieces of glass underneath the button. Dad would catch the thread on his side and sew through another button opposite mine on his side of the glass. The buttons pulled tight in this way held the two pieces of glass together. If we didn't have any replacement glass, we just nailed a board over the open space for winter.

Things that fell apart didn't get fixed. The ringer on the washer broke, and we scrubbed clothes on a scrubbing board. But Mother kept us clean. Even if I had just one dress, it was washed and pressed and sponged on Saturday to be ready for Sunday.

She used to have to work even when she was feeling too poorly. I can remember as a kid her making bread and sitting me at the table beside her with a handkerchief to wipe her nose. She had a cold but she had to make the bread.

I don't think Dad ever appreciated how much Mom did. I know when she made that little coat for Donny, all she wanted was his arms around her to thank her. All she wanted out of life was a little bit of appreciation and kindness. And somehow or another, she just didn't always get it.

At one point Ellie came to the end of her tether.

There's things I don't even like to think about. I came home from school and Mom wasn't there. I said, "Where's Mom?" And Dad didn't know. He had the little boys with him, and he was looking in the closet at the clothes that were hanging there and, as I think back on it now, it hit me what was going on. He was white in the face, and he was looking to see if she'd pulled out.

It must have been eight o'clock or so. Dad had got our supper and we were sitting there, and she walked in with a big smile on her face. "Oh, she'd gone to see Mrs. Smith and she'd stayed for supper." Well, I found out later that they had had some kind of disagreement. It wouldn't be an argument because she would never talk back to him. He took the two boys and went over to George Lynn's in Spallumcheen to get some feed for the pigs or something, and I guess she couldn't take it anymore, and she walked the nine miles to Armstrong to see my sister, who was working in the hospital at the time. Miss Hayhurst was the matron then, and she came upstairs and said, "Ruth, I'll take over for you. Your mother is downstairs."

And Mother told Ruth, "I just can't take it any more." She had met Dave Lawson on the way as he was going home (actually, the men were always good to Mother – I think they knew how difficult Dad could be) – and he had said, "Oh, Mrs. Hilliard, you'd better come on back with me." And she told him, "I just can't take it any more, Dave. I'm going to leave him." So, of course, the men talk. And he must have told Albert Hayhurst, and then too with Miss Hayhurst being there, the men would know what happened.

Ruth didn't know what to do. She couldn't do anything, in a way. Then that night Bill Parker, who was courting Ruth at the time, came in the cutter with his horse Jenny to see her, and he said, "She'll have to go back with us. You can't keep her here." So the two of them took her past where we lived and away up to Henry Hill and then turned the horse around and came back, so Dad would never know that somebody had brought her home. And that's what she said when she came in: "Oh, I went to see Mrs. Smith and I stayed there for supper." And she never let on to us kids. Ruth and I traded stories about a year later – she told me her side of it and I told her mine. But those were the kinds of things that went on. A woman was just a woman, you know. The man was the boss and the woman kept her mouth shut.

The occasional opportunity to practise his trade, however, gave

Brock a deeply needed boost in morale and lightened the atmosphere at home.

Dad was taught to be perfect. As a lineotype operator, he wasn't allowed any excuse for making a mistake. He had to put the letters in – all backwards, of course, so the paper would print right way up – and he was good at it.

One bright spot I remember in those past years was when the Armstrong Advertiser used to phone – Mr. Jamieson, senior – and ask Dad to come in and help them out because they had the telephone directory or the IPE [Fair] prize list to do. (He was called in by the previous owner as well.) Young Bill Jamieson, who liked to drive a car, would come out to Deep Creek and pick him up. They paid him in cash and he stayed at the Armstrong Hotel, of course, until the job was done, as he had no way of getting back and forth. When he came home again, he brought some <u>cold, sliced ham</u> – oh, man!! – and I had it in my lunch as long as it lasted. Was that ever wonderful – cold, sliced ham folded in a piece of waxed paper!

And maybe because he was associating with other people and got in the way of behaving himself – like he used *to be – whenever he came home, everything was hunky-dory for a while. Later on, when Jim Jamieson was qualified to take over the lineotype work, Dad wasn't needed there anymore.*

For many families in both Spallumcheen Municipality and Deep Creek, the social activities at Hullcar Hall provided a respite from the hardships of earning a living in poor economic times. From the parcels of used clothing from her sisters, Ellie outfitted Janet.

Oh, we had the most wonderful times in Hullcar Hall! The fathers would bring their young people. Mr. Hayhurst and my father would sit up on the stage and play cribbage. We had a dance every two weeks. One dance was played for by Mr. and Mrs. Glen of Enderby, and Laurie Field played the banjo. The next time the Graves family would play, and they had four or five in their band. We had quadrilles, square dances, seven-steps, one-steps, two-steps, three-steps, waltzes. Somebody called the dance and the music went with the dance.

Janet is humming. *Seven steps forward and seven steps back, and then change to a waltz.... Everybody knew what music to play for each type of dance. And it didn't cost the girls anything! They used to bring a cake. I remember one time, a girl said, "Oh, gosh, they thought that my boot-box was a cake. I got in for nothing tonight." After the dance was all over, they auctioned off any food that was left to the bachelors.*

The number of single men was both a blessing and a curse to the young women of the times. Indispensable at dances, as marriage prospects they needed to be both resident in the vicinity and able to earn a living.

Everybody went to see their girlfriends on horseback – that was fine – but if it went beyond that distance, they never got there. So you had to find somebody within your own little area to marry. There were several farms around us where a brother and sister had never married and were living together. I don't suppose any of these people ever got as far as Vernon. I was fortunate my parents knew Mr. and Mrs. Garrett, and they took me to Vernon for a couple of weeks every summer. If it weren't for them, I would never have got to Vernon. And lots of people never did.

The Women's Missionary Society also held its meetings in Hullcar Hall – *Mother was president* – and the Literary Society met there regularly. *I recited there, people played the piano, and we had a speaker from town. The topics were to do with English literature, more or less. Miss Ford, one of our teachers, spoke one night. My father spoke one time on 'Poems of Yesteryear.' (I have all his schoolbooks from the 1800s.)*

Dan Martin had married T.W. Platten's daughter. They boarded the school teacher, Miss Taylor, of Hullcar School. He was on the

Hullcar Hall executive and took a lot of interest in it. One night when we were at a Literary Society meeting, Dan Martin was there. They discovered they didn't have a coffee bag, and the hall was miles from anywhere. Dan pulled out his shirt-tail and dared somebody to take the butcher knife and cut a piece off the bottom of his good white shirt. Somebody did. "There's your coffee bag," he said. They said it was the best coffee they had ever tasted!

At the Christmas concert each child got a net sack of candy with a Japanese orange in the toe. One Christmas my mother organized the concert – songs and skits and dialogues – and made all the sacks. We had a great big tree that touched the roof of the place, and it was all decorated with beautiful baubles. I don't know where the Barber boys, Eddie and Leslie, could find such a huge tree. Onstage there was a cloth screen that unrolled on pulleys – with wings to make it wider – all painted with trees with coloured leaves. If you had a light behind it and the audience in darkness, you could see a road that curved off into the distance under these lovely trees. I often wish I could talk to the people who are restoring the hall and tell them. This beautiful screen – I can see it just like yesterday. The last time I saw it, a heater had leaked black liquid streaks down it and I felt sad.

Interestingly, Janet doesn't recall any wives at these do's, only the husbands and young people. She also notes that some wives in Deep Creek appeared in public only rarely. Presumably, women stayed at home with younger children. Families tended to be large, not only because farming was labour intensive but also because birth control information was covert.

Of course, in those days they didn't know anything about birth control. That was just coming in when my sisters got married. I can remember, as well as can be, hearing the two of them whispering about it. Ethel had come home after many years; she was engaged to marry Charlie Harwood of Vernon, Joe Harwood's son, and she was working for Dr. Tennant in the hospital here and living with the Tennants. I remember her telling Ruth: "You know, Mrs. Tennant *sent me to her bedroom several times for no particular reason. Her package of Lueco [lubricant for inserting a diaphragm] was sitting on the bureau and I know she sent me there purposely to see it, but half the label was torn off! I couldn't read it!"* Mrs. Tennant was trying to tell Ethel about birth control without speaking about it! So they were just starting to talk about it in the 1930s.

Male doctors could be reticent in discussing sexuality with their patients, and parents tended to be close-mouthed on the subject. *After Mother had Ethel in Salem, Oregon, she had a miscarriage. Her doctor sent her to a lady doctor to get something to give her a rest from having more children for a while. When I had my menstruation, Mother said, "We don't talk about things like this."*

Both infant death and death in childbirth were not unusual in these times, and family members tried to help out when these circumstances arose.

Aunty Florence had married Arthur Foster and they had one child, Catherine. When she got pregnant the second time, her doctor expected that as a nurse she would need less supervision. Baby Enid was born dead and she died shortly afterwards. Catherine told me, "Of course, I was told to go and see my mother before she died." Aunt Olive decided that, as she was unmarried and the next oldest after Florence, she should keep house for Arthur and look after Catherine. She did so for three years and then they were married. Olive's niece became her stepdaughter.

Farming and logging accidents also claimed a share of victims. One memory again involves Dave Lawson.

We had dirt roads, and in the fall the soft spots would freeze solid into deep ruts. So in the springtime the men would stand on a float dragged by a team to level the ruts. One spring as he crossed the road on his way to the spring for water, Dad met Dave doing roadwork, and for some unknown reason, the chain was fastened to the horses from the rear of the float instead of from the front. Dave got off the float and said to him, "You know, I don't like riding on this thing."

While Dad was up in the bush at the spring, he heard a noise. He came down and found that the horses had bolted and tipped the float over on Dave. He tied up the horses and got him down to our place. He was unconscious. When I got there, Dr. Van Kleeck had come in his car. While waiting for the doctor, Mother had given Dave some brandy, as she always had some in the cupboard for herself – Three Star Hennessy – to medicate her bronchitis. We were all told, when she was really bad, to put one teaspoon of brandy and a bit of sugar in hot water in a cup and give it to her. It picked her up a bit. Dad never touched it. Dr. Van Kleeck told Mother, "You did the right thing normally, but because he was unconscious, he might have choked on it."

When Ethel still lived at home, she had special cause to be fond of Dave Lawson.

One time the haymakers were at our place, and Ethel was helping get their dinner. That girl – everything she held, she dropped, or she broke, or she did something – she was that kind of kid. She was straining the potatoes in the back kitchen at the last minute, and somehow the pot slipped out of her hands and went upside down on the board floor. Just that minute Dave came in the back door, and he never thought twice: "Get a bowl quick. Get a spoon." And between them they picked it all up except for the bits right on the bottom. "Now get a broom and sweep that up." And all through the meal he kept saying, "Gee whiz, these potatoes are good," and winking at Ethel. He was a really good guy. I remember after a taffy pull at school, Ethel rolled a nice one around a stick and sent it to him.

I could talk to Ruth about anything – unload all my troubles – but Ethel and I used to antagonize each other. When I wanted to talk to her about the old days, she'd say, "I don't want to think of those things!"

We'd be all ready to go somewhere, and Ruth would decide she needed to press her dress, and we'd be late. Ethel was always on time. She was very tidy. As a kid I'd be snipping pictures out of Eaton's catalogue. "Your snips are all over the floor!!" So I'd get into the woodbox and snip my pictures and glare at her.

One year Ethel walked to Hullcar School by herself because Ruth had graduated, and I was waiting until Hillcrest School was built. She'd get home so tired and have to wash supper dishes and do her homework. One time the dishwater got cold, and she placed the dishpan on the stove to warm the water so she could finish up. She was draining the cutlery in an empty lard tin and she put it on the stove too. The handles on the cutlery were imitation ivory, and the lard tin got so hot the handles melted and caught fire. Ethel just left everything and went to bed.

When Mother and Dad came in from the barn, Mother saw what had happened, and she said to Dad, "Go in and talk to her." So Dad went, and I guess he told her not to worry about it. So for the next few months we ate with cutlery that just had a long metal shank at the top – all that was left of the handles.

Had Douglas and Donald been the eldest instead of the youngest children, the Hilliards' attempts to make a living from farming might have been more successful. Brock needed strong backs, and adult sons might have mitigated his authoritarian streak. Instead, still a schoolgirl, Janet became the mainstay of both her parents.

Mother was a very industrious woman but she hadn't the strength to back it up, so I washed the cream separator, I packed the water, I brought in the wood, I scrubbed the floor, and then I went out in the field and helped Dad. I cranked the handle to sharpen the mower blade, and learned how to coil the hay in haycocks so it would lift off in layers when it was piled on the wagon. I never liked working in the loft because you had the hay being thrown at you and you would sink up to your knees – you had no footing – and you had to pitch it evenly around the mow so that in winter you could fork it easily down the hole in the ceiling to feed the cows. As a growing girl, I was often left to care for my brothers. If Mother and Dad were late getting home, I remember how nervous I became when the coyotes howled – there were hundreds of them in those days and they came for the chickens at night.

Her Aunt Olive's visit, however, made clear the painful difference between their lives, especially her mother's life, and the lives of their eastern relatives.

Aunt Olive's husband had passed away and she came from the east by train to visit. Ruth, married, drove over to the Salmon Arm station in her little Model T car and brought her back. Well, I know Mother and Dad had cleaned up the place as best they could. They had painted the inside walls of the house with Kalsomine. It was a dollar a box. It was a type of whitewash, and every time you touched the wall, it would come off on your finger. And they had stippled little pink designs on the Kalsomine with a sponge above the boards that ran halfway up the walls, and Kalsomined the ceilings. I fixed everything all up outside, what little flowers we had around. I know Ruth brought up some toilet paper for my mother because all we ever had was Eaton's catalogue; we rubbed it between our hands to make it soft. And I remember she brought her some bowls because we had our porridge on a plate, and the milk ran around the outside of it.

I remember bringing Aunt Olive in the front door, which we hardly ever used, and when Mother took her out into the old lean-to at the back, she said, "Oh, this is my summer kitchen, Olive." I'll always remember that. She made everything sound so nice, and it wasn't nice, it was terrible. "This is my summer kitchen." And here was this darn old shack. But she was like that in everything.

While Aunt Olive was there, she asked me to sleep with her. That made things easier, you see, because Mother and Dad took the boys' room and I could sleep with Aunt Olive in their bed. The next morning it was pouring rain and, of course, we had a chamber pot, but instead she got herself all dressed and went out into the leanto where the rain was just pouring through the cracks in the roof. Mother followed her out there.

My dad, if he'd wiggled, could easily have fixed that roof. We had cedar in the bush and he could have made shakes without it costing him anything. But he didn't do it. How embarrassing it must have been for my poor mother! Olive said, "Old shed leaks like a sieve" and went down to use the privy. I said, "Well, there was a chamber pot there." And she said, "I can't get down that far." She was old, you see.

Watching the family dynamics was difficult for Janet. *The sense of being the poor relatives* humiliated her. Brock may have found the situation equally galling, particularly in an age in which a measure of a man's worth was his ability to provide adequately for his wife and children. Janet identified with her mother – she too was working her heart out. Her father's attempts to improve production, however, tended to dissipate in failure.

Mother's cows were Guernseys and Jerseys and they gave a lot of milk. Dad bought a red polled bull because he didn't want calves with horns. When I look back now, what we got was nothing! The cows didn't give much milk and they weren't fat enough for beef. And he had those darned things standing there eating hay all the time. Fred Murray came out and offered him ten dollars for a cow, which was the average for a beast in those days. Dad wouldn't sell. "We'll eat them first!" So Murray went up to Hayhurst and he sold him a cow, so it wasn't worrying Fred Murray any. And that ten dollars would have helped out in so many ways. We just kept on working and getting nowhere. I'd help him with the hay – we had fields and fields of hay – and then it seemed all we did was put it in the mangers and get nothing for it.

Dad's overall pants wore out. So you'd cut off a piece from the bottom and put a patch on the knee. Then you tightened the shortened leg and that's how you wore them. To begin with, Mother put the patch underneath the hole and mended around it. Well, he didn't like that. She had to put the patch on the top and sew around the edge. Well, when that wore out, you had to put a patch on top of the patch! And this went on until – really and truly!! I felt like saying, "Why don't you sell one of those darn cows and get yourself a pair of pants? It would be easier on Mother and she wouldn't have to be worrying about this." But you never talked back to Dad. I think actually we were all scared of him.

I was about fifteen when we got a few sheep, and at the end we had accumulated about 125. They were my job. I had to take them out to pasture on the grass along the road because they nibbled their own pasture pretty close. I used to get up about half past four in the morning and take them out before the milk truck got there. When the truck came, it was time to bring them home. In lambing time you sometimes got triplets and the third one had to be bottle-fed. I might have seven or eight of these pets by the time lambing season was over. Even after she was weaned and grown, one of them would come every day – jingle, jingle, jingle – to the back door for a little bowl of apple peelings or potato peelings. In the end we sold that herd to a man by the name of Smith out at Falkland, and I hated to see my pet sheep go. They walked them all the way from Deep Creek to Falkland, and my father got $100 for the lot.

Janet discovered she was fond of pigs. *To my way of thinking, pigs are not dirty. You put bedding and straw in their sty, and they always had their toilet in one corner.* Always. *You fed them 'chop' and buttermilk and a lot of milk. When I was about eleven, a little pig was given to me by my brother-in-law, Ruth's husband. It had three legs and a little stump for the fourth, and I guess he didn't want to be bothered with it. I looked after that pig and sold it for the tremendous price of twenty-five dollars.*

I sent to Eaton's for a coat with a fur shawl collar. Mother said if I went and asked my father, he would get me a hat to go with the coat. It took me a long time to get up my courage because I found it very, very difficult to ask for anything. I had looked after the sheep *all summer long and worked on the farm, and I felt I shouldn't have to ask for a hat. Mother must have told him, "Janet needs a hat," so I got the hat. I think it cost about four dollars.*

By the time Janet graduated at the top of her class from Hillcrest School and Douglas finished grade one, the Great Depression was proving that things could indeed get worse.

I loved my school years. I was always reading and thought it would be nice to train for a teacher. One or two students in my class went to high school in Armstrong and worked for their board. Another boy and I tried correspondence courses from the Department of Education in Victoria. It's pretty hard to do it on your own. Some teacher that knew my sister said, "Tell her to take Latin." Well! Everything the same except for the endings!! Strange as it may seem, I was poor in math but got very high marks in algebra. I couldn't believe the results when they came back. Geometry wasn't too bad. Literature and composition I liked. I had to take chemistry and had the kitchen table all covered with apparatus – turning things blue and pink. Eventually I just let it slide.

Ellie's bronchitis became asthma and she was often bedridden. Unable to control the circumstances that were keeping the family poor, Brock's temperament worsened. Janet was overburdened with responsibility. The attitude that the father was the master of the house alienated her, and Ellie was hard pressed to keep the family on an even keel.

It seems to me that when a man gets to a certain age he begins to get difficult, and my dad was difficult – very difficult to live with all of a sudden, and I was a teenager. I got along with him all right and I worked around outside with him, but I used to feel sorry for my mother because she did everything she could possibly do to help him and make things easier for him than they already were. We had no money. At one time she sold eggs to Fred Murray for six or seven cents a dozen, and she'd be out milking cows day in and day out in that dirty old barn. Sixteen dollars for one month was the biggest cream cheque I ever saw from all those cows, and that wasn't much when you had to feed three kids and buy their boots!

When I was about fifteen or so, we had a lot of clucky hens. I decided to set every egg I could find under these clucky hens. As a result we had a lot of roosters, and I would clean them for Mother and give us something nice to eat in the summertime. I was very glad I did that because it made things easier.

She got down to where she didn't have any clothes. She was very particular about being nicely dressed, and it must have been hard on her not to have anything good to wear. Eventually Dad bought her a dress before Christmas, but she had to raise the front and put in a piece because her neck got thin as she grew older. I remember her cutting it up in strips years later and, with some grey, making a stub mat out of it. Nothing was ever wasted. She had one pair of shoes, and she had to wear them every day, and she'd polish them over and over. Oh, God, it was awful. It was just awful.

She'd worn the same winter coat year in and year out, and she needed a new coat. Well, Dad never seemed to wiggle himself to <u>do</u> anything about it. And he growled…. And he grumped…. So she bought two little pigs and kept a book of her expenses, and he'd go into town and get the chop for the pigs. And she'd get up at six o'clock in the morning – she always was an early riser – and she'd go out and feed these pigs – and she'd feed them at noon and she'd feed them at night. And she went on doing that until they got big. Now, there was no reason in the wide world, if *she* could do that, why *he* couldn't do that too and get her a coat.

Eventually she got the money, and I remember her sending to Eaton's and getting the coat. She didn't say anything to him about it because he'd get mad. So, of course, we kids said, "Oh, why don't you save it and open it on Christmas." Well, I should have known better. When Christmas time came, she cried because she realized the amount of work she had put into this disappointing coat. It spoiled her Christmas.

My sisters were all for Mother, so they took her to Vernon and got her a coat that had a nice fur collar that went all the way round, and you wore a scarf in the opening. Well, I didn't like the coat – it was a pale grey and the fur was grey, and I had seen her in things that looked better on her. But she was happy with it and that's all that mattered.

Brock's fears and prejudices also made life harder for the family than it need have been. Refusing to sell his stock at Depression prices, he nevertheless made little use of it himself.

He never sold anything to make money – that's what used to get me. And nothing was ever butchered, you know. The women up and down the valley learned how to can meat. But my dad refused to eat it. Mrs. Hayhurst and Mrs. Lawson, they'd brown it on both sides in a pan, and then they'd pack it in the jar, pour the fat over it, screw on the lid and process it for three or four hours. And nobody ever died. He thought he might croak! And then Mrs. Hayhurst had a canning machine – a new thing. You could cut the lid off a can three times and put a new lid on. Brock wasn't convinced. Yet killing and canning beef and poultry would have varied their diet and made meal planning less of a chore for the women.

Mother made our meals out of nothing. I used to help Ruth a lot when she had her children. I'd walk down and stay with her. Her husband used to butcher for Fred Murray – it was Murray and Parker then – they bought their farms together when Bill Parker came home from overseas. I remember him bringing in this big liver one time – you never got anything for the liver and the heart – and I guess Ruth was so sick of 'doing something' with the liver that she said, "Janet, take this out in the wheat field and throw it away." I remember thinking, "Oh, Mother, if you could only have this." I almost cried when I dumped it into the field and, of course, Bill never asked her where it went.

Brock and Ellie were now in their fifties. The Depression showed no signs of remission. Brock's frustration deteriorated into a loss of interest in the farm. This strange apathy frightened and enraged his daughter.

He got lazier and lazier. When the cows needed milking, he'd sit after supper – it would be ten o'clock, and eventually he'd go out with a lantern to milk. The odd person would come in the evening, and we hadn't done the milking, and we'd have to do it after they had gone home. It was absolutely ridiculous. And I'd say to Mother, "You're not going out there. I'm old enough. I'll go out." Well, I got smart after a while and, without saying anything, I'd pick up the milk buckets after supper and hike for the barn. Of course, he couldn't let me go by myself, so pretty soon he'd come out, and in that way I'd get the milking done.

Then when winter came on, he'd sit down after breakfast. "Oh, let me have my paper and my smoke." And he'd have a pipe and read the paper. And all the time the darn barn needed cleaning out, or something else needed doing. Instead of going out after breakfast and getting the jobs done and then *sitting down, he didn't.*

The manure heap sat there. He could have put it on the land but he didn't bother. He lost the respect of the other farmers. It was just terrible.

Brock had always been restrictive in allowing Janet social outings on her own. *On Hallowe'en, for instance, he wouldn't let me go for the simple reason that I might be involved in tipping over somebody's privy, or something. I'd go to bed early, but I could hear the others laughing and giggling as they went up the road.* Now a young woman, Janet chafed under his rules and longed for opportunities to join her friends in laughter and fun.

Albert Hayhurst had four girls, and if a bunch of us went up there: "You have to be back by ten o'clock." Well, there was no way! I went once to a thing like that, and we would have our fun, and then at ten o'clock the hostess would make tea and serve something or other, and there was no way I could be home by ten o'clock without having to say, "Excuse me, I have to go home now," and looking like nothing on earth! I got so I wouldn't go.

I think Mother felt bad about it, and if ever I was invited out, she'd try to make me a new dress out of something that she had. I remember when I was going out with Bob, she'd say to Dad: "Cut Janet's hair." When I think about all the things she tried to do to help us – never thinking about herself....

For a change of scene and a little money, Janet began doing housework for the neighbours. *I would walk a couple of miles and iron and wash the floors and such, and I'd get fifty cents and lunch or dinner.* However, when she was nearly twenty, Janet heard about a live-in job prospect in Kamloops.

At that time we had a teacher called Ethel McKim at Hillcrest – it was just about ready to close – who said there was a man in north Kamloops whose wife had died and left him with a boy. Kamloops was a long way off. But the average pay was ten dollars a month. *It would be a whole year before I could afford to go home, of course, because a train ticket cost five dollars, half a month's salary. I wasn't looking to leave – the boys were beginning to get to a place where they would soon have been a help. But I decided to go. The man picked me up, and he picked up two bales of hay somewhere, and then he picked up something else for somebody else – that kind of transit business.* Janet was just another package.

I didn't last very long there – about a month or so – he said he didn't need me anymore. Later I heard that the girl who had preceded me had become pregnant. She left and went to work for Dr. Tennant, who had moved to Kamloops. Of course, after a while he noticed her getting a little large.

Friends of my father – McAuliffes – whom he had boarded with in Greenwood had moved to Kamloops. They used to come by about once a year. So when I lost my job, I went there. Someone visiting Mrs. McAuliffe said, "Oh, I know someone who needs some help."

So I went to the Pollards. Mrs. Pollard and the children were going to Edmonton for the summer to be with her sister. Her husband was an engineer for the Canadian Pacific Railway.

Oh, I had a wonderful summer! All I had to do was walk the dog – they had a Great Dane – and cut the sweetpeas (he wanted that done), and take any orders that came by telephone: "Call Billy Pollard at 2300 hours," *and I was supposed to light the stove to have a cistern of hot water ready for him when he came home from work. So with* those *jobs, you can imagine what a fine time I had!! I got eight dollars a month for that. And in the evenings I made quite a few friends.*

When Mrs. Pollard came back, she and her husband went off to the Coast for a week and I looked after the children. Then a jeweller and his wife had a baby, and I gave them a hand for a couple of weeks. Then Mrs. Pollard heard that Dr. and Mrs. Willoughby needed help with their new baby, David, but when I phoned, the job had been filled. However, her friend nearby, Mrs. Corbould, was in need of someone, and I went to work for her.

After a summer at the Pollards', the Corboulds were a decided anticlimax. They had six children and Mrs. Corbould had been raised in London, England. She wanted things done the English way.

I had to do curls every morning – just so – and I had a great big elephant bone brush to do them with. Mrs. Corbould was so organized – not crabby – but I could tell you what we would be doing every second of the day: At half past five the little children had their supper – breakfast cereal – in the kitchen, and at supper hour the two eldest girls joined their mother and father in the dining room. Meanwhile the little ones played a while and then were put to bed. *And on it went.*

I was there for about a year. It wasn't an easy place – I had to get up early – I was spoiled. One cold winter day she told me to scrub the porch – the North Thompson was all ice! So was the porch when Janet finished. *I said to her, "I'd like twelve dollars a month." She was paying ten. She said, "I don't mind if you're worth it." So I always worked hard because if you didn't, there was always somebody right there to take your place. And if you got your room and board and something extra, you were all right. You had your evenings off to a certain extent. Nevertheless, I gave her notice and moved. The little girl who slept in my bedroom still writes me every Christmas.*

But always the line was distinct. You were the servant. I'd had so much of that at home – we were the people that mother's sisters sent their clothes out to every two years – and Mom was glad of it.

I went back to the McAuliffes. She was an invalid in a wheelchair. I had dropped to ten dollars when I went to her but the work was much easier. Then my brother-in-law came to see me – he was over for the Kamloops Bull Sale – and he said it was time I quit working with old people and came home.

The feeling seemed to be that she was missed, and that life had more to offer than scrubbing other people's floors and minding other people's children. When Janet came back to Deep Creek in the autumn of 1935, she was different from the girl who had left. She had made the best of the work situations that had presented themselves and been independent for nearly two years. *I found the atmosphere much more acceptable in every way.*

Bob Coldicott was interested. *I knew him. He was ten years older than I was. He was always hunting deer. He said he could remember me singing 'Star of the East' at Hullcar Hall. That winter I started going to dances there.* Her father would no longer be driving her.

Bob decided to make his move. Wisely, he began by dealing first with Janet's father in a matter of business and putting some money in his pocket. *Around about January Bob took a hunting trip over Pyott and Beddington's hill and came down in Deep Creek. He*

193

asked my father if he could buy some hay from him. That started it. We were married that fall, October 7, 1936.

The Coldicotts had been homesteaders in Spallumcheen.

My husband's family cleared that piece of land in Knob Hill where Dr. Rutherford lives now. It was all covered with bush. Now, of course, it's all broken up into small areas. They built the barn first, and then that winter when Bob was a little child, they had no house and the snow came on. My husband always said, "I don't know why we couldn't have lived in the barn. The barn was nice and warm." But for some reason or other, his parents were scared stiff of fire and wouldn't put up a stove in the barn and when they went to bed, put the fire out as a precaution.

That summer a lady had brought her son up from the Coast and put up a tent on a wooden form, just about where Mariposa Nursery used to be. Her son was inclined to tuberculosis and they thought it would be drier up here for him. When winter came on, they went back to the Coast, but she told Mrs. Coldicott if she liked she could have that tent. And the Coldicotts lived in the tent – his sister Dolly and Bob and the parents – all winter. That's where Bob started. Then the parents sold the property to Floyd Hunter and moved over to Lansdowne.

Janet's wedding was momentous. The eastern relatives were involved, as they had always been, Brock was amenable, and Ellie had the chance to fuss over her daughter. Janet's bridesmaid was her friend Marjory Moffatt, whom she had met at the United Church young people's group in Kamloops, where they had gone on treasure hunts and put on concerts.

When Ethel married, she had asked me to be her bridesmaid, but I couldn't accept because at the time I didn't have anything suitable for a dress. When my turn came, I asked Marjory, and she came on the CNR in the morning and stayed all day with me, and we put her on the night train going back.

In a corner of the old Hudson's Bay store in Kamloops, there was a ladies' store called Joyce's. Joyce was a milliner and made hats. Marjorie had a green dress for the wedding and she went to Joyce for a hat. When Alice drove me to Cranbrook in March [2003] for Marjory's 90th birthday, I said to Marjory, "Do you remember Joyce wove two colours of ribbon and made a 'chapeau' to match your green dress?" A wedding photograph shows her sporting a close-fitting cloche. *When I waved goodbye this time, I knew I would never see her again, and I think she knew it too.*

Momma took me to Hudson's Bay in Vernon to buy the dress. Dad must have had some money coming – he was secretary for the Typographical Union of Printers for years and years – he had books from them that just covered the table. Somehow or other there was money for the dress. It had a train and you held it up by a loop over your little finger.

When Mother wrote back east to tell the aunts, my only cousin, Catherine, wrote that she would like to send me her veil. It is a floor-length veil, and the day is breezy. In the photograph it floats like a mist behind her head. She carries a trailing bouquet, frail strands drifting down the front of the dress. *I don't remember what the flowers were, but there were also little bits of flowers here and there on the fern. It was beautiful. Bob got them in Vernon at the florist's down the hill by the courthouse near the tracks.*

We were married by Reverend Boothroyd in the United Church in Armstrong. There was a wooden arch in the driving shed behind the church – there was no hall then – and Emma Wahl, who used to live here and worked for Fred Murray, got it brought into the church for the wedding. (She was an equestrian and so was Bob, so she did it for him too.) We had gone out to Florence Smith's who lived up Hullcar way and picked sugar maple leaves and covered the arch with them. And we took some out and put them in our old house too.

After the service we went back to Deep Creek. Aunt Olive in

Ontario had got her maid to make a whole box of tiny cookies in individual papers like chocolates. They were wonderful. And they had come all that way without damage. Mother had made some pretty salads, and she and Ethel had baked a three-tiered wedding cake. She knew a man named Mr. Rolston, a baker in Vernon, and had asked him to ice it. A fellow came into his shop looking for a job. "Well, there's a cake in the back. Let's see what you can do." So of course he made it fancy because he wanted the work. [Following the reception] Bob and I went over to Salmon Arm and down to Vancouver and across on the ferry to Nanaimo [on Vancouver Island] where his parents had retired. His sister was at the wedding.

They returned from their wedding trip to the Coldicott farm at Lansdowne and made an attempt to earn a living there.

Bob's parents gave the Lansdowne property to us when we married because when they sold the Knob Hill property there was still some money owing on it, and Bob kept paying that off for them and worked hard for them. We had eighty acres, and a well, and an outdoor privy. The property was on a hillside and the only piece he could make use of was right inside the gate. He seeded barley there and I think we had one crop. Then he bought another thirty acres across the road, but it still wasn't enough to keep us going.

So he turned the car in on a truck and went up in the bush behind my dad's place and started hauling logs. When he came home on weekends – he had somebody working for him up in the bush – he would haul me a barrel of water to do my washing for the week, and then I could pack the water in buckets from the well for drinking.

Alice was born on August 20, 1937. In 1940 Bob proposed that the family relocate to Armstrong. *He thought that we could better ourselves and it would be better for me. So we had a sale of all the equipment and brought in $1000 – enough to put down on this seven acres on Wood Avenue. It was listed at $2000. We had to let the taxes go for three years – at the end of three years the City could foreclose – and instead we made the payments. We couldn't do both – we had* to let something go. At the end of three years we owned the property, and Bob had made enough money hauling logs for Mr. Leduc to pay the taxes. Oh, gosh!

We sold the farm to Harry Ruby, a Welsh miner. That's why he came out to British Columbia, and he worked at the open pit gypsum mine in Falkland. Everything was in order – the rope was there – but he fell over the edge of the mine and was killed.

Janet lived in the house on Wood Avenue until November, 2003, when she relocated to Tiffany Lane. *Our son Frank was born in Armstrong on April 5, 1941. Bob died in 1993. Alice and I nursed him at home. He was a sweet man – no trouble.*

Ellie died in 1940. *The boys were still at home and she was cooking for the three of them. They had never been taught to help out with housework. I was visiting Mrs. Parkinson with Alice, just a toddler, and I was told that Mother had been taken to the hospital in Armstrong. When I arrived, Ruth was at the head of the bed holding the oxygen mask to her face. I think she was in a coma. She didn't know she was dying. So it wasn't a long drawn-out affair as far as her death was concerned, but living with bronchitis and asthma had occupied long, weary years.*

She didn't have proper food. When I look back compared to what we have today, it makes me ill to think about it. We lived on potatoes and beans – scalloped potatoes and potato soup or a big baked potato; baked beans and bean soup with a little cream in it. She always found something to fill our stomachs. I used to wonder how she could do it. Of course, the chickens didn't lay in the wintertime, and I remember her giving me twenty-five cents to get some eggs from Henry Hill. I think she just got to the stage where she longed for an egg.

After she died, Dad and the boys lived on at Deep Creek for a couple of years. Douglas assumed the duty of cook and bottlewasher, and Donald worked at a small sawmill on the Beadle property. Then

Dad returned to his trade, had a sale of the farm goods, and moved to Penticton, where he was employed by the Penticton Herald. He made a deposit on a house and Mother would have loved it. It was a low house covered with vine and had a kitchen, a living/dining room, three bedrooms, and a big porch on the front. It would have been so nice for her. It had an indoor toilet. He had under two blocks to walk to work. Why he didn't do it earlier I'll never know. He just got to the point, I guess, where he couldn't manage on his own and had to pull out.

Before Brock left Deep Creek, he gave Douglas a chance at a job. *Dad favoured Douglas – always did. Douglas was a plodder. He was quiet. He didn't show initiative. As a child he'd sit at the end of the table when Mother was baking and say, "What can I do, Momma, what can I do?" Donald, on the other hand, was more like Mother – always making birdhouses or slingshots – busy at something he'd thought up himself.*

Ethel's husband, Charlie Harwood, was an electrician. They felt sorry for Donald because he was so anxious to better himself. So Charlie said, "If there's an opening at Edgar Electric where I work, I'll see that Donald gets a chance."

I wasn't living at home then, so this is hearsay, but apparently an opening came. They phoned up and said, "Would Donald come down?" Of course, he was working at that bit of a sawmill. So Dad said to Douglas, "If you walk to Armstrong to catch the train, I'll give you the money for a ticket to Vernon." So Douglas turned up at Edgar Electric. Charlie said, "It was Donald we asked to come." "Well, he couldn't come because he's working at a sawmill." They weren't too pleased but they hired him. That episode was another of Dad's little quirks – it just wasn't cricket.

Later on, Charlie went into business on his own, and this time Donald got his chance. So both boys apprenticed as electricians. Later they moved to Penticton to be with Dad until such time as they were called to fight for their country. Douglas and Donald enlisted in the army: Douglas in the Reconnaissance Corps and Donald in the Tank Corps. They both served in Europe.

Douglas had to crawl on his hands and knees within enemy lines carrying a radio. Apparently this job was something they couldn't order you to do. As Janet recalls, the selection of the man was the luck of the draw. *They put all the names in a hat and pulled out Douglas' name. In the course of the reconnaissance, he raised up a little and got shot across the back. After that, his nerves became very bad. War does terrible things to people. He married a girl from Penticton and worked at maintenance in a big sawmill in Port Alberni. They had two sons. I was with him when he died.*

Donald was killed on D-Day – June 6, 1944. His tank was hit. The family received a letter saying that he had been killed in action. His body lies in the military cemetery at Beny-sur-mer, France.

Brock died in 1953. One last story about him twinkles in Janet's memory. *Aunt Olive and Aunt Ethel moved out to Calgary when Dad was working there before he and Mother were married. He took them to see a show. Of course, he never looked to see what the show was about, and it was a little risqué for those days. Ethel was absolutely horrified, but Olive nudged Dad and whispered, "I don't care if you don't."*

Looking back on her life in Deep Creek, Janet acknowledges a debt to her mother. *We were poor in money, but poor in other ways I never felt because Mother knew what was appropriate. She seemed to have that knack – she always knew what was correct. She'd talk to us and tell us.*

We always *had a tablecloth – even if it was only four flour sacks sewn together. We never used just the oilcloth. She taught us how to lay the table and always to put the knife with the cutting edge towards the plate. I remember once I went to a girl's place and her mother asked her to set the table. She was annoyed she had to do it, and she put the cup on the wrong saucer. "Well, that's good enough." When I* came home, I thought I'd try that trick, but it didn't last five minutes with Mother. "You're not going to do that," she said. She never let us give up on ourselves, and she never complained.

One time I had an invitation from a teacher to visit her one particular weekend in Salmon Arm, and she phoned to ask, "Would it matter very much if Janet came the following weekend?" Well, I was all excited to go at the original date, but Mother said, "Maybe it's not convenient for her to have you this weekend." She always considered the other person. She had guidance from her relatives, but most of it came from inside herself. Most of it, I think, is born in a person.

Ellie believed, for example, that childhood innocence should not be spoiled by frightening images of death and interment. We were never allowed to go to a funeral, but she'd sit and tell us all about a funeral from one end to the other. The first funeral I ever went to was her own.

Janet also remembers aunts Claribel and Olive with love. They are another real bright memory. They were so good to us. They'd send out so many nice little things for my brothers – kites to make, and erector sets. My brothers used to attach a belt to the sewing machine wheel to get all their little windmills going! Aunt Claribel lived to be ninety-eight. We used to write back and forth and were close.

Janet's artistry and love of nature enrich her life; her former garden on Wood Avenue was a rainbow of tranquil space. A member of the Presbyterian Church in Armstrong, she submitted, anonymously at first, a monthly column entitled 'Nature's Way' to the St. Andrew's *Messenger* and accompanied each one with her own illustrations. Some samples of her reflections follow:

> I had my window open at night recently and was fortunate to hear the mating hoot of two saw-whet owls. They will be nesting very soon. There is a ravine nearby where a few trees still remain to attract them. Years ago I was wandering around the back of Rose Swanson

Mountain and I came across one asleep on the branch of an old stub. He does not have tufted ears, is brown in colour, and is more striped rather than spotted down the breast. Only the pigmy owl is smaller. I put my hand out and touched him. He opened his eyes, gave me a good peck and a dirty look for disturbing him, and then went promptly back to sleep until dusk of that day.

From my dining-room window I can see the leaves on the big maple tree beginning to show a change of colour which reminds me it is nearly the month of September, the beginning of autumn. The Anglo-Saxons called it Gerst Monath, Barley Month, and that describes it beautifully. It is the golden month, one of warm, still and mellow days. Corn has been gathered, apples are ready for harvesting, squash and pumpkins are ripening on the vine. Before we know it, Jack Frost will be stealing in with icy fingers to give us a nudge to gather up what's left in the garden before month's end.

Dusk was falling as I took my usual chair to watch the night close in. There is something very homey and comforting about sitting on my back porch watching the bats fly to and fro through the waning twilight, and there comes to mind a fitting conclusion to my day, the first verse of Thomas Gray's 'Elegy written in a Country Churchyard':

> The curfew tolls the knell of parting day
> The lowing herd winds slowly o'er the lea,
> The plowman homeward plods his weary way,
> And leaves the world to darkness and to me.

[Janet Marion (Hilliard) Coldicott died peacefully at her home on May 1st, 2004.]

Janet Hilliard at age twenty in Kamloops

Chapter Four

Poets, Painters, and Ploughmen

Russell Carleton 'Rusty' Freeze

When Dad and Mother wrote to each other, their letters were always in poetry.

>A package of tobacco
>Sure makes me smile with glee
>When from the dear old girl at home
>Is sent with love to me.
>>Eyes so blue
>>Fond and true
>
>Look at you thru Smokeland
>>Wish you joy
>>Without alloy
>
>As it's curling upward.

James Russell Freeze scribbled this poem on the back of an envelope in response to a gift of tobacco from his wife, Edie, who was living with their children on a homestead in Salmon River Valley during the First World War.

World War One was James Russell Freeze's second war.

When the Boer War started, Dad, although only nineteen, joined the Strathcona Horse, the requirement being that you had to be able to ride and shoot. Lord Strathcona and Mount Royal, the Canadian High Commissioner in London, equipped this regiment and paid all expenses.

It took six weeks to get to South Africa, and a lot of the horses, including Dad's, died on the way. Since Grandma Freeze had made a couple of the older enlisted men promise to look after Dad, after disembarking at Cape Town, they went out one night and stole a little Basuto pony for him, roached [cut short] its mane, and generally changed its appearance. The next morning the Boer farmer came looking for his horse. The men were put on parade, and he went down the line, but he didn't recognize it. Dad rode that horse all through the war – it was one of the toughest horses he ever had.

Rusty Freeze has a wooden cigar box inscribed as follows:

S. Davis & Sons, makers of good cigars for over half a century. Winners of the Gold Medals (Grand Prix) at Paris in 1853 and Centennial in 1867 in competition against the World.

Rusty no longer smokes – *these boxes were common in those days* – but he keeps some treasures in it. One of these is a dried eucalyptus leaf from South Africa on which his father wrote to Rusty's grandmother back in Calgary:

> Go where I will on land or on sea
> My mother's dear voice I can hear:
> "Oh! God bless my boy, I can trust him to You,"
> The words of dear Mother's prayer.
>   Your loving son
>   Trooper J.R. Freeze

Trooper J.R. Freeze did a significant amount of travelling on his Basuto pony. A second item in the cigar box is a letter from him written on the cartridge paper in which his ammunition was wrapped. He appeared to be using blue crayon and he wasted no space. He had been in South Africa for approximately six months.

Newcastle, June 20, [1900]

Dear Mother,
    No doubt you are surprised at not hearing from me before this but I have not had a chance to write you till today. We have been away up in Zululand for a while back scouting, but we returned to Durban and entrained for here. Gen Buller is about 20 miles from here at Laing's Neck [Nek] and we are going up to him tomorrow. We passed through Ladysmith yesterday morning and saw the battlefield of Colenso and

Tugela River. I don't see how Buller ever relieved Ladysmith as the Boers held a very strong position. They held a line of hills about 7 miles broad which completely surrounded Ladysmith, and if the British had held the position that the Boers did, nothing could have driven them out. The battlefield is covered with graves where many a poor soldier lies buried. We passed the bridges that were blown up by the Boers but they are all fixed up now. The main body of the Boer army is about 5 miles from here but word came into camp that they were all split up so I think that the war is nearly over. Perhaps by the time you receive this it will be over and it is nearly time it was. Well I suppose that you will think that this is funny writing paper but [it] is the only paper I can get so you will have to excuse it. Do not be surprised if you do not hear from me for some time because I do not think that we will be where we can post a letter from. Hope you can read this some time. Goodbye. Your loving son, J.R. Freeze.

James Russell brought back with him a small, square, metal snuffbox – *he probably got it from a Boer* – and a beautifully painted card of the port of Cape Town, Table Mountain in the background. It is dated October 29, 1900, and attributed to the city's mayor in grateful acknowledgement of military service to the colony. He also brought home a meerschaum pipe with General Buller's face carved into the bowl, and a small quantity of gold from the Rand.

Boys from the prairies and BC knew what gold was and how to wash [pan] for it. Dad saw the men running around with their mess tins so he took his and washed all night. Next morning they were all made to line up and hand over their gold. Well, Dad managed to keep some and brought it home and had a pair of cufflinks made. Somewhere along the line they were lost except for one small piece. Mother had a ring made out of it with Dad's initials on the inside and mine on the topside. I couldn't wear the thing – it felt too heavy.

When Dad came back from the Boer War, the boat stopped in London, and Edward VII had the men shown all over the Tower of London. They saw the Crown jewels – something they would never have got to see otherwise.

Rusty's cigar box holds several photos. One picture he took himself in Nova Scotia of the original Freeze home. It is a large, white frame building set among flowering bushes and lawns. It looks cool and substantial.

The Freezes migrated to England from Friesland in Holland around 1500 as weavers, but William and his father Samuel were stonemasons. It was said of the Freezes that they were born with a stonehammer in one hand and a songbook in the other. By the time the family tree proliferated in Canada, the stonehammer had been replaced by a plough, and the songbook by a paintbrush and a poem. William built the white frame house in Amherst Point, Nova Scotia, in 1772.

The house was originally close to the water, but it was relocated on rollers half a mile inland. Twenty teams of oxen were used, and the women stayed inside the house and cooked meals for the men while it was on the move. When the oxen arrived at the hole dug for the new basement, six teams walked on the left side of it, six teams walked on the right side of it, and the middle eight teams walked down into the hole and up the other side. Of course, the teams on the sides were much higher than the teams down the hole, so they dragged those eight teams through the air until they reached ground again on the opposite side, and the house followed the teams and settled over the basement.

William's grandson John had seven children including William, Isaac, and Bertram James. B.J., as he was called, was Rusty Freeze's rapscallion grandfather. *He was a drunkard. He used to get the DTs and see snakes.* In an alcoholic interpolation of the story in which Jesus exorcised an evil spirit into a herd of swine, *he used to threaten to throw Grandma over the wall into the pigs. Grandma was Martha Arnold, a relative of Benedict Arnold – who sold information to both sides during the American War of Independence from Britain – and a cousin of the American poet Will Carleton.* At some stage deviltry and poetry slipped into the genes.

The family started moving west – first to New Brunswick where Dad was born, then to Montreal. About 1883 they got to Alberta. Isaac had come out ahead and opened the first grocery store in Calgary. Until the railroad came through, he brought supplies in by Red River cart. He left his wife to mind the store and went off to the Klondike for a couple of years. I don't think he ever mined for gold – he mined the miners – he played cards. The fire that devastated the main street in Calgary left his store standing, perhaps because of its name.

B.J. and Martha Freeze had nine children of whom only three survived. They lost three in three weeks – Willie, age seven; John, age three; and Owen Sanford – not unusual in those times. One picked up lye off the floor when they were scrubbing and ate it. The three that grew up were Aunt Matty, Aunt Bertie, and my father, James Russell.

Rusty's cigar box discloses another photo – a spare, clapboard house that is marked with a small white X and stands in a barren, unfenced yard where a cow and a pig are rooting.

Dad's father had a homestead out on the bald prairie about ten miles from Calgary. The house was struck twice by lightning in one year. That X shows where Grandma Freeze was standing next the house when her little daughter came up to her. Grandma bent down over the child, and the lightning hit her and ripped her back open and killed a calf and a dog. She was in bed for six months. Later that year they had company and Grandma suddenly hustled everyone out of the kitchen, and the lightning struck the house again, but this time no one was hurt.

A photo of B.J. reveals a tall dark man in riding gear and a soft felt hat, one leg propped nonchalantly on a chair in the yard.

Both Grandpa Freeze and my dad were around five foot ten, I guess. Grandpa liked to imbibe and Kootenay Brown, of course, did too. John George 'Kootenay' Brown was a notable figure – an Irish-born adventurer, army scout, trader, and trapper. *One night they met in a bar in Calgary, and Grandpa brought Kootenay Brown home with him for dinner. I guess Grandma wasn't too impressed with the state of the two of them when they got to the house. She was a big woman and had a tongue and wasn't afraid to use it. Kootenay Brown said, "Don't worry, Mrs. Freeze, come fall I'll get you some huckleberries." That fall two four-gallon coal oil cans arrived full of huckleberries. They used to cut the tops off coal oil cans and use them for buckets.*

Dad was one of ten children that went to the first school in Calgary. He used to talk about how, as a kid of ten or twelve, he had to go with his father in winter the forty miles to the Foothills to get wood or dig coal, almost freezing to death in the process, because B.J. never planned ahead. As a result, Dad would never attempt to farm on the prairie. He would never even go back!! (Years later Dode [daughter Dorothy] and Jim persuaded him to take a trip to Calgary with them.)

The cattle just ran wild in those days – no fences. Dad said you could ride for forty miles and never touch a fence. He used to ride for ten miles to some little bluff so he could get sticks to whittle – something to do, I guess.

With Isaac already established in Calgary and B.J. fond of the amenities there, the family abandoned the homestead and moved to the city. *William got drowned while attempting to ford the Bow River.* B.J. went back to his original trade as a painter and paperhanger, and when James Russell returned from the Boer War, he joined his father's business. Perhaps in rebellion against his father's drinking habits, he enlisted in the Salvation Army and played in the band. In this way he met his wife, Edith Lilie 'Edie' Gamble.

Grandpa and Grandma Gamble were Methodists. He used to run a windmill flour mill in England, and he moved out to Regina [Saskatchewan] to work at the Bell Farm. A big hailstorm came up and ruined the crops and the Bell Farm went broke. Mother was just six years old when they came to Regina. As they arrived, they met a trainload of soldiers returning to Ontario after having put down the Riel Rebellion.

Mother became a Salvationist and played a guitar. There was a Salvation Army excursion by train across the prairies to Banff [Alberta], and they picked up Salvationists all along the line. Mother and Dad met on the train. They met only three times before they were married.

He went back to Regina to see her. He had got himself a new suit, and he hired what he thought was a fancy rig with a high stepping trotter to take her out for a ride away from her family. Instead they gave him an old plough horse. When he got out in the country, he soon discovered the reason. The buggy wheels started to pick up the grass and prairie gumbo, and he had to get out in his courting best and scrape them off before he could turn the horse around and go back home. Grandma Gamble allowed them fifteen minutes' private conversation after she and Grandpa had gone up to bed.

It must have been long enough for James Russell to propose marriage. They were married in 1905. *For the day of the wedding he had had a new suit made in Calgary, and the sisters of the bride-to-be wanted to see what it looked like. So on the evening before the wedding they persuaded Dad to show it to them. He opened the box and the darn tailor hadn't sewn the pieces together. So they rushed around and got someone to finish the suit in time for the ceremony.*

My sisters Marjorie and Janet were born in Calgary where Dad was making a living as a painter. In those days all paint had a lead base, which was hard on his health, and he was subject to enteric fever [a type of dysentery] from his time in South Africa. As a result he was skin and bone. One day he saw a poster in a real estate window with a little guy lolling under an apple tree: 'Come to the Okanagan; a fruit grower has time to read.' *Grandma and Grandpa Gamble had already moved out to Armstrong (they had a house on*

Rosedale Avenue near the highway), so Mother and Dad sold the business and followed them here.

The little man under the apple tree was a fantasy.

All Pleasant Valley Road was planted to orchard at one time. They moved onto ten acres of orchard just south of the high school on the left hand side. Nice and flat up there – ten acres of clay – and frost!! They were frozen out four years hand-running, and they sold the piano that Mother had brought with her from back east and used the money for heaters. I still remember those things – round with holes and standing on four legs. They burned coal briquets [compressed coal dust] in them to make smoke to keep off the frost in winter and the bugs in summer.

The cigar box displays a scene in the apple orchard. James Russell has stopped for a moment to rest on a wooden bench, his dog Don lying at his feet. His friend and neighbour Eddie Rochester holds a horse – *horses did all the work*. Behind them a dirt road runs back along a row of apple trees. A half-barrel holds flowers – *something Mother would have planted*.

Dad had the privilege of finding the first coddling moth in the Okanagan. I guess someone threw a rotten apple with a coddling moth in it out of the train. So the Department of Agriculture bought all his apples that fall and burned them. That was the only money he ever made from his orchard. Feeling flush, he went ahead and bought a second ten acres, and they went broke and lost the twenty acres. They foreclosed on him. After that, you could never get Dad to grow another apple tree, no way!!

The only recourse left to the Freezes was to secure a homestead.

Dad had never farmed in his life, but what were they going to do? Dorothy had been born in Armstrong, and Mother was pregnant again. They moved to Yankee Flats in the Salmon River Valley and homesteaded on a 'bench' about two miles above the river. 157 acres of bush, three acres cleared, a little log cabin (no ceiling in it so they put up cloth), two miles to water that they hauled from the river uphill in a barrel. They dug two wells but they were both dry. The property was covered with huge pine and fir trees and open underneath, just like a big park. One of my fondest memories is the sound of the wind sighing through the pine.

In order to get a little money, settlers cut trees into logs and hauled them on sleighs to the river, and then logging crews drove the logs down to Salmon Arm on the spring freshet. The price they got for the logs was three dollars for a thousand board feet – if they could collect the money. Bridges in those days were suspension bridges – no piles – so that logs could be driven down the river without obstruction. Salmon River is classed as a navigable river on that account.

Dad told the story of the first time he tried to load the logs on the sleigh. As each log was about three feet through, it could not be loaded by hand; he had to use a decking line and, handling the team, roll it onto the sleigh. Being alone, he had no one to stop the log, and it rolled off the other side. This happened three times before he realized he had to chain a stopper on the bunks.

James Russell finally got the sleigh loaded up and began the drive downhill towards Salmon River. *One of the horses dropped dead. I know the exact spot where it happened.* He had no money to buy another horse, so he asked his brother-in-law Albert Giles – a smart Englishman – Bertie's husband – for a fifty dollar loan. Albert worked in Los Angeles for International Harvester and was Bertie's second husband. Bertie at fourteen had married a man much older than herself and then had left him and gone to live with Albert. Scandalous in those days! And so was fifty dollars for a horse! Albert thought the world of Bertie and made my dad the loan. (Aunt Maddy was down in California too.)

As if to complicate matters, on May 10, 1915, Edie gave birth to a set of beautiful twins – Eleanor and Russell Carleton. Six weeks later James Russell enlisted in the First World War.

He was patriotic – it's how they were in those days – he waited until we were a little older before he joined up. For some reason Grandpa Gamble called us Tillie and Nebbie. And when Dad had to put on the enlistment form the names of his children, all he could think of in our case was Tillie and Nebbie, so that's what he put down. Tillie is anyone's guess – Tillie the Toiler? – the family has no idea – but Nebuchadnezzar was king of Babylon.

Dad left Mother with five kids, a horse, and three cows to look after and haul water for. Mrs. Sharp was in the same boat, so to speak. Hum, her husband, had also enlisted, but she only had four kids, and they were a little older than we were. Their house was only a shell and very cold, so they moved in with us that first winter. Our sister Janet was given the job of looking after Eleanor, and Marj, the job of looking after me. We were always very close until her death. To this day the two families are also very close – Eleanor married Norris Sharp.

The cigar box offers two photographs from this period. The first shows Edie holding the reins and walking alongside a horse hauling a wagonload of wood. *She'd cut big, old, dry pine for the winter – dead pine, still standing. It made a good hot fire.* The second is a winter scene in the yard behind the house. Edie and Mrs. Sharp are at the woodpile on opposite ends of a crosscut saw sunk in a log that is two and a half feet in diameter. Edie is wearing a tuque and scarf, a three-quarter coat and heavy, ankle-length skirt. The children are not in sight.

One time, although I was too young to remember much about it, Kathleen, the oldest Sharp girl, was going to scrub the floor and had a pot of boiling water on the floor in readiness. She picked me up and danced around with me. I guess I got dizzy and sat down in the hot water and got badly scalded. Mrs. Sharp grabbed me and stripped off my clothes or it would have been much worse. Norris

Sharp had gone to town, and the phone had just been installed at Heywood's store, so Mother was able to phone Armstrong and get Norris to bring out some sort of oil to put on my burn. I was in bed for about six weeks. In those days you never went to the doctor. You lived or died as God dictated. Besides, Mother figured she knew more than most doctors, unless it was old Dr. Van Kleeck.

Another time we were going for water, and I was sitting down on the floor of the wagon and had my hands spread on the boards to brace myself. The empty barrel was dancing around in the wagon and it landed on my finger and pulled out the nail. I lost more than one nail in one way or another.

Childhood was indeed perilous.

We were all in the democrat ready to go somewhere, and the girls were fooling around. Eleanor fell out and landed on her head. Mother grabbed the brandy bottle (which she kept for medicinal purposes, as both she and Dad were teetotallers) and soaked Eleanor's head with it until, as the girls tell the story, she became tipsy.

We were just learning to talk when we got the measles. In the course of it, Eleanor got an infection in her ears. Grandma Gamble snapped her fingers beside Eleanor's head and announced, "The child's deaf." It was true. Eleanor was much smarter than I, and it is to her credit that she has managed her life so successfully.

In these days personalized postcards were popular. One such was taken by 'Harold Smith, Military Photographer, Vancouver and Vernon, B.C.,' on August 24, 1916, at the army camp in Vernon. In front of a tent seven men are sitting or standing. All wear army fatigues and bush hats. One of them is James Russell Freeze.

Dad was a crack shot – he could have entered the Bisley [England] competition for marksmanship – and he wanted to be a sniper. But when he got to England, he happened to meet an officer he had known in Calgary. Knowing Dad's background, the fellow said Dad was just the man to be in charge of running the camp at Aldershot, so he was made a Sergeant Major and stayed there 'til the end of the war.

Two further artifacts report on James Russell's overseas tour of duty. The first is an invitation to a dance. (Lancers were a branch of the British cavalry.)

The Canadian Forestry Battalion Orchestra requests the pleasure of Sgt. Freeze and Friend's company at a Dance on Tuesday, Sept. 18, 1917 at the Constitutional Hall, Egham, from 8 pm – 12. Programme:
8 dances: waltz, one-step, valeta, foxtrot, Lancers, three-step, military two-step, waltz.
Interval and two extra dances.
Grand March and Lancers, waltz, barn dance, one-step, valeta, two-step, foxtrot, Home waltz.
Tickets: double ¾ [pound] Single 1/8 [pound] including tax. Engagements' side to be filled in for each dance.

The second is a pretty, commercially produced card inscribed by the sender:

With best wishes for a Long and happy Life Free from Cares and Heartaches, From your loving Daddy. Corporal J.R. Freeze 687820, 172 Battn, Canadian Expeditionary Force.

Edie decided not to spend a second winter on the bench and moved in with her parents. She brought with her their most valuable possessions.

The second winter [1916/17] we went to live with Grandma and Grandpa Gamble in Armstrong – five kids, a horse, and three cows. No way was she going to get rid of those cows – they would be the start of the herd. Two were purebred Holsteins – Nancy and Betsy – and Janie was a cross – a blue cow – kick the hell out of you!

Janet and Marj tell the story of that Christmas. They wanted Santa to bring them each an Eaton beauty doll. Christmas Eve came and they were sent upstairs to bed. Mother's sisters were entertaining their boyfriends downstairs. There was a heat register in the floor of the bedroom, and the girls were peering through it to see if Santa had come yet. In their excitement they knocked over the chamber pot and the contents ran through the register and dripped beside the Christmas tree on Grandma's new carpet. Needless to say what the result for the girls was – but Santa did not mind and left them their dolls anyway.

In the spring we went home. Mother left the bench property, however – she was getting a remittance from the Army – and rented the Morgan place down on the Salmon River. It had a good barn and a lean-to shack on it, and a good spring of water about a hundred yards away.

Edie and the children remained on the Morgan place until James Russell returned from England at the conclusion of the war. Then the family relocated for six months to Vancouver. *The cattle were farmed out.*

When the war was over and Dad came home, he had to go to Vancouver as an outpatient at the military hospital in Shaughnessy because he had a bad ear. There were no antibiotics then. We went down by train. It was the time of the great flu epidemic, and I remember the people on the train all wearing masks. We were lucky, as none of our family got sick.

We lived in a house on Quebec Street. As part of his rehabilitation, Dad took a course in carpentry and made a chair. I remember being pestered by the bragging little kid next door whose dad owned a car: "My daddy is going to take me for a ride around the block when he gets his spark plug fixed." He never had it fixed as long as we were there.

Across the street there was a vacant lot covered with bramble bushes. One day we twins found a hole in the bushes and crawled through. In the centre we found an old chicken house and played there all afternoon. *The family thought we were lost and hunted all over for us until we crawled out.*

There was even some thought given to the idea of staying in Vancouver permanently, as job prospects seemed promising. *Dad got a job as a painter. One day Mother saw him working on the outside of a high building and announced we were going back to Armstrong.*

They bought the Morgan farm through the Soldier Settlement Board, not quite 160 acres – mostly bush, very little cultivated – about three acres. Dad cleared it all by hand with the aid of stumping powder and an axe. I can remember it took him one full day to chop down one big cottonwood tree. Some of these trees were seven or eight feet in diameter. Stumping powder was very dangerous. Some people got blown up because the fuse was slow – they might think they had not set the cap right and go back to check. Charlie Schweb got blown up with it – mangled his face.

And they tried to get the herd going, but all they were getting were bull calves! They eventually got up to twenty cows. In time they built a larger house for themselves and a small one for Grandpa and Grandma Freeze. A photo showcases the grandparents' house ringed on all sides with piled logs, some sawn into chunks ready to be split – a year's supply of firewood.

In 1919 Rusty was four, too young to go to school, and enjoying himself on the Morgan place.

Although he was six years older than I was, Doug Heywood and I were great friends. I used to watch for him when he came home from school and get behind him on the saddle on his grey horse, Dolly, and go to look for the milk cows. Everybody's cows ran wild on the range – the land wasn't fenced. We used to pay twenty-five dollars to the Indian Agent to let us run the cows on the Indian Reserve. On the Reserve there is a big high knoll – it was kind of public property – hardly any Indians around there – and it gave us a good view. As the cows could be five or six miles in any direction, you had to be able to guess where to look for them.

We didn't brand them but we had bells on them and everybody's cows had a different bell. You knew which sound belonged to which herd. The horse got to know the bells, and when you stopped to listen, it would prick its ears and listen too. Sometimes the horse could hear the bells when you could not, and it would turn its head in the direction of the sound, and if you went that way you would be sure to find the cows. If the neighbour's cows followed together with yours, you'd bring them home too. Doug and I had some close shaves, but we got out of them ourselves and never bothered our parents with the details. We were expected to be responsible.

One time I wanted to drive Dolly, so he let me sit on the front of the saddle and take the reins. As soon as we were on board, she took off under a branch sticking out from a big fir tree. She went under it and we went off! Thereafter Rusty resumed his accustomed place behind Doug.

Another time we were driving the cattle alongside the river where there was a kind of water hole. The cattle went through all right, but in the particular spot the horse picked, she bogged up to her back. Doug swung off over her head and got to firm ground. There was a little tuft of grass in the centre of the bog and I slipped off her hind end and stood on this tuft. We managed to get the old mare out, but we might have lost her in the sinkhole. A small boy on a small tuft in a bog, and a ten-year-old performing the rescue – more might have been lost than the horse.

In 1919 when the Freeze family returned from Vancouver and settled on the Morgan place, it was named Morgandale after the original owners. *The area is known today as Heywood's Corner (the name changed when the school was built) – about ten miles west of Spallumcheen at the junction of the road to Armstrong and the Salmon Valley Road to Salmon Arm.* The Freezes and other families petitioned the province to build a neighbourhood school at Heywood's Corner. James Russell added a personal plea:

> Morgandale [1919]
>
> Recently a Petition has been sent you from part of the ratepayers of Salmon Valley School District asking for an assisted school in this part of the district on which my name will be found. This matter is a serious one for me and means one of two things: Either I will have to leave the farm here if we do not get this school or I will be able to stay here and do my duty as a Canadian if our petition should be favorably considered. I may say that I have answered the call of my country twice and served in the Boer War in the Strathcona Horse 1900-1901 and served from Sept. 15, 1915 till Aug 23, 1918 in the present war, and further have answered the call of the country by going back on the land with my wife and five children and at present am engaged in trying to [turn] a piece of bush land into cultivation. While I am satisfied with my present mode of life I refuse to bring up five children without an education, and furthermore I do not see the justice of their having to walk three miles to school. I have been forced to rent a place one mile nearer to school than my own, and since last fall three of my children have been attending the school already here, but I want to live on my own place, and having obtained a small loan from the Soldiers' Land Settlement Board I will have to move there in the near future. Another returned man's place joins mine and he with two children is similarly situated. We have 14 children here all of school age and plenty more growing up. All that will be needed is to divide the district and let us have an assisted school at this end of it. You may think that this is rather a strong letter but the matter is a vital one with us, and as Canadians we feel we have a right to a school within walking distance for our children. Hoping to hear from you favorably in this matter,
>
> > I beg to remain,
> > Yours truly,
> > (signed) J.R. Freeze

The farms around us were bought through the Soldier Settlement Board. The Sharps, for instance, had bought a farm one-half mile north of us. So the settlers got together and built a one-room school just north of Heywood's store. I can remember them building that school about 1920. It was about 300 yards from our place – we used to run home for lunch.

L.J. Botting was the first teacher and came from England. It seemed to me all we learned was English history – the dates when the kings lived and died and how many wives they chopped the heads off. They live a pretty tame life now compared to those days. Not much on Canadian history, of course. He was a good teacher.

They had a son called Stanley – he'd been in the First War – he could draw anything – a bucking horse, a girl – anything you'd want – a few scribbles and there it was! I'd have given my ears to be able to draw like that. And an elocutionist! He could recite 'The Cremation of Sam McGee' or 'The Highwayman' and make your hair stand on end. During the war he married another Botting, and I remember him telling us she crowned him with a pan of hot onions. Surprising the talent that was around.

Then the kids grew up and they closed the school. I guess I was in about grade five or six. Edie decided to stage a protest. *The Salmon Valley School was up by Ernie Schweb's on the Salmon Valley Road – about a mile or two. But Mother got her dander up – we weren't going to go – she was going to teach us at home. She kept us home for six months – she spent hours. Then she gave it up and we went to the Salmon Valley School after all.*

When I got to grade seven, I couldn't see. And Miss Kenny used to fill the board with this neat, small writing – she'd spend hours after school putting everything on the board for us next day – what we had to learn and everything we had to do. (Mr. Botting never put anything on the board – we got it out of books.) You don't like saying in front of the other kids that you can't see, but I finally did and Miss Kenny moved me up to the front. But I was still having to squint. I said to Mother, "I can't see the board." "Oh, there's nothing wrong with your eyes!" So I passed into grade eight on trial. Miss Kenny left and went to Victoria, I think. And I got glasses when I was about thirteen or fourteen.

In the meantime families had kids that came of age, like the Duthies, who had two or three. Another family moved in with about four, and younger families had kids, so they re-opened Heywood's Corner School at Christmas time and hired a teacher. I went back. Teacher boarded with us. Once Mr. Petrie came for a visit and in the night he started to snore. Teacher came and woke Mother: "The pigs are under your window!"

I was good at composition – never very good at spelling – poor at math. Elizabeth Sharp was better in math than the teacher. "Biddy Sharp, you help him." So when I came to town and tried my exams, there was all this stuff I didn't know. So I failed grade eight. By this time I was beginning to lose interest in school – the only boy in the family too – and I left to help my dad farm.

It was 1929 just as the stock markets crashed. Prices for farm produce went to nothing and there was no hope of living in town to continue schooling. My grandparents were in their eighties and too old to have me. Anyway, I was needed on the farm, and we at least got enough to eat, which couldn't be said of the poor devils that rode the rods from one part of the country to the other looking for work.

One thing that I was thankful for was that my parents bought me a set of Books of Knowledge. How they were paid for I will never know, but I devoured them from cover to cover. I learned about the history of the earth, the history of Greece and Rome, and the classics, and they gave me a basic knowledge that I would never have got in any other way.

Rusty's do-it-yourself attitude never deserted him. Problems were puzzles to be solved in imaginative ways. He was never idle – always looking for something inventive to do. He designed and built many types of machinery. One was an improved tuber unit that cut potatoes into four pieces for seeding and deposited each piece a foot apart in the row while the one-person crew sat aboard and fed the potatoes from a hopper.

The wheels were about a metre in diameter, and I had to figure out how far they would travel and how to space the seed pieces when they dropped onto the belt. When the four pieces of a diseased potato come up in one spot, they are easier to see. Before potato-planting machinery appeared, the 'eyes' for seed were cut out by hand and planted from a communal bucket. *We used to take the tuber unit around and plant potatoes for the neighbours, and they would come and help us when we needed them.*

By the time I left school, Dad had cleared the farm, but these old stumps were left all over the place – you could run over them with a mower. You watched and got to know where they were and raised the mower blade. Potatoes grew pretty well, but during the Depression they were worth nothing. We just left them. We had the cream cheque and that was it.

There was mail delivery between Falkland and Armstrong. The mailman picked up the cream along the route and delivered it to Armstrong. (It was then taken to Vernon.) He also picked up in Armstrong what people needed – any woman that wanted some thread or bread, or whatever.

We didn't have running water at that time. We had a hand pump in the house to bring in water from a well. It was called the sandpoint method. You drove a two-inch pipe with a point on the end of it, enclosed by netting to keep out debris, down into the ground – you couldn't go farther than twenty feet, as the hand pump wouldn't lift the water any higher than that – and you kept pumping to see if you had hit water. The water table was close to the surface – generally at about five feet. The water wasn't that good – it was full of iron. We used it for washing clothes. Eventually we put a cistern up on the hill, pumped water from our running spring up into the cistern and let gravity run it back down through a pipe to the house for drinking water. We built a little house over the running spring and kept our butter and cream cool in there.

On one ordinary winter afternoon, Edie's quick thinking and

strength of character prevented a misunderstanding that might have had serious consequences.

One incident I'll remember to the day I die. Dad and Grandpa Freeze went out to the yard to cut some wood. They lit up their pipes, got on each end of the crosscut saw and started to work. All of a sudden there was a loud bang, and the end of Dad's pipe blew off. He was sure he'd been shot at.

He'd had an argument with another person in the area who was trying to get lanes through the farms in the valley so his cows could get to the river for water. Since there already were roads about every mile giving him access, Dad had said no. The news then got back to Dad that the man had been bragging that he was going to "get that Freeze" for blocking him.

I can remember like it was yesterday. Dad came into the house, his face as white as a sheet, grabbed the Ross .303 rifle off the wall and started to load it. Nobody was going to shoot at him and live to tell the story! Mother grabbed hold of the rifle and kept talking to him. She said if it was that man who had shot at him, if she jumped on the pony, she could beat him home; and if he was already home, they would know for sure it wasn't him. This is what she did and, sure enough, the fellow was in his yard sawing wood.

James Russell was unconvinced. *Dad got the men at the sawmill to come and help him look for tracks in the fresh snow but they couldn't find any. Then Dad remembered that when he had been helping a neighbour kill pigs that morning, a .22 shell had misfired and he had put it in his pocket. He checked and it wasn't there. He realized that somehow it had got inside his tobacco pouch and, before he started to saw that day, he had tamped it into his pipe, lit up, and the shell had exploded.*

Dad got on the horse, rode to the man's place, told him what had happened and apologized for what he had thought. But if Dad had been killed, everyone would have blamed that man. It was quite a lesson for him, for never again did he say he was going to get somebody.

Rusty's father was a full-time farmer now – no war, public or private, to divert him from the task. Instead, his eye saw the beauty in his surroundings and his heart responded with poetry. *I can remember when he wrote this one. We came in after coiling hay all afternoon – dead tired. It was in the '30s.* The poem is untitled.

This afternoon I spent at work – no matter what you say –
After all this rain I had to coil a field of clover hay.
The hay was damp and heavy – and I was feeling blue,
Felt just like throwing up the sponge, as we farmers sometimes do.

I started in at 1 p.m. and finished just at 5
And worked hard every minute just as sure as you're alive.
I said before that we had had a darn long rainy spell,
And I noticed – as I started – that lovely clover smell.

It seemed to scent the whole darn field with a perfume rich and rare,
And it almost drove away the blues to breathe that scented air.
Then I saw the leaves of all the trees were washed and fresh and clean
As if they'd just been painted many lovely shades of green.

Then a breeze sprang up from somewhere and it came singing by –
It caused the leaves to dance and play and helped the hay to dry,
Then a flicker started tapping on an old, dry cottonwood
While blackbirds hopped around the field catching big fat worms for food.

Salmon River seemed quite happy as it sang its murmuring song –
And it invited me to take a drink to help the work along,
Then a flock of Mallard ducks whirred by – flying up the stream,
And I watched them 'til they dropped from sight behind a wall of green.

Then someone on the road hallo'ed on their way home from town,
They told me how the rain had knocked their own alfalfa down,
And while I rolled a cigarette and rested for a smoke,
They told me how the farmers all were quickly going broke.

But while I smelled the clover, and the birds and trees seemed glad –
I couldn't think that everything was so darned awful bad.
And I thought –
"While I can smell the clover – hear the droning of the bees –
Hear the murmur of the river – see the twinkling of the leaves –
See the raindrops on the willows – smell the perfume of the hay –
Just so long I'll keep on farming – even tho' it does not pay."
And while I thought I looked around – the last windrow was done –
It was time to milk the cows again. The afternoon had flown.

James Russell also recorded his impressions in oils. In his home Rusty displays his father's canvases beside his own. *He was a better painter than I ever was.*

In 1934 when Rusty was nineteen, a new teacher was hired for Heywood's Corner School. Her name was Minnie Kohut. Small, pretty, and educated, she was twenty-five years old. Rusty was smitten, but Minnie thought he was too young. She liked her freedom. She had her own car. Nebbie was undeterred.

Minnie was the daughter of Wasel and Katherine Kohut. They had emigrated from the Ukraine and farmed at Togo, Saskatchewan. Minnie took her teacher training in Regina and Vancouver and taught school on the prairies. When her parents found the winters too cold, the whole family, including Minnie's younger sister, Sophia, moved to Hullcar and bought a farm.

Minnie taught quite a little gang at Heywood's Corner School. In the photograph Minnie is grinning beside a clutch of seventeen children, several of whom are as tall as she. *We were married on July 12, 1940.*

We moved into the little house originally made for Grandma and Grandpa Freeze. The main part of the house was about twenty by twenty feet. The attached lean-to had been built over a big stump. As the house settled over it, the floor buckled in the centre and sloped down on all sides. So we tore off the lean-to. The stump had won.

Our son Rossie [Russell Owen Sanford] was born in April of 1941. He was named for me and for the third of Dad's three little brothers who had died within weeks of each other. Rossie died in November, 1945. The little boy had been born with a fatal condition. The 'soft spot' at the top of his head was missing, and allowed no room for the bones in his head to grow in the normal way. *In these days it could have been fixed.* The parents suffered along with their son. To their regret they had no more children.

I remember I was in Victoria on one occasion and I had a morning to spare. I wandered around in a churchyard and saw a gravestone with the names of five children, all from one minister's family. It happened all the time.

Penicillin saved me or I'd be dead long ago. We were digging potatoes and I got a flu and dysentery. Finally I had to give in and go up to the house. Dr. Haugen came out – someone phoned from Heywood's Corner store – and he took me back to Armstrong Hospital, making a couple of stops along the way. I was given an intravenous drip and went into shock. The fellow in the next bed went for the nurse and she came and jerked it out of me. I was asked for the name of someone to come out and stay the night with me, and I told them to phone for Min. She came and Mother came with her. I was delirious all night – the flu had turned into pneumonia – and they poured the penicillin into me. After five or six days, Dr. Haugen told me, "You are one of the sickest people I ever saw that lived."

By this time I had about a six-day growth of beard and I wanted a shave, but I didn't have the strength. So Min and Tina, who used to live at the Corner [Heywood's], undertook to lather me up, but it wasn't working worth a damn. I looked to see what they were using and it was toothpaste! I was so mad I suddenly had the energy to do it myself! In all the years Tina worked at the hospital, whenever she saw me she started to laugh.

The Morgan farm had been renamed Glenwood. *Mother liked the name but it was quite a common name. There were other*

Glenwoods and other names prefixed with 'Glen.' Glenemma, for example, was a little district halfway between Armstrong and Falkland where there used to be a school. It was a stopping place for everybody. There used to be a hall there too – a log building – but it was taken down when they put the highway through. Where that little cemetery is located just above the road – that's Glenemma. It was named after Emma Bell – one of the original settlers. Stanley Bell lived there for years and years after Emma's death.

With the hard work of Rusty and James Russell, and the energy and focus of Edie and Minnie, Glenwood prospered. James Russell was elected to the first board of directors of NOCA in 1932 – *each farmer paid fifty cents to belong* – and served in various capacities for twenty-five years. When he resigned in 1957, Rusty took his father's place on the board.

You were elected by the area. The function was to run the creamery. The creamery was in Spallumcheen, down by the height of land between here and Enderby, on Creamery Road. We had a manager – Everard Clarke – right from the start. When the original creamery started up and had a hard time selling their butter, Pat Burns [Burns Meats] took it over and sent out Clarke to manage it – just a kid but an aggressive worker. When the creamery burned down in 1927, the plant was moved to Vernon, perhaps because of better facilities there. NOCA enlarged to SODICA, Shuswap Okanagan Dairy Interior Creamery Association.

Rusty became particularly interested in the growing and commercial marketing of good quality potatoes. In the 1940s he was instrumental in forming the Salmon River Potato Growers' Association, which lasted until the late 1970s. Fields were devoted to both seed potatoes and commercial potatoes. The growing of seed was regulated by the provincial government, which sent inspectors to evaluate both the product and the methods of production. A newspaper report of the 'Fourth Annual Heywood's Corner Field Days' in 1950 reflects both the scope of the enterprise and the enthusiasm of the participants:

The officials present were C. Hamilton – field inspector for Salmon River Valley District; C. Hilliard – Interior Vegetable Marketing Board, from Kamloops; and H.S. McLeod, district inspector for the provincial government. Rusty Freeze was master of ceremonies, and seventy members of the Salmon River Potato Growers' Association attended.

The group visited five farms in the morning and four more in the afternoon. These included the farms of A. Schweb, W. Schweb, A.D. Heywood, N.J. Sharp, and E. Needoba. In addition to viewing the fields of potatoes, the group witnessed a sprinkling display at E. Needoba's, inspected large pumping outfits at both E. Schweb's and the Freeze farm, and surveyed an array of equipment: tractors, power diggers, planters, six-row custers, and power graders.

Wives served both lunch and evening refreshments to the seventy members in a shady spot near the river on E. Needoba's farm. C. Hamilton gave a speech on crop conditions, pests, diseases, weeds, and certified seed. The visiting three-man team then named the winners in various categories and presented the prizes. For freedom from disease and insect pests: N.J. Sharp – table lamp; C. Schweb – 5 gallons of oil. For best cultivation and crop management: E. Needoba – tractor tire pump; R.C. Freeze – 10 pounds of grease. For best all-round field: R.C. Freeze – 2 sacks of 5-7 dust; C. Schweb – case of soft drinks. Mrs. W.C. Tucker presented chocolates and cigarettes to the women who had prepared and served the food.

The manager for our potato growers' association was the wife of one of the growers. We developed a market in Kamloops for our Salmon River Valley brand and did really well. They took all our potatoes – mainly Netted Gem – at so much a ton. We went through the Vegetable Marketing Board and did well on the commercial potatoes as well as on the seed. We were very fussy about our grades. The growers all agreed to produce top grade only, so we had a good quality potato. Then we gradually went out of seed potatoes, as the commercial market was more attractive – less work and higher profit.

The annual Potato Growers' Field Days, however, continued. In September, 1964, the *Cream Collector,* the monthly magazine put out by SODICA, recorded this one:

A field day on sprinkler system design and operation sponsored by the Agricultural Engineering Division of the B.C. Department of Agriculture was held on September 9 on the Freeze farm. The system has been in operation for many years and so is of practical use: application rates, evenness of application, effect of spacing, nozzle discharge, effect of pressure variation, and methods of scheduling.

Shortly after the end of the Second World War, Rusty and his father became involved in a project which, years later, saw the creation of BC Hydro.

It's a story that only I know because I'm the only one left that took part in it. Right after the war, about 1945 or '46, there was no rural electrification, no electricity to the farms at all in our area. The directors that built SODICA arranged a meeting in Vernon and invited the manager of the little company that ran the Shuswap Falls power station, the bank managers, and all the farmers they could gather together for the purpose.

The manager explained to the meeting that the power station was at full capacity in supplying power to the local towns and had neither the capital nor the resources to bring electricity to the farms. The costs would be prohibitive. Then Dad and a fellow by the name of Stephen Freeman, who had been a CCF [Co-operative Commonwealth Federation] candidate in the previous election and who lived in Coldstream, proposed a resolution to the group that the provincial government be asked to take over the company in order to bring electricity to the farms.

The idea was startling. Farmers needed electrical power in order to modernize production, but the idea of government's involving itself in business appalled some people. As proponents of the resolution, James Russell and Stephen Freeman made *a dynamic presentation*. The meeting spoke for and against the resolution. As one of the instigators Rusty spoke in favour.

The resolution passed and was forwarded to Victoria. Within one week the government had taken over the power company and agreed to provide rural electrification to the area. The government formed an advisory committee made up of some of the businessmen in town, some bank managers, and some directors of SODICA, including Dad, and went ahead and built a bigger dam at Whatshan Lake to produce the necessary power.

The reason for the quick action was the timing of the request. The Hart government – a Coalition government of Liberals and Conservatives – was facing an election. It was being strongly opposed by the CCF party, which had been prevented from forming the government only by the formation of this coalition. Rural electrification was the issue the government needed to guarantee a win.

They started with the bigger farms at Grindrod and carried on towards Salmon Arm and then along the Salmon River Valley. The whole valley went from being dark to being light. Once this area was complete, they moved into the Cariboo. The BC Power Commission just hooked the little power companies all up. It was quite a saga. Prior to that, each individual company just extended the power line farm by farm, if they could afford to do it.

They didn't get to our place until 1949 or '50 – it was a team effort and had to be done in an orderly way. Digging post holes and putting up poles was all done by hand and provided work. My nephew Don Needoba, who was in his late teens, got a job and could have stayed on with the company, but he said, "I'm going to be a farmer."

It was quite a sight to drive along the valley at night and see all those farms lit up and know that you had helped to make it happen. The farmers made money because they were able to put in refrigeration and irrigation equipment, and modernize their farms. The bank managers made money because they were making loans to the farmers to make these improvements. The electrical companies made money because they were putting in the equipment on the farms. And see what it did for the housewife! A lot of the farms had those Delco systems – 12 or 24 volts that would give you some light and that was all – you couldn't have a fridge and you couldn't have a stove. A lot of people couldn't have running water because you needed a pump to raise water from the well. Everybody benefited.

The process begun at the meeting in Vernon was completed under W.A.C. Bennett. *When W.A.C. Bennett became premier in the fifties, he fought another election on the issue of taking over BC Electric, which was in the Vancouver area: "Those godless socialists were going to ruin the country!" But within months of his victory, his government took over the company, amalgamated all the power sources into BC Hydro and began to build bigger dams. He made a deal to sell water and power on the Columbia River to the Americans, which I didn't particularly like, but it allowed for the development of the province. It couldn't have taken place otherwise.*

You have no idea what the roads were like in those days – all washboard. Then 'Gaglardi and God' supplied hard surface on the roads and transportation went ahead. (Gaglardi, a preacher, was the minister of highways.) To give Bennett his due, he had a vision for the province. BC Hydro was a legacy for the people, and it galls me today to see it in danger of being dispersed.

A natural evolution for Rusty was to become interested in politics. In 1950 he ran in a provincial election as the CCF candidate for the Shuswap against a Coalitionist rival and discovered he was an excellent public speaker. His platform included free treatment of cancer and arthritis, low rental housing and rental subsidies, the removal of the sales tax from necessities, free textbooks up to grade nine, junior vocational colleges in several centres, farm co-operatives of all kinds, and two weeks' holiday with pay for workers. Too radical for the voters, he lost at the polls.

I believed in the Co-operative Movement – people getting together to accomplish objectives. My vision had the people within the community work co-operatively to do the things they wanted to do together, and expand the network to the cities and the municipalities. The job of the government was to give them financial backing and expertise – advice for management – a crucial component – not like today where Big Business is taking over and running everything: Dairyland absorbs Armstrong Cheese, absorbs SODICA, absorbs Fraser Valley Milk Producers and becomes another big conglomerate.

Dad was a reader of philosophy. Bill Selder, a United Church minister, used to come around and they'd talk until the small hours of the morning. I can't say what religion I am. When I was about five or six, I was going to be a minister. In the summer we used to get these student preachers. They'd preach in the schoolhouses at Heywood's Corner, Yankee Flats, Silver Creek, Falkland – four or five places. One preacher was named Redmond. I really liked him. I think he had quite an influence on my life.

One of these itinerant ministers was an eccentric son of a gun. One time Mother had a big party at our house and he was there. Stanley Botting came in dressed like a woman and got down on one knee and proposed to him! Those characters!! I wonder if our school system produces people like that anymore. I'll never forget Stanley telling me once about a girl he fell in love with: "She had the eye-s-s-s-s of a Medusa!" In Greek myth Medusa's slightest glance turned the unfortunate man to stone.

One time he went to do some work for an old bachelor named McKechnie – no relation to the McKechnies here – and the bull treed them on top of a haystack. McKechnie said to Stanley, "I'll tease him and you slip down the other side and run for the barn. Bring back a couple of pitchforks." Stanley got to the barn all right, but he didn't stop – he went home! He told me he saw McKechnie in town a couple of weeks later, and the old fellow never mentioned the incident.

On January 8, 1955, James Russell Freeze died suddenly at Glenwood. He was seventy-six years old. *I was sawing logs in the yard one afternoon, Dad watching me and smoking his pipe. Suddenly he slumped down. I got him into the house and Dr. Haugen came out and wanted to bring him into the hospital. But Mother was bound and determined he was going to stay at home and she would nurse him. He died that evening of a brain hemorrhage.*

In an editorial in the *Vernon News,* Frank R. Harris remarked on his wide-ranging and, for the times, eccentric interests. Besides community contributions, such as, the school board, the Armstrong Co-operative Society, and the promotion of irrigation, James Russell was an artist, a poet, an environmentalist, an agnostic, and an active supporter of the CCF party since its inception in 1933. The editor seemed baffled by the apparent contradictions in his nature:

> ... A socialist for many years, he was [nevertheless] proud to have served the cause of Empire in the Boer War, and the cause of liberty in the First World War.... Attracted by the teachings of atheism, he nonetheless numbered members of the clergy among his friends, and the last rites were held in church. [Bill Selder came from Vancouver to conduct the service.] Many people of different temperaments knew him as a friend.... He had an extraordinary capacity to see the other point of view....

The death of his father signalled a change in direction on the farm. Always on the lookout for a new initiative, Rusty slowly began to sell off the dairy herd. *The herd was on ROP and we had a gold medal dam. We sold a heifer and she became another gold medal dam. There were very few in Canada.* The farm acquired a new name – Russlea – and Rusty began to raise purebred Herefords. In the 1960s a newspaper article from the magazine *Country Life* records his success:

> Japanese cattle buyers say the best Hereford bull imported to Japan for many years came from B.C... the R.C. (Rusty) Freeze herd, Salmon River... [which was] in a shipment of Herefords from B.C. three years ago of forty head of registered Canadian Polled Hereford females and one bull. The cattle were selected from Karl Freding Ranch, Penticton; the R.C. Freeze Ranch, Salmon Arm; and Kelowna Ranchers Ltd., Kelowna.

Selling that bull to Japan was one thing I was proud of.

Rusty's Herefords were also successful at the local agricultural fair, the Interior Provincial Exhibition. In 1972, the date of the final Livestock Parade, he led his Grand Champion female with bull calf at foot around the oval to well-deserved applause. Minnie's vegetables and flowers were also consistent winners year after year, both as individual performers and as part of the Salmon River Valley District displays.

Another of her interests was in maintaining a record of weather and rainfall. A copper vial inside a small cylinder captured the rain, which was then poured into a calibrated glass vessel for accurate results. For twenty years she volunteered these records to the Atmospheric Environment Service and in 1981 received a plaque in thanks.

When Edie died in 1974 at the age of 95, she was something of a celebrity. Her garden was praised as a miniature park and, an excellent horsewoman herself, she had over the years supplied the flowers for the annual Falkland Stampede. Blind since 1960, she had made friends with her disability and retained her independence. On her 85th birthday she gave an interview to the *Vernon News:*

"When I first went blind, I made up my mind to accept it and it was the best thing I ever did. Of course, I sometimes get turned around when I walk in the yard and have to be set straight. But I can still tell the difference between a flower and a weed." She took courses given by the Canadian National Institute for the Blind and learned to type. She knit afghans and slippers by the bushel and scrubbed her own floors – *"I measure out the areas I have done."* Given a next time, she said she would choose to be a photographer.

As a potato producer and member of the Salmon Valley Potato Growers' Co-operative, Rusty in the 1970s became a director on the BC Interior Vegetable Marketing Board and within a short time, the chairman. His abrupt resignation in 1974 caused a stir.

In order to have consistent quality, especially in potatoes, I felt we had to have a central facility in the Okanagan-Mainline area for packing, shipping and storing vegetables. I had a thing about those old-time packing houses – they robbed the Chinese right, left and centre and only gave them enough to eat – their costs were high and they thought only of themselves. A single, central plant in our area would reduce shipping costs, raise standards of produce, provide district workers with more seasonal employment, and increase acreage for vegetable growing. Well, the board wouldn't go for it. And I felt strongly about it. So I resigned as chair of the marketing board.

After that, the board got second thoughts. They decided to buy a wholesale place in Vancouver and were talking about moving the office down to Vancouver. I didn't like the look of the wholesale company they had their eye on, and then the place burned down!

He had no time for regrets. In early 1975 Rusty was appointed vice-chairman of a provincial marketing board – called a 'super-board' – to examine decisions by district marketing boards and hear appeals.

In 1981 Rusty and Minnie sold the farm and moved to a house on Wood Avenue that they had designed and he had built. Minnie became a regular volunteer at the Hospital Auxiliary Bargain Bin, and Rusty, a rapid and prolific painter. He took lessons and joined the local Paint and Palette Club. He supported financially the construction of the Art Gallery attached to the Museum and, to honour the Freeze family, one room in the gallery was named the Freeze Gallery.

You really don't have to have talent to paint. It's just a matter of sticking to it. The one thing I've got that some others don't have is persistence – a 'don't give up' attitude. That's my strong point.

Freeze's Fine Art Gallery occupied the old Mac Crow house on the corner of Okanagan and Wood Avenue for a number of years. He framed pictures – *I didn't charge for labour* – and sold his own art along with collections that his sister-in-law Sophia owned, she having sponsored artist émigrés in Vancouver for years. He and Minnie continued to exhibit in the fall fair the vegetables and flowers that made their place productive and beautiful.

In 1992 when Canada celebrated its 125th birthday, Rusty and Minnie were among the twenty-eight persons in the riding of Okanagan-Shuswap to receive a 'Canada 125' medal given to recognize contributions to country, community, and fellow citizens.

In September, 1995, Minnie died of cancer. *When I painted, all my pictures were black.*

The following year at the Seniors' Activity Centre, he met Jessie Johnson, a widow and the matriarch of an extensive family of six children and several grandchildren. They were married in a large, cheerful family wedding on November 2, 1996, and moved into a new house designed with plenty of space for their hobbies – *Jessie likes doing a lot of crafts*. Rusty also discovered he enjoyed buying and renovating property and then renting or selling it to friends and family. Converting an old house next door to the Museum and Art Gallery into The Brown Derby restaurant was an early project for the couple.

In sustaining an active interest in politics, Russell Carleton Freeze exhibits Edie's pragmatic will and James Russell's idealism. He expresses these traits in the following letter to the editor of the *Armstrong Advertiser* in the early 1990s at the time of the debate in Canada as to whether Quebec constituted a distinct society:

Distinct Society

Have you ever walked in the deep woods on a clear, still fall day, stopped to listen and there is no sound, not even the sound of the wind sighing in the pines, and you wonder, Will silence be the only thing left in Canada fifty years from now? Then, suddenly, the silence is shattered by the chattering of a squirrel scolding you for invading the privacy of his domain, and your mind snaps back to reality; but the image continues to haunt you, and you vow to do all in your power not to let this happen, as you ponder, What is the real language of Canada?

Is it English? Is it French? Or the language of one of the many ethnic groups that go to make up this great mosaic that is Canada? Then you come to realize that the language and distinct society that we are losing in Canada bit by bit, insidiously, is the honk of the wild geese as they fly to their nesting grounds in our north, the cry of the loon echoing across a lonely lake, the plop of a trout as it jumps just for the sheer joy and exuberance of being alive, the bark of the coyote as he talks to his mate in the frosty February air, the various sounds of spring as the many forms of life go busily about the task of renewing the species, the crunch of unpolluted snow under your feet on a frosty morning, the sound of happy, healthy children shouting and laughing at play.

This is the real language and distinct society of this country that we are in danger of losing by the destruction of our forests, the fouling of the air, the pollution of our lakes, rivers, and oceans, the damaged ozone layer, the advancing deserts.

Surely we can agree that we are all entitled to speak one of the official languages of this country wherever and whenever we choose. Surely it is the right of a person to nurture and keep alive the customs and language of their forefathers. Surely in this shrinking political world the more languages a person can speak, the greater their own personal enrichment, and the better their understanding of the greater problem of the survival of the species that faces us.

Let us in this beautiful and bountiful country of ours, which is the envy of so many, unite together and declare war on pollution and save the real language of the country. Let our epitaph be "The world is better and more beautiful for your having been here" rather than "All was beauty before you came."

Rusty Freeze on Granville Street, Vancouver, in the 1940s

Chapter Five

Friends and Fortune

William McLeod 'Mac' Thornton (and Barney)

McLeod subdivision was named after my grandfather Murdock McLeod, and I don't think he lived in Armstrong more than three years. And I don't know where my father met my mother. It might have been in Edmonton [Alberta] or it might have been Armstrong. When you're young, you're not interested in all the relations. You don't think to ask the right questions.

The connection of the McLeods and the Thorntons to the Spallumcheen subdivision east of Armstrong is conclusive. However, oral tradition supplies some conflicting details. For example, one source says McLeod Road was named for Murdock McLeod's son John. Yet 'Squeaky Jack,' nicknamed for the timbre of his voice, lived on Back Enderby Road. His father, on the other hand, resided on the property he had bought in McLeod subdivision, even if only for a short period. Since local people remembered John McLeod well and Murdock McLeod likely not at all, Mac Thornton's claim on behalf of his grandfather may be the correct one.

Mother's parents were both McLeods. Her father, Murdock, was born on the Isle of Lewis in Scotland and came out here to work for the Hudson Bay Company. He could speak Eskimo, and us kids used to ask him to say Eskimo words. He was a Scots Presbyterian – I think the worst word he ever said was "Gosh." I think my grandmother was born in Ontario. They were early settlers in Edmonton. They came from Winnipeg to Edmonton in a covered wagon. Both my McLeod grandparents lived to be eighty-four. Mac himself is now ninety-one.

There's a school in Edmonton named after my grandfather. I was invited to the dedication and wasn't able to go. My wife and I were shown around later and there's a picture of the old boy in the school. There's a street named after him too, but he had nothing to do with the McLeod Trail – a different McLeod.

One of my mother's sisters was among the first people involved in the Edmonton Old-timers' Association. I think she knew everybody in Edmonton. I remember once I visited her, and she wasn't home. One of the neighbours told me she was at the fair. We went along over there and found her talking to a bunch of people. Somebody walked by and she called to him by his first name and introduced us. It was the lieutenant-governor.

In 1905 the McLeods with their family left Edmonton for the Okanagan and settled in Spallumcheen on the forty acres that later became known as the Lamb place. Benjamin Arthur Thornton and his two cousins, Robert and Syd Thompson, were in the community around the same time.

I think there was an epidemic in England in the real early 1900s, and Dad and his two cousins came out here because the Canadian government was encouraging immigration. When Dad arrived in Canada, he spent time in Ontario, and I remember him also talking about living in Edmonton. Then the three of them came [farther] west and settled in the Armstrong area. Their initials were RAT, SAT, and BAT – Robert, Syd, and Ben. My dad was Ben.

Dad came from Calverley, Leeds, in Yorkshire. Mat. S. Hassen gave me an atlas of Yorkshire and the place names were 'Thornton this…' and 'Thornton that….' He went 'round to see the family during the [Second] War. He maintains one of the brothers was seven feet tall. I know they're tall. My dad was too. Mac himself is well over six feet, lean and fit. I remember Dad telling me about his seven-foot brother. There were six or seven of them in the family.

I made a family tree, all scribbled out in handwriting, and it only went back to 1600 or 1700. Meredith, my son Brian's wife, is quite artistic and I said to her, "How about making something out of this?" So she did it all in old English script and the odd thing is – it looks like a tree. I was always going to track it back further but I never did.

When Mac's maternal grandparents, the McLeods, decided in 1908 to leave Armstrong and return to Edmonton, they sold their farm to Ben Thornton and his cousins. *They bought the [Lamb] place together – the three of them owned it. They built a hewn log barn on it that's still standing. Our first farm was very small – twenty acres.*

The land was in two parcels: Ben had twenty acres and his Thompson cousins, the other twenty. Having met either in Edmonton or in Armstrong, Ben Thornton and Dollina McLeod were married. Their first three children were born on the Lamb place.

There were six of us – I was the oldest. I was born on June 23, 1913. Jack was about a year and a half younger, then came Margaret, who died when she was twelve, then the twins, Jim and Kay, and finally Barbara. As kids we had a pet barn owl. I remember some of our friends trying to catch it: the youngest Phillips boy – his dad had a store – and one of the Fuenfgelds – Fred – who lived on [what was later called] the Lockhart place.

Because his holding was small, Ben Thornton took on another job. *For a period of time my dad farmed during the day and worked the night shift at the powerhouse on Davis Creek. He got seventy-five dollars a month for that job.* This powerhouse supplied electricity to Armstrong.

In 1918 when Mac was five years old, the Thorntons moved to Back Enderby Road to live on the sixty-acre farm that had belonged to Dollina's brother, John McLeod.

I remember when the First War ended. Very few people had radios in those days. Josh Blackburn [Blackburn's Transfer] sent a fellow on a grey horse around Back Enderby Road to tell the farm-

ers that the war was over. I can see that horse yet! My brother was three and a half, and we were walking across the field and someone was blasting stumps and he said, "That's the Germans!!" How the hell would he know? One thing I remember about the war – sugar was rationed. 'Lasses in our porridge!

Ben Thornton set about improving the family's living quarters, and Mac was soon busy with school chums.

There was a frame house on the place, and Dad built an addition of solid brick. Then he laid brick veneer over the frame house [to unify the effect]. There was a big old barn too that I think had been constructed back in the 1880s. It was closed in at the bottom and open at the top underneath a galvanized tin roof. We never had any trouble with the wind blowing through the open space, but a few years ago I saw a clipping from the Armstrong Advertiser with a picture of a monster barn flattened right out by a windstorm, and I recognized it!

We had a well about fourteen feet from the house. It was the hardest water – pure lime – lovely water to drink – but we had to haul water to do the washing because you could never make any suds. I think they used to put a marble into the bucket to try and collect the lime. There was no electricity until 1938.

I went to Mountain View School above Martin Meggait's place on Back Enderby Road. There were about nine or ten kids. The teacher was Miss Inglis who married Wilf Smith that owned the livery stable in town. Wilf used to drive her to school in the sleigh in winter and in the democrat in summer. It was a leisurely way to get acquainted and good advertisement for his business. *When I was selling insurance, I did quite a bit of travelling in BC. I was in Terrace, I think, and a guy came over to me and said, "You're Thornton, aren't you?" "Yes, who are you?" When he told me, I said, "Your mother taught me in grade one."*

Over the summer holidays Mountain View School burned down.

So for two years we went to school where the Odd Fellows' hall is now. The teacher was Miss Fraser – John Fraser's daughter. Having lost their neighbourhood school, the children had to be transported to Armstrong to attend the old elementary school at the corner of Bridge Street and Pleasant Valley Road. John McLeod drove them.

Uncle John had a 490 Chev – I saw one in the Automotive Museum in Langley. It was called a touring car – curtains and everything – a two-seater. How did all those kids get in it? They didn't wear seat belts, for one thing. *I can name the families who rode with him: Jim McCallan (a very good friend of mine); Frank Poole must have adopted nieces of his – two girls; the Wilson family – one of them; then Nina and Charlie Graves, me, and Uncle John. He drove us for two years. In winter we went in a sleigh and in the spring, in a democrat. The roads, of course, in those days were mostly mud, and I can remember when I was older riding a horse and hauling the school bus up Larmer Hill on Back Enderby Road. Jim Phillips eventually lived in the Larmer place. He had the grocery store in town – Phillips and Whitehouse – bananas hung up on the stem, a big cleaver to cut the cheese.*

All the local schools had to be closed when the consolidated school opened in Armstrong in 1921. Two of my uncles had buses – buses were all privately owned – not owned by the school board. Uncle John's bus was a Model T truck – I think Uncle Bill's was a Model T too – we sat along the inside on benches. When it was raining, they let the vinyl curtains down. There was a running board at the back where you stepped up to get in, and us kids would get outside and ride on it. Conveniently remote in the driver's seat, Mac's uncle may have been unaware of his external passengers.

I remember riding on the running board one day and then climbing onto the roof. The fellow who boosted me up was Ken North – his father was a manual training teacher at the Brick School. He became a sergeant in the Vancouver Police Force. One day he was parked on duty and I went over to talk to him. "Ken, what would you do if you saw some kid riding on top of a school bus?" "I don't know." "Well, you sure as hell saw it happen! You shoved me up on top of Bill Biggs' school bus!" The roof was made of slats – luckily I wasn't very heavy.

Ken North became a type of amateur wrestler. I boarded with somebody in Vancouver who had something to do with the sport, so I always went to the matches. I can remember one night in Ladner one fellow threw the other fellow out of the ring and then chased him up the street with an axe. Stradiotta was the 'Bad Guy' – he used to do some weird things.

I finished school at the end of grade eight – school didn't make much impression on me.

Ben Thornton had developed a Holstein dairy herd and shipped pigs spring and fall. He supported the Interior Provincial Exhibition and also did his stint in municipal politics.

With three boys in the family, my dad was involved in the fair as long as I can remember. He was a director and president of the IPE during the war. I sure did my volunteer work there!! He was also on Spallumcheen council. I remember one time they were horse-hauling gravel for the roads, and they could barely make it up the hill on Back Enderby Road. They asked Dad if they could hire me and the horse to help out. Dad said, "If you're dealing with him, that's all right, but you're not dealing with me." No conflict of interest!

When Mac was fifteen years old, his twelve-year-old sister, Margaret, died of peritonitis from a burst appendix. The following year at the age of forty-eight, his mother died following an operation for goitre disease, probably as a result of pneumonia. Dollina left a family of five children, the youngest still a preschooler.

In those days they didn't know how to fix goitre trouble. I was talking about it one day to Betty Hopkins – our farm backed on the Hopkins place and Betty was related to us by marriage. She told me she always remembered her dad saying to my dad, "Ben, I don't know how you can tolerate this," and Dad told Jack Hopkins, "You take one day at a time." Mother's sister was in Calgary, so my aunt and uncle took the girls and brought them up. The youngest one, Barbara, later came back and went to high school in Armstrong.

When I finished school, I helped my dad on the farm, but with three boys in the family there wasn't always enough work for us all. So in 1931 I went to work for Bernice McCallan's father, Hilliard. (I had a phone call from Bernice on my 90th birthday.) I worked on their farm for a dollar a day – ten cents an hour – room and board for thirty dollars a month.

One spring Hilliard rented me two or three acres of bottomland along Davis Creek because I wanted to grow certified potatoes. But Davis Creek always flooded in the spring. It flooded the potatoes. I replanted them. It flooded again and I lost them again. Twice in one year was too much for me and I gave it up.

Boys generally found ways to enliven their dull moments.

Our family and 'Sawdust Billy' Smith's family were very close. One day Jack and his brother Archie got up on top of a loaded boxcar of lumber that was sitting on the track in town and slipped the brake. The boxcar happened to be on a slope and, of course, it ran off the rails and upset. 'Sawdust Billy' came running out of his office in the mill yard, hauled off his belt, and took action. As a kid when Jack laughed, he always smacked his knees. A while ago I visited Jack in hospital and reminded him of that escapade, and he laughed and smacked his knees!

Hallowe'en was another opportunity for high jinks.

In the old days a favourite Hallowe'en prank was taking gates off the fences. A bunch of us came to this place on Back Enderby Road that had a pole gate. We couldn't lift it off so we just yanked it off. Up the road a ways a fellow saw us and asked us not to do anything to his farm, and he wouldn't tell anybody what he had seen.

251

But he must have told the Broughtons that we were in the area that night.

Police Chief Barnes came around to our place. Dad and I were out in the yard and he followed us into the house and issued a summons to court. As I look back, the odd part of the court session was that Chief Barnes didn't seem to be prosecuting us – he was defending us. Dr. Van Kleeck's father-in-law, a fellow by the name of Groves, was the magistrate then, and I remember him looking over his glasses and saying, "Case dismissed." That was my only run-in with the law – a couple of parking tickets in Vancouver.

I remember another Hallowe'en night. Not too far from our farm were two families, one of whom was named Ball, and he was deaf. I don't think they loved each other much, so we took the wheels off their wagons and exchanged them – put each of the wheels on the other fellow's wagon. Ball found out what had happened and came over to see my dad. He told him we were going to have to put the wheels back where they belonged. I guess he didn't want anything to do with his neighbour, that's all.

Mac sounds somewhat envious of the wider variety of Hallowe'en pranks available to the youth who lived in Armstrong.

Of course, we didn't go to town. The kids in town took a horse-pulled road grader and dragged it up the steps of the old high school, which was next door to the Rec. Centre. They pulled the principal's gate up the flagpole at the elementary school, and then McFarland shinnied up the pole and tied the end of the rope to the top of it so nobody could winch it down again. Tommy Aldworth was the principal – a colonel in World War One – and when he was teaching, all he ever talked about was the war. He was a great old guy. I always figured he was fair because more than once he should have given me the strap. Was Mac that bad? I never shot anybody. I never stole a car. But the teacher had me up into Tommy's office often enough. He didn't have an office – just a desk in the room.

Mac, however, never lacked for friends.

A bunch of us were seventeen or eighteen years old. There was a beer parlour in the Armstrong Hotel, but they wouldn't let us in. The age limit was twenty-one. So we used to go to Vernon because they didn't know us. Those were the days of the National Hotel and the National Restaurant in Vernon. One day we tied the local BC policeman up to a telephone pole because he'd been giving us a hard time – put his own handcuffs on him.

In a photograph taken on a summer afternoon, a cluster of five young men decorate a rail fence in the Thornton yard. They are dressed with casual flair in shirt and pants, and three of them sport soft felt hats. Mac hunches atop the tallest rail – even there you can see his height – Irwin Trudel leaning back beside him; a young Jim Thornton perches up behind a youthful Art Nash. Older brother Sid Nash in white trousers and stylish pullover poses nonchalantly and grins; like Fred Astaire he looks to be a good dancer. They all appear ready for fun. *There were nine Nashes. But I was at Frank Hassard's one day and* sixteen *of them sat down to the table; one of the boys was away.*

Although Mac left home at the age of twenty-six, his connection to families and events in Spallumcheen is lasting and constantly renewed by visits, telephone calls and synchronicities. *Except during the War, there wasn't a year that I didn't come to Armstrong.*

Martin Meggait is an old-timer born in Spallumcheen; I was talking to him the other day. One of his sisters, Ann, was an X-ray technician. When my daughter was about three years old, we were visiting people in Vancouver and she fell downstairs. The doctor sent her to have an X-ray. Ann Meggait was the technician. I got in touch with her by phone about a month ago and she reminded me of this story:

There was a fire in Armstrong in early 1933 that burnt several businesses including the Okanagan Hotel, Shepherd's hardware, and Safeway. Safeway in BC had their fiftieth anniversary about ten years ago and I knew the manager in Vancouver where we dealt. I said to him: "You've got a sign up there that says Safeway has been in BC for fifty years. I think you're wrong." "What do you mean?" he said. I told him, "The first Safeway in BC was in Armstrong and they never re-opened there after it burnt down." I had with me the Armstrong Advertiser – you know the section 'Looking Back – Fifty Years Ago,' and I think the date given for the fire was several years before this anniversary celebration. "Here," I said, "read this." So he sent it to Head Office to get them caught up on their own history.

I saw that fire. Safeway, I guess, had been in Armstrong a year. Martin Meggait's mother was expecting, and in those days the doctor came out and delivered the babies on the farms. Meggaits phoned our house because they couldn't get through to the doctor – the fire downtown had burned the lines. They wanted to know if I would ride to the next farm – Hopkins – three-quarters of a mile away, I guess, and try phoning from there. It must have been about two o'clock on a cold January morning. I can remember riding that darn horse too. I had to get him through the gate that separated our farms – take down all the rails and put them back up again. Hopkins was able to make the call. Ann Meggait reminded me that she was the baby born that day.

Always on the lookout for some adventure and extra money, Mac worked the summer of 1934 at Douglas Lake Ranch. *Hec [Hector] McKinnon and I went up and lived in a tent with Mat. S. Hassen. There was a bunkhouse there but it was pretty crummy and held older fellows than us. Woodward's sold the ranch in the '90s for $100 million. It was worth one million then. Today we could probably have bought it at the old price!*

In 1937 the Depression was at full strength and Mac, like others, was scrambling to find sustainable work. *Armstrong was a famous place for truck gardens – celery, lettuce, potatoes. Armstrong in the twenties was called the Celery Capital of the World. Even in the '30s*

Armstrong shipped celery to Hawaii. One day I was talking to Frank Marshall and he told me it was hard to get good help. I said, "How about we go into partnership? I'll supply the labour myself or hire any extra that's needed, and you supply the land."

I worked with him for about three years. We harvested annually two crops of lettuce – one in the spring and one in the fall. I remember Ted Poole owned the packing house, and he wanted us to ship by consignment to Toronto. That meant we'd get whatever the market price was at the time of sale. I said no. Frank said, "Oh, let's try it." "Okay," I said, "you own the land." We shipped it and went to Poole to get paid, and I think we got nineteen cents a case – four dozen heads of lettuce to a case. A few days ago I paid $3.14 for a head of lettuce in the grocery store. I told the vegetable manager about what we had got that fall and he looked at me as if I was crazy.

The market was dead. And you can't leave lettuce in the ground too long. One year things were good – we made good money on celery. A friend asked if I could loan him $800 to buy a car. I didn't have a car myself – had to cadge a ride. Anyhow, I loaned him the money – nothing signed or a damn thing. Where did I get $800? Growing celery and lettuce. I had to put in long hours. Start at three or four o'clock in the morning cutting lettuce before it got dry. I remember Bert Fletcher lent me his truck to cart lettuce to the packing house and didn't charge me for it. A dollar is a dollar.

Mac also grabbed the chance for a second job. *When West Canadian Hydroelectric put the power through Marshall's and up through Lansdowne in 1937, they contracted out the work, including digging the holes for the poles by hand for one dollar apiece – good money too! My brother Jack took on the contract for Back Enderby Road but he had to give up because he hit rock. But I dug the holes through Marshall's where the ground was nice and soft. I remember when I lived in Vancouver, an accident sheared off a power pole, and it flattened my tool shed and fence. A crew was replacing the pole with power tools. I walked over and told them about digging* holes with a shovel for a dollar a hole. They looked at me as if I was crazy.

In 1939 through the community network, Mac was presented with an unexpected opportunity.

Buckerfield's seed operation was located in Vancouver. They had the franchise for Rennie Seeds. The manager, Dick Horrex, was related to Hilliard McCallan and had grown up in Armstrong – his parents still lived here – and he was visiting them. He said to me, "How would you like to work for us in Vancouver?" "Sure would! When are you leaving?" "Tomorrow." So Vancouver's where I landed.

I stayed with them for a couple of years. We packaged garden seeds, and we bought clover seed from farmers and cleaned and bagged it for sale. Later on for about six years I worked for a company that installed fire sprinklers. I installed them from Alaska to Oregon. Then in 1949 I began working in the commercial insurance business. I retired twice – the first time in 1977 – and started the next day to work for a different company. I finally quit for good in 1983.

Between the years he worked at Rennie Seeds and the years he sold fire sprinklers, Mac served an abortive term in the Canadian army. World War Two had started the year he left Armstrong.

I was in Vancouver in an anti-tank unit. In Shilo, Manitoba, they were looking for volunteers for Signal Corps. I think there were about 6000 personnel in that camp and they never got one volunteer. So our artillery unit put up a list of 200 names including mine and we were given a course on Morse Code. I said to the officer, "I don't think I'll make a signalman." He said, "Thornton, we think you will." We wrote the test, and I was one of seven that got picked from the 200. I had learned it in cadets at the Brick School. Tommy Aldworth would have been pleased. We used flags mostly back then. I didn't really like it, though, and I thought I could fail the test, but I guess they thought I'd failed it too easy.

In Kingston, Ontario, I was in the Signal Corps waiting to go overseas, and the place was packed. I was given the job of sweeping the floor of the hut, and I was sick. I was sitting on the bunk and this officer came in. "What's the matter with you?" "I don't know, I think I'm going to die!" "You'd better go to the hospital. Get in my jeep – I'll take you."

One day one of the nurses said there was a colonel wanting to see me: "He says he knows you." It was Ted Poole! The first thing he said to me was "How come you get a private room and a private nurse in an army hospital, and I have to share my room with a major?" I said, "Teddy, old boy, it depends who you know."

Probably I was the only private in the Canadian army to have that fancy treatment. I was discharged out of the army in 1943 before I even got to Europe – six months in four different army hospitals – pleurisy. They must have thought I was going to be too expensive – my temperature was 104 degrees for a long time and I was in an oxygen tent. As a matter of fact, four or five other fellows had pleurisy – a couple died and one ended up in the sanitarium [tuberculosis]. I was supposed to go with three other fellows to New York City for New Year's Eve, but I never made it. I still remember the number on my dog tag though – K65917.

Fortunately, the only war injury Mac received was at camp. *I got my finger caught in the trail of a twenty-five pound gun and had to go to Brandon, Manitoba, to get it X-rayed. I still have the scar.*

Having been given a medical discharge from the army, Mac located and on April 4, 1945, married Lillian Sanderson, whom he had known in Armstrong. *Lillian's mother was a Simpson, an old family from Nanaimo. Her father had a butcher shop on Railway Avenue in Armstrong. He worked for Pat Burns.*

Pat Burns had begun as a drover/buyer in Alberta. He was fostering the retail meat business by acquiring butcher shops. His cattle buyers went around the countryside buying cattle and pigs that came on the market – usually once a year – whatever stock the farmers wanted to get rid of – and then he'd sell it in his butcher shops.

Joe Sanderson's job was to build up the butcher shop in a town and then sell it off and move to the next town. The other butcher shop in Armstrong at the time was Fred Murray's. A very odd thing about Murray and Sanderson – I guess you'd call them competitors but they were good friends. Fred Murray was always involved in sport and so was Joe Sanderson. Armstrong was a big hockey town. Fred Murray played hockey and Sanderson coached. I have a picture of the team and there's only one of them living. Fred's daughter Margaret was probably one of the first people Lillian's sister Millicent met when she came to Armstrong, and they kept in touch all their lives. Fred Murray was a very good friend of my dad's too.

Lillian's father died in 1936, and she and her mother moved to Vancouver Island. I walked into Cunningham Drugs in Victoria one day and Lillian was working there. Their meeting was not entirely accidental – the network still operated. When they married, Lillian was determined to stay put.

My wife said she had lived in McLeod, Alberta, and in seven different towns in BC. She had moved eight times! So we lived in the same house in Vancouver for fifty years. We bought it in 1950 and sold in 2001. I had paid $7500 for a forty-six foot lot. There was no garage. I don't think the inside was even painted. A twenty-year mortgage was guaranteed by the government – National Housing – at four and a half percent for twenty years. When I sold it, I figured I had made practically $5000 every year. I wanted to sell it quick – didn't want a lot of viewers coming and going – and I sold for $250,000.

I talked to some of the neighbours later, and they said the blinds were always closed. I knew an inspector in the police force and told him, "I think you smoke it!" He found 460 plants – a potential million dollar operation – and dammit! I never got in on it!!

For ventilation they had cut a hole in the living-room floor. Except for the bedrooms, the flooring throughout was three-quarter inch oak. So, of course, the next one who bought the house had to tear it down. What hurt me most, though, was that Vancouver has a bylaw that any tree that grows over nine feet tall has to be replaced. We had some beautiful trees – a Japanese maple – all gone.

Mac lives in Port Alberni in Abbeyfield close to his daughter and son-in-law, Sandra and Ted Gilbert. He maintains close connection with family and friends, not forgetting the people and places of his youth. In fact, friends who grew up together tended to find each other again when they left home.

Tom Aldworth, the principal of the elementary school, lived close to us in Vancouver. Frank Everett was a Vancouver policeman. Another Armstrong boy, Elmer Hassard, was captain of the Vancouver Fire Department, and several others were in the department with him: Vance Young's boy, Bunny, and Don Sugden, for example. Don was the first Armstrong boy taken prisoner in the Second War. He was held for four years and escaped twice. Both times the fellow that was with him was shot. Don came home.

When I had to quit driving because of my poor eyesight, young Mat. [Matthew Robert] used to chauffeur me to Armstrong for visits and special occasions, including the Year 2000 Reunion for everybody who had ever lived in Armstrong Spallumcheen. I thought I wouldn't know that many people any more, but I came anyway. In the first few minutes that I was wearing my name tag, about a dozen people came over to speak to me. I was surprised at how many old friends were still around. I [even] talked to Dr. Haugen. And then I realized that these were the second generation! I was talking to Dr. Haugen's son and he was a doctor too!

On that trip I left my lawn bowls for the Armstrong Lawn Bowling Club. I'd bowled for about fifteen years in Central Park in South Burnaby, and I didn't use them anymore. The Armstrong club needed them and I wanted to leave a trail.

Each time I visited Armstrong, I'd buy two or three sides of bacon from Askew's. They had their own slaughterhouse in Salmon Arm and cured the meat themselves. The other day I bought some store bacon in Port Alberni – I felt like taking it back.

Mac's ninetieth birthday party was a celebration.

When you make 90, it's a little slower. Turning 65 was a lot different – I stood on my head that day – I had more people that I knew. That's the trouble when you move to a new town, especially when you're older. I meet people but they're all younger than me. But I had a nice time at my 90th though. What surprised me is the number of people that knew when my birthday was – a dozen people phoned me. I'm still getting calls. I had a call from my sister Kay in Australia. Barney got a bag of ribs from my birthday supper to come home with.

Barney is a little grey poodle that brings joy to more than Mac. Everyone knows Barney.

I was in the dentist's office: "Where's Barney?" One of the girls in the bank: "My mother's in the care centre. She just loves Barney."

The care centres are Echo Lodge and Fir Park Village, which Mac and Barney visit together several mornings a week. *They had their eleventh anniversary: "Be sure and bring Barney." There were fifty or sixty people there and only one dog.* Barney had his photograph taken on a cushioned chair. Mac has a copy. He also has a Certificate of Appreciation presented to them on that occasion:

The residents of Echo Lodge proudly present this certificate to Mac Thornton and Barney for their regular visits to our Village and their friendship to the residents. March 7, 2003.

I never had any regrets – I always had a buck – still have. If I'd gone to school longer, my grammar might have been better. When I was in the insurance business, I said something to my boss about it – he was an engineer, actually – and he said to me, "Mac, it's all in the library!"

Mac Thornton, left, and friends on the Thornton farm

Chapter Six

No Time to Rust

John Rawleigh Boss

My birthday is registered as November 6th. The doctor came out and stayed the night at our place in Nova Scotia, and he asked in the morning if anyone had looked at the clock when I was born and nobody had, so it could have been the 7th. Maybe that's why my life has been confusing.

My grandfather's name was John, but he said, "A boss should never be called John." My aunt suggested I be called Rawleigh. I think they were looking for a name and might have been using Rawleigh's baby powder. So when I started school, I said to the teacher, "John Rawleigh is my name. Which name do you like?" And she said, "Rawleigh." So that's the name I put first. It's a name that can't be shortened.

The family name attracted heavy humour – *"Are you the Boss?"* – but when Rawleigh's father, William Charles Boss, married Rawleigh's mother, Flora Bella Beaton, he devised the cheerful pun: *"Well, I was the Boss until I took a good Beaton!"*

Like other old-timers in the Okanagan, the Boss family wandered far afield before William Charles settled in Armstrong Spallumcheen. On this continent the American Civil War of 1860-65 split the family.

Back in the early history of the Boss family, three members immigrated to America from England, and two of them came to Canada with the United Empire Loyalists. Our line settled in Nova Scotia near the New Brunswick border – what they call Amherst Shore. The ocean was just a few yards away. The other brother settled in Athol, or what is called Springhill. You know the singer Anne Murray?

She's from Springhill, and I've heard it said that her mother was a Boss. We didn't have much connection with that branch – in horse and buggy days you didn't have the transportation.

William Charles and Flora Bella grew up in the same community, where fishing, mixed farming, and logging struggled against poor soil, a short growing season, and testy weather. *In Nova Scotia the land is very poor – you're lucky if you get a good crop of hay – you couldn't think of getting two crops – and in order to get that one crop you had to use fish for fertilizer – fish, seaweed, and manure. When you think of the price of fish today in the stores, it's hard to imagine they threw fish on the land. Back there in the early days, you didn't have main road fences as you do here because, being near the ocean, the wind changes direction and in winter the snow drifts, and if the road was blocked with snow, you just drove your horse around the blockage through the open fields.*

Well, Dad had a yearning to see what the west was like, and in 1906 he and two brothers, his father, and a sister and her husband came to BC. They discovered Armstrong and Dad fell in love with it. He accumulated quite a bit of property here. You know the house on Wood Avenue [3495] straight across from the bottom of Schubert Road? He built that house in 1908. Another parcel he owned was up on MacDonald Road [4262] – what later became known as the Lindsay property. Dad and his relations were here for three years and then went back to Nova Scotia.

In fact, William Charles owned more property than the family realized, and over the years he was quietly generous. This type of community spirit built Armstrong Spallumcheen.

In 1977 when the Baptist Church had its 70th anniversary, they invited my mother and presented her with a Bible. [They said] that in 1907 Dad had donated the land on Becker Street to build their church. Mother hadn't known anything about it because the family had always gone to the United Church. Dad owned a second property too – perhaps Gordon Grey's – there's a picture in the Museum of the house but it's not identified. We figured it must have been in the same part of town as the Baptist Church. Dad couldn't really remember because Armstrong was pretty much in the bush in those days. From 1907 until our family came in 1923 – sixteen years can make a lot of changes.

Behind Armstrong Elementary School there was a strip of land known as the old tennis court. Dad was the one that graded it off to make the court. Now it's a parking lot. He also started clearing the land for the park. At the time there wasn't much done – just some clearing in the back. It wasn't until after the [Second] War that the swimming pool was put in. During the war they quit making so many things – everything was directed to war production – and no two-inch pipe could be found anywhere in Canada to complete the pool. We happened to have quite a few hundred feet of it for irrigation, so we were able to contribute it to finish construction of the project.

Home again in 1909 from his western reconnaissance, William Charles waited for Flora Bella to come of marriageable age. Sixteen years older than she, he had known her family before she was born. *Dad and Mom always got along – I never heard a cross word between them in my whole life. On a farm all kinds of things can go wrong, but he was the type of person that always left the problems outside the door when he came into the house. There were frustrations but he'd just accept things as best he could. Mother knew what was going on – they would discuss things – but there was no controversy. They got along so well together.*

In Nova Scotia we had a mixed farm with a small sawmill at the back of it, and horses were used to do the work. About 1909 Dad jumped on the back of one of them to go home from the sawmill, and just as he did the animal bolted and knocked him off. His foot caught in the harness, and he was dragged and it did some damage to his hip. So he was not in a very good state for a while.

William Charles was still recuperating when he received bad news about his land purchases in Armstrong. He believed he had made arrangements for the taxes on his properties to be paid during his absence.

My memory isn't good here because I was just a kid listening to these stories, but apparently Dad trusted a local businessman to look after his affairs. Word trickled back to him that the land was going to be sold for taxes. If taxes aren't paid for two years, the property goes to a tax sale. And he was at the other end of the country. So he came back to Armstrong in 1910 and was able to retrieve his property in time. Then he stayed on to straighten things out. During that time he built the Lindsay house and then sold that piece to a fellow by the name of Jack Henson, but he kept the twenty acres just across the tracks [4304 MacDonald Road] west of the Hensons. (Hensons eventually wanted to move to the Coast so they sold to the Lindsays, who came to Armstrong in 1935 or '36.) Dad went back to Nova Scotia in 1912 and got married. We kids were all born in Nova Scotia.

Chandler and Noland came first, then Rawleigh on either November 6th or 7th, 1918, and finally Violet.

I remember Mother used to feed the mill crew – it wasn't a big sawmill – and she'd have us fed and in bed before the crew came in for their supper at 5:30. So we were used to going to bed early! I remember when we came out here, one night the Gussie Schuberts and the kids were up visiting – and I can still hear my brother say, "Oh-h-h, it's ten o'clock at night!!" We'd never been up that late before.

When Dad decided to come back to Armstrong, he came out in the spring of 1923 and built a house on his MacDonald Road property to be ready for the family's arrival that fall. My mother was reluctant to move because she was so much younger than Dad, and for her it meant leaving her relatives behind – she'd be 3,000 miles away – but she came. We arrived on the 22nd of October. It was a very bleak day and there was snow on the ground. "Is this the wonderful Armstrong?" But she made the best of it and eventually grew to like it as much as he did. He never went back to Nova Scotia, but my mother visited her family a couple of times.

Mother lived past 100. Her mother lived past 101. The last time my mother was back, my grandmother was 98. They had to walk about a mile across the field to church, and Mother really had to move to keep up with her. My grandmother was never sick. In her 90s she was still taking the sheep's wool and making yarn, and every year at Christmas Dad got white socks and white mittens. Between her 101st and 102nd birthday, she lay down on either a Good Friday or an Easter Monday and went to sleep.

Although he was only five years old at the time and unable to make a choice for himself, Rawleigh feels that the family's move to Armstrong was significant for him. *Actually, my mother's parents didn't want me to come with them. I was my grandfather's favourite – his pet. They wanted me to stay behind with them. If I'd stayed in Nova Scotia, I wonder how different my life would have been. And my first year in Armstrong was a pretty disastrous one. I came down with whooping cough, measles, bronchitis, and pneumonia – one after the other – and I almost didn't survive.*

But that very first Christmas we spent in Armstrong, we had the MacDonald family for Christmas Day, and that tradition went on for sixty-five years without a break. The MacDonalds lived on 160 acres right next door to us. Miles and Granny MacDonald had three children – two boys, Neil and Don, and a girl, Flora. Neil was the oldest and later married one of the Hassard girls. Don took over the family farm, and Flora married Joe Erickson and they bought a place on Otter Lake Road [1768] just past Walbridge – the two-storey house with the red barn up behind it – the old Albert Evans place. (A lot of these old-timers were jack of all trades. I'm pretty sure Evans also built the old Glaicar place that burned down on Grandview Flats.) Jack Jamieson [Armstrong Advertiser] took a picture of my mother and Flora on the anniversary of our 65th Christmas together.

It was a wonderful neighbourhood. There were the MacDon-

alds, the Hensons, who owned the other half of our property, the Nobles, Harrops, the Walbridge family on Walbridge Road, and the Schuberts, Gussie senior and Gussie junior. The Schubert property extended on both sides of Otter Lake Road. Gussie senior lived east of the road and when Gussie junior married, they built a house for him on the corner of Otter Lake Road and MacDonald [4214, currently Harrison]. Gussie junior's wife was a Timberlake and they had five children – Bert, Trevor, Shirley, Audrey and Norma. Bert was killed just before the end of the Second War – his leave was cancelled for some reason and he was sent back in. A friend, Hugh Ehlers from Salmon Arm, saw him die and came to visit the family. He met Shirley at that time and they later married.

William Charles realized that he needed more than the twenty acres he owned, and he began a series of deals and relocations to improve his prospects.

The acreage wasn't big enough to support a family, so we leased an 80-acre parcel on Walbridge Road – what we always called 'the old Russian property.' That was before the rails were laid on the CN track, but the right-of-way was there, so we used it as a shortcut to the leased land. I don't think the rails were laid until 1925 or '26. The CP, of course, was here quite a bit earlier [1890s]. Then we leased part of the Schubert Ranch – the bottomland. They didn't want to sell their ranch – they wanted to test retiring in Victoria – so in the late '20s we took a lease on the whole ranch and moved down. The Schubert house that is now on the O'Keefe Ranch – I lived in that house for three years.

We had maybe fourteen or fifteen milk cows, and Mom was very good at raising chickens – we used to have 1000 chickens – and Dad had a good many pigs because in those days if you couldn't sell your potatoes – I've seen potatoes go for $5 a ton – well, you'd have pigs to feed them to. I've seen the price of pigs drop to one or two cents a pound. I remember one time Dad had to slaughter some pigs and bury them because he was losing money feeding them.

The Schubert Ranch presented its own problems. *Back in those days the creek that ran through their property to Otter Lake would flood in the spring and that whole meadow south of Otter Lake Road would be water. Actually, it would flood when the weather was still cold. From the Schubert Ranch right into town would be a solid ice sheet, and I've seen hundreds of people skating on it every Sunday – come to a line fence and just step over it. Later with the dredges it was easier to dig drainage ditches, but in those days you had to dig them by hand. It was a big chore. Two of the three years we were there, the crops were flooded out on the meadow and one year there was drought – so Dad got the bee in his head to raise celery and head lettuce.*

In 1929 he bought the Stickle place – a twenty-three acre parcel two and a half miles northeast of town on the road to Enderby. It was after the bend in the highway on your left just before you reach the railway tracks. There was no home on the property, just an old Chinese cabin, so he also bought from Ed Johnson the thirty-eight acres across the road – bottomland with a little log house and a log barn on the hill. That was the Home Forty, and we lived in the log house until we built a new home in 1946.

Dad had a philosophy – it was tough on us at the time, but looking back, it made sense. So often as kids, you hanker for that dollar to run and spend, but he always said, "Get your farms paid for first, *and then when you spend money, you're spending your own and not somebody else's." That's why we went through that Depression time without having those dollars to throw away. We wanted to get all the farms paid for, and then when we built the house, it was* our *house.*

The original Boss home on MacDonald Road, however, was kept in the family for another fifty years.

When we first moved down to the Schubert place, and Don MacDonald got married, he rented the house from us until he got his own built on this end of the old MacDonald farm [currently the Arneson place, 4312]. Don's son, Norm MacDonald, the postmaster, also lived in that house for a good length of time. Miles and Granny MacDonald lived at the other end of the property underneath the mountain. Don's wife, Corinna, was a Fraser, and the Frasers were old-timers. Harry Fraser was one of the first schoolteachers in Armstrong, and he lived in a house on a little farm on Mill Street where the police station is now. He was already an old man when we were growing up. Harry's wife was a Schubert. Corinna was their only child and a smart businesswoman, and Dad had a reputation for being honest. She said Dad was the only person she didn't ask to give her a receipt. After the MacDonalds moved into their new place, Dad turned our old farm over to his younger brother, Ivan, but he spent most of his time with us. We raised celery and head lettuce for a good many years. You can grow two crops in a year.

Rawleigh and his brothers were expected to do their share of the farm work. When Rawleigh was in elementary school, however, he discovered he had a special aptitude for track and field, high jumping in particular, and by the time he reached high school, he was setting personal records.

Elementary school kids did their training – the fifty-yard dashes and the high jump pit – roughly where the Armstrong Play School is now. High jumping was just something that I seemed able to do. I had a good leg spring. Once upon a time I could stand and jump over a 4-foot 2-inch barrier without running at it. I had that potential. But I always felt I had to specialize. I would broad jump only if it was after the high jump. High jumping came first. In fact, the high jump was a good warm-up for the broad jump. My parents never discouraged me, but I always felt if they were going to give me a day off work to compete, I'd better do something right. I had to win in order to get an excuse for another day off.

The old high school I attended was just above Hassen Hall where the Youth Centre is now. In the early fifties it was condemned, but it was so well built they had a job tearing it down. They built a new junior/senior high school there, and it fell apart and later they had to demolish it, but the old building was solid. When I first started high school, you took four years in three, which was pretty rough. When I was entering grade 10, they brought back the four-year course and have had it ever since. Once I remember they had a grade 13 for a short period of time – I forget just what year.

Although Rawleigh found classes burdensome, in the high jump pit he appeared to do naturally what others needed regular coaching and sponsorship to accomplish. However, he lacked both the disciplined support and the apt advice that a coach could have given him. As a result, despite achieving outstanding height in his jumps, he regrets that he never received credit for breaking a Canadian record.

You've got to be in the right meet at the right time. When I was sixteen years old, the Canadian juvenile record for age sixteen and under was 5 feet 9 inches, and for age eighteen and under it was 5 feet 10 inches. I went into a senior competition in Vernon where both the Canadian senior champion and his younger brother, who was my age, were entered. They were from Trail, and Trail sponsored their athletes.

The Canadian senior champion was jumping about 6 feet 4 inches. At the time I couldn't match that, so the big battle was between his younger brother and me for second place. He was doing the western roll, and the style of the western roll is supposed to give about six or eight inches more height than the scissors. I was still doing the scissors. We both could clear the 6 feet but neither one of us could clear the 6 foot 1 inch. We tried and tried, and the crowd got fed up after a while and let us take some time off, and then we went back at it again. I always remember Mac Lynch – he was a high school teacher's son and a mile runner – and he came over and pep-talked me into clearing the 6 foot 1 inch. The other fellow couldn't do it.

The following year this younger brother set a new Canadian junior record at 5 feet 11 inches. But because my win [the previous year] had happened in a senior event, it didn't mean anything – I'd just come second. When I got back home, all the credit I got was, "There must have been an awful big sag in the crossbar!" But at the time I had jumped three and a half inches higher than the Canadian juvenile record.

To give himself an even chance, Rawleigh learned the western roll. But he was still bedevilled by the lack of consistent coaching. *A fellow called Jack Lynes, who was the Valley physical education instructor, taught me the basics of the western roll and I switched over from the scissors. But I had no official coach to see that I carried on doing things right.*

One heartbreak happened in my last year in high school – I had a once-in-a-lifetime chance to set a Canadian high-school high jump record. One of the judges was a real smart aleck – thought he was being a big shot. If your feet or hips didn't reach the crossbar in advance of your head, it was called a 'dive.' I wasn't diving. I was taking too acute an angle and so my head was reaching the crossbar just ahead of my feet. "Oh, that's a dive. You've got to jump it again." "Jump it again...." "Jump it again...." And every jump I made was a 3-3 decision of the judges. When you are a teenager, that experience can wear you down. I won the event, but I didn't jump high enough to set a record. A week later on the 24th of May I jumped in Enderby – the standards were 6 feet 2 inches and the crossbar was on top of the standards, and I easily cleared that height.

The climax came when Rawleigh attempted to qualify for the 1937 British Empire Games in Australia. First he needed to enter officially sanctioned competitions and win. *When it came to entering the trials, you had an opportunity to list your past performances. In Enderby I jumped 6 feet 2 inches, but I couldn't list small meets like those because they weren't sanctioned by the British Empire Games Association. So how many track meets would I be in that I could list? That was a black mark.*

My chance came down to the BC championships in Nanaimo in 1937 and I was entered in the high jump and the broad jump. I'd never been to the Coast before. My high school Latin teacher met me when I went down on the train, and I stayed at their place all night, and she took me to the ferry. It's a different climate, and you've got to get used to the change. I won the high jump and was third in the broad jump. They didn't dare dig up the ground there, as the meet was held in a park, so the broad-jump pit was two feet of shavings on top of the ground. You had to clear two feet of shavings each time you made a jump. So you can imagine I broke no records there!

Coming back on the ferry from Nanaimo, I happened to be talking to a young fellow that had competed with me, and I said I wanted to stay over in Vancouver, as a couple of important meets were coming up. He said, "My dad's in Toronto at a meeting, my mother's in the States at the races, my grandmother's looking after me, so you can come and stay with us." That was just a gift from heaven and I was there for several weeks.

I won the high jump at the Hastings Park Community Club, and I was entered in both the junior and senior classes in the Caledonian Sports. That day I heard that the Pacific Coast champion was entered in the senior meet. I won the junior meet at about 5 feet 10 inches or something – that wasn't the Canadian record – but I was saving my energy for the senior meet – the Men's Open – because I thought the competition with the champion was going to be so great. And that was my stupidity! If I had had a coach, he would likely have said, "Go for height now and you'll set a Canadian junior record." I jumped over 6 feet and won the senior event, but it wasn't a senior record – you lose a lot of stamina jumping once and again an hour later – and they wouldn't count that jump for the junior event. So I lost that opportunity. Looking back over these things, you don't realize at the time your lack of knowledge.

Although Rawleigh had not recognized his chance to set a Canadian record, his wins at the Coastal meets had given him the provenance he needed to enter the trials for the Empire Games.

So when it came, I was in the track meet in Vernon on Labour

Day, and the trials were the following week in Vancouver. I jumped 6 feet 4 inches in the Vernon meet. Then I quit jumping that day because I didn't want to overexert myself. So I don't know how high I could have gone if forced to do so.

Those trials were the only time since age sixteen that I was defeated. The Pacific Coast champion wasn't that good but I was scared. I know my uncle had said to me, "You don't want to go to the Coast. Vancouver's a bigger city." The implication was that athletes in a bigger city can jump higher than the ones from smaller centres. I'd already proven him wrong.

In those days the rules were so strict. For example, a cousin of one of the high-school teachers who used to compete with me was a world champion swimmer. As she was travelling by boat to the Olympics, somebody took her photograph when she was holding a bottle of coke. They accused her of advertising Coca Cola and kicked her off the team. Such stories as these did nothing for Rawleigh's confidence. I suppose I could have been disqualified for having gone to meets in Enderby, Vernon, and Oyama because they weren't sanctioned as amateur events. They always had goods as prizes – they couldn't have money prizes. I don't know what would happen if you were a six-year-old and somebody gave you two bits for winning a race at a picnic!

I travelled to the Coast and went to the trials, and I was doing okay. In high jumping your mental attitude is extremely important. It's one of the most precise sports. Pole vaulting would be similar to it. A race you run as fast as you can. Broad jump – you run and then jump as far as you can. High jump – you have to guide yourself as you're going up, and some people, if they could jump 6 feet, wouldn't start jumping until the bar was set at 5 feet 8 or 9 inches. Me, I started lower than that and gradually warmed up. I'm not saying it was right or wrong, just the way I did it. When it comes to this level of competition, they more or less start away up there, which I wasn't used to – no time to warm up.

But I was up around the 6 feet and then panic took over: "What if I win this and we don't have any money to send me to Australia – it's going to be pretty embarrassing!" Where would I get money back in the thirties? There just wasn't money around. The government of Canada sponsored the basic expenses but you have to have something of your own and I just plain didn't. So I chickened out. I think I jumped 6 feet and the winner jumped 6 feet 2 inches and went on to the British Empire Games, and I'd jumped two inches higher than that in Vernon the week before. It is sad looking back on it. I'd have loved that trip to Australia too. And they quit having the Games when the [Second] War came. So that's why, when my son Roy came along, and I was more affluent, and he was active in sports, I was able to see he got to all these places.

Rawleigh's ability to high jump, however, did not go unnoticed, and an opportunity presented itself to leave Armstrong and the farm to pursue his talent. *The Vancouver Police Department had a track club and wanted me to join up because they had weight throwers and sprinters and broad jumpers but no high jumpers. They wanted me to become a Vancouver policeman and be on the team. But I didn't follow through. The Depression was still on and times were tough. I don't know how my life would have changed if I had become a Vancouver policeman....*

Rawleigh's demonstrations of superb high jumping were not quite over. The Dominion Day festivities in each town offered various entertainments and often included sports competitions.

Years ago July 1st was an important day in Armstrong. I recall Dad telling the story that on July 1st, 1912, a Wright plane touched down at the fairgrounds in Armstrong for the celebrations, and he had the job of guarding it. The Armstrong [Spallumcheen] Museum has a picture of that plane, so I guess his story is correct. The plane has two long, flat, rectangular 'wings,' one fastened above the other with struts. The lower wing is on the same level as the open-air seat from which the pilot grips a vertical steering wheel on what resembles an early, iron-wheeled mower.

I jumped 6 feet at the Dominion Day celebrations, 1940, in Lumby, and I never jumped again until July 1st, 1946. In 1946 I had developed something wrong with my back and I was going to a chiropractor. He said, "Your back isn't in very good shape – if you take three months off work, I think you might be all right." So I followed his advice. But when one of the other patients asked him how I was doing, he said, "If that man thinks he's going to work again, he's got another think coming." I went back to work the next day and have been going ever since.

A few months after [my return to work] it was July 1st.... With high jumping, it's a strange thing. The height that you can jump on the last day of the fall, you can still jump on the first day the next spring. But if you go ahead and jump that high, your muscles will pay for it! I went in the Dominion Day track meet in Armstrong and that day Brian Weddell, the Okanagan Valley high school champion, jumped 5 feet 11 inches. In order to win, I had to jump 6 feet and I hadn't jumped since 1940. I sure paid for it in the next twenty-four hours, but I could still go out and do it!

I couldn't train anymore but I was invited to officiate at track meets in Kelowna. The Jack Brow Meet was held at the end of June – people from all over BC went to that one – and I had been asked to be one of the judges. But I snuck down my spikes and shorts and said, "What would you say if I competed?" I think I was 34 at the time. They said, "Go ahead." I won it. Two other kids were in it – one was 16 and the other, 17, so I was older than both of them put together. I haven't jumped since.

Rawleigh was now fully involved in the family farm. In purchasing the property, William Charles had chosen a good site for a market garden.

You can be near a mountain and your land can be dried out and gravel, or you can benefit from the mountain seepage. We were very fortunate in that upland area to benefit from the mountain seepage. The bottomland was sub-irrigated – the water is just below the soil and you don't have to irrigate. In a hot summer the top inch of soil would be dry but you could brush that away, take a handful of dirt and squeeze moisture out of it. Around Armstrong there was a lot of bottomland, and the moisture in the soil went down from two to four feet; out in our area the moisture went down in some places as much as fifteen to twenty feet. So we were growing three good crops of hay without irrigation, and one year when there was an early spring and a late fall, we got four. It was unique because just across the valley on the other hill, they'd be lucky if their second crop was a foot high.

A creek ran beside the main road past our place, and the creekbed was so soft you could push a pole down through it by hand. Over the years at different times, I've seen a cow or horse fall into the creek and be sucked down until only their head and neck was showing. You'd have to hook a team on to haul them out. They must have had tough necks! It was real muck. That was ideal stuff for growing celery and head lettuce.

When the CPR was put through in the 1890s, they didn't have cranes. One old railway man, Bill Aslin, said that when they were building the line, one of the engines toppled over and they didn't have any means of raising it back onto the track. So it gradually sank, and somewhere between our farm and Stepney that engine is still under the ground. The bottomland went down that deep.

We used to pasture our dairy herd in the bottomland. We had it divided into sections and when one pasture got eaten down, we'd open the gate into another. One pasture had no access to the creek and we'd dug a well there. One summer it dried up and we dug down looking for water. And about four or five feet below the surface, we found the remnants of a birch tree with the bark still on it. How long ago did that tree fall and all the debris pile on top of it? Perhaps hundreds of years ago.

The bottomland presented some difficulties to the highway

crew that was changing the location of part of the roadbed in the late 1940s.

The original road to Enderby was the Lansdowne Road – a country road that turned up the Jake Lauer Hill, went across on the high country and came down again near Stepney Road. The road was crooked and dangerous, so they decided instead to go straight [along the present highway] and up the hill. They were going to raise the road and take it over the railroad track, and they brought in heavy machinery on that bottomland – big carry-alls – to bring in the clay and gravel. A carry-all is a piece of heavy machinery that has to be towed by a big bulldozer, and the combined weight was too much.

Dad tried to reason with them but "We're engineers and what do you know about it?" They hauled clay for three days and three nights and they didn't raise the road much, and the weight of the machinery pushed up the creekbed so that instead of the water draining off the land into the creek, the water was running back onto the land. And the weight of the machinery pushed the railway bed over and popped the hydro poles and fence posts.

Eventually they had to listen to Dad, and he said, "Take those heavy machines off the road and use trucks instead to top it up with clay." The clay would pack down, and then the gravel put on afterwards wouldn't immediately sink. Years ago when you watched a truck going along the road, you could see the road raise after the truck went by. We gave them a hill of clay and we got a wonderful lane. The trucks were going in and out, and when the road sank down, they just kept adding clay and gravel. It did us a double favour: we had a lane that lasted a good many years, and we got rid of the hill of clay and had a better view.

When they got the road constructed just past our place, they put up road signs: 'Don't go any farther!' The road was all broken up – just muck. Dad saw one guy get out of his vehicle, throw the sign in the ditch, drive through and sink. I wish we had five bucks for every time we pulled somebody out: "Thank you. Goodbye!"

Despite the difficulties associated with bottomland, Rawleigh expresses a fondness for it. *In the early days where it was real boggy, they used to build what they called 'corduroy' roads. They would lay trees down and put the clay on top of them. By the time the trees rotted underneath, the clay would be packed down hard enough to take the traffic. Down behind the Anglican Church the amount of clay and fill they brought in to destroy that beautiful bottomland! Someday they will regret it. When the world gets hungry, that's the type of land that feeds people.*

The Boss farm supported the Interior Provincial Exhibition.

As kids we were active in 4H [Junior Farmers]. I had a dairy calf in the fair one year that placed ninth out of ten, but she turned out to be one of the best milk cows we ever had! But we also had a lot of calves that got first place but didn't make good milk producers. Years later, if a kid wanted a 4H calf but wasn't able to raise one around home, we'd lend him one, and he'd look after it and bring it back after the fair.

In the history of market gardens in Armstrong, you read about the Chinese growers but seldom hear that there were other important growers too. [Yet] we were part of the early days of market gardening. Actually, when celery and head lettuce were prominent, there were three growers – Frank Marshall, Otto Lane, and ourselves – and I suggest that these three together had the greatest acreage [under cultivation] and produced the most crop. Marshall had twenty acres, Otto Lane had ten acres behind the fire hall and another ten or so of bottomland farther back towards the hill at the end of Keevil Road, and we had twenty-three acres.

As you go out of Armstrong, Wong Chog had the farm just across from the Liquor Store, and there he had a minor packing house where he sold his own vegetables. He and Lee Bak Bong oc-

casionally entered vegetable classes in the fair, but Marshall, Lane, and Boss regularly entered classes of celery and head lettuce along with vegetable displays. You were supposed to have six potatoes or six carrots, for instance, and you'd have five that matched and one that didn't! It was a friendly competition, though, among the three of us – if they beat us one year, we'd try harder the next. I couldn't say the same for the ladies entering the cooking competition. Mother was a good cook but she would never enter. She didn't want to get involved in any animosity – some of the women were very competitive.

Knitting, sewing, cooking, and art entries were located in the Rec. Hall, and in the old rink just behind it were the vegetables. In a little corner of the rink, the United Church women served lunch. [At the time] Tuesday was Preparation Day, and Wednesday and Thursday were fair days. Promptly at six o'clock on Thursday afternoon, they closed the Rec. Hall and cleared out the tables to hold the dance. Quite a few hundred people used to come. The fair was where you met people you hadn't seen in a long time.

We always maintained our membership in the IPE and we used to pick it up just before the fair. Suddenly, a new executive decided that you had to buy it [earlier] and we didn't know. So we lost out on perpetuating our membership down the years, and we just bought passes. 2003 marked the 80th consecutive fair that I attended. I started going to the fair in 1924 and never missed. We came to Armstrong too late for the one in 1923.

As a grower of market produce, the Boss farm was subject to the regulations of the vegetable marketing board. Rawleigh has mixed feelings about the usefulness of marketing boards, and at the time found government inspectors both ignorant of and insensitive to farming concerns. Over the years as the Bosses adapted farm production to suit changing market demands, Rawleigh's feelings on this subject remained the same.

The custom was to keep a few cows to put the groceries on the table, and your vegetables were supposed to be a cash crop to build up the farm. Of course, it was hit and miss. But when you think of what a head of lettuce or a stalk of celery costs today, the marketing board tried to force us to grow lettuce for ten cents a dozen. Actually, we could make money at twenty cents a dozen. People could always come to the farm and buy lettuce and celery, but when the marketing board didn't buy any more that season, we couldn't sell to any other market. So what are you supposed to do with it? One year we had to dump sixty wagonloads of lettuce that we hadn't sold [in order] to clear the ground for the second crop.

On the bottomland at our farm we had three root cellars, each 24 feet by 100 feet and a few logs high – just to keep the frost out. [One year] two of these were solid with celery sticks. That's a lot of celery. We sold one fifty-pound crate for fifty cents. The rest lay there and rotted. Then the stores started bringing it in from California at thirty-nine cents a pound; they said the US season was longer and guaranteed a better supply. The same thing happened to the fruit growers, and it gradually froze these people out. The Chinese left too; only a few, like the Jongs, stayed.

The MacDonalds used to take a truckload of produce up to the Cariboo where their fresh vegetables were very popular. Uncle Ivan had a regular route in Vernon. He'd load the back of his car with celery, lettuce and other vegetables and peddle them. It was a good living. But then the marketing board said they couldn't do that any more. That's one thing I like about the Farmers' Market – people can come there and sell their own produce.

Rawleigh remembers one benefit from growing vegetables.

We used to let the department of agriculture run test plots on the property – there was an agriculturalist and a horticulturalist – so we had a lot of visitors coming to the farm. We didn't get any money out of it – they didn't pay rent – but if they found anything new, we knew about it before anybody else did. For example, in hot weather lettuce had a tendency to 'tip burn,' particularly if you grew it in sandy soil, and they tried to find a strain that was resistant to tip burn. We became the first ones to grow the green celery that we buy today. The original celery was banked up with soil by hand in order to leach the colour out of the stalks and keep them white. It was an awful lot of work, and the celery was stringy. Even so, it took years before green celery became popular.

Then when the War came along, there was a need for vegetable seeds – Europe was out of production – so we went into growing vegetable seeds. Vegetable seed, other than lettuce and radish, takes two years. You grow your carrots, turnips, and parsnips one year, transplant the vegetables the second year, and let these vegetables go to seed. Radish or head lettuce, that's a one-year thing. But by the time head lettuce broke out into seed, the fall rains would be setting in, so it was a lucky year if you could produce lettuce seed. We had over twenty acres of vegetable seed – it got us on our feet.

We belonged to the BC Seed Co-op. Take carrot seed: You were guaranteed payment for 500 pounds of carrot seed to an acre. If you produced more than that, the surplus was placed in a seed pool and you were paid when it sold so it didn't go to waste. We used to hire help from the neighbours to weed because you couldn't allow weed seed to get mixed in with the crop. Mary Meggait was weeding one day and this young fellow came up and said, "I'm here to inspect your carrot seed. Where is it?" Mary looked up at him: "You're standing in the middle of the field." He didn't even know what a carrot seed looked like. So much for government inspectors!

Nature was more precise in selecting her targets. *After a few years diseases came along and created problems. Parsnips, for example, got a pestilence called webworm; it would get in and sap the vitality of the plants and the seeds would shrivel. Turnips had a weevil that would get inside the pod and eat the seeds. Carrots had thrip – something you couldn't see but [that] undermined the germination. One year we had to burn 800 pounds of carrot seed.*

When there's a scarcity, there's no problem making a sale.

However, after the War was over, Europe started to get back into seed production again. So the seed co-op hired a professional to find markets in the US. He didn't supply us with new markets – Europe got the markets – and the seed co-op went out of business. Our family lost several thousand dollars, which was a lot of money in those days. So since the vegetable seed industry was phasing out, we saw the need to increase the dairy herd instead, but for that we needed more land.

Gradually over time two forty-acre parcels and a ten-acre parcel became available in a convenient cluster abutting the farm and facing onto Mountain View Road.

Broughton, an old Englishman, wanted to sell out; a couple of years later Lawson, quite a horseman, decided to move to the Coast; and when my eldest brother, Chandler, got married to Jean McNair, one of the old-time families here on Lansdowne Road just north of the highway, we sold the 160 acres we had on the mountain next to Meggait's – it had some mining holes on it and a slightly used lime kiln, but only ten or fifteen acres cleared that we used mainly for pasture – and with the money we bought the Watson place for Chandler, a ten-acre farm with a house on it. On some of these parcels we had to do some land clearing. Land was a lot cheaper then but wages were lower too.

We gradually built up to over forty milk cows, a Jersey herd. Originally we were shipping cream to Vernon. For shipping cream the Jersey was your cow because the butterfat was higher – 4.5% to 5% – whereas Holsteins might be 3.5% to perhaps 4%. The Jersey animal is also a smaller animal and cheaper to feed than a Holstein, which we called 'a white elephant.' You could fit more Jerseys in the barn.

Rawleigh became the herdsman by default. *I sort of drifted into that part of it. We had a mixed farm. Chandler was more interested in machinery and naturally didn't want other people monkeying around with it. Some people don't like milking cows. It was easier* for me to milk than to fuss. We had fifteen or sixteen to milk before we got milking machines, and I worked in the field when I wasn't in the barn. But when you get up to forty cows, they take a lot of time. It wasn't loafing barns in those days, you had to clean up the barns, so when I was through with the chores, I inherited the business end of the farm as well.

Over the years the production of Boss milk and cream progressed through several changes.

The milk cans held eight gallons each and we would fill eight or ten each day. We separated the milk by hand. It was a big boost when we got the electrical separator. Actually, once upon a time we had the biggest electrical farm separator in North America. I remember it was a DeLaval and it was featured in a national magazine. In the early days Nelson Griffith hauled the cream cans to Vernon. The manager of the Vernon creamery [North Okanagan Creamery Association], Everard Clarke, said he used our cream to make the butter he entered in the national butter contest where he won several championships. Clarke also had the DeLaval dealership.

Then when the Armstrong Cheese Factory went into the whole milk business, we switched over from selling cream to supplying milk to the cheese factory. Eventually we got a bulk tank and strained the milk into it, and they weighed it at our farm. In those days to adulterate milk one way or the other was a criminal offence. Nowadays you can buy skim or 1% or 2%, but that was illegal in those times.

When we went in for whole milk production, Holsteins were better than Jerseys. But it was hard to put a big Holstein into a Jersey stall in the barn. (You didn't have milking parlours in those days.) So we did some crossbreeding of Ayrshire/Jersey and Holstein/Jersey to get more milk plus hopefully a better test. What you'd like is the Holstein amount of milk and the Jersey butterfat!

As William Charles aged, he played a smaller role on the farm.

Flora Bella, much younger, was still energetic. Vode Boss supplemented the labour force.

Dad would go out and work in the garden for two or three hours, get tired, come in and have a cup of tea, lay down for a few minutes, and go out again. He was a tall, thin man; he never ate much. He was the head of the house but he wasn't domineering. Mother, on the other hand, had the same stamina as my grandmother. In her 70s she was still coming out to help in the barn. I was running three milking machines, and it was handy to have somebody moving ahead and washing the cows' udders – not too far ahead because that brings the milk. She was a good hard worker.

Dad's brother Vode always lived with us. He was a sort of hired man, and he and Dad got along well. He had a bad leg and he limped. He was Mr. Fix-it and very handy when something broke. In those cases he used a lot of haywire! He and Dad died a few months apart when Gary was just a baby.

Raising cattle, of course, carried the bovine brand of frustration.

I remember in 1951 or '52 we sold an old Jersey bull for $323 – and I thought, "Gee, that sounds good," so instead of knocking the bull calves on the head as usual, I kept twelve. When they were little, they drank a lot of fresh milk – we fed them skim and kept the cream – we had our own grain and grass. Anyway, when they were between 2 and 2 ½ years old, we shipped eight of them to the Coast and got a cheque back for $319 for the lot. To make it worse, that money was classed as income and we had to pay income tax on it!

Rawleigh had unknowingly compounded his error: *When we separated the milk to feed the calves, I used to add the cream to the whole milk we were sending to the cheese factory in order to increase the butterfat content – 15 pounds of cream from every 100 pounds of milk. Well, the butterfat content in the milk never increased one speck. We should have sold the cream separately, and at least we would have got some money for it.*

The government would tell you how much something cost to raise; for instance, they used to say it cost $165 to raise a calf to a milk cow. I suppose if you bought everything – milk, hay, grain – that's what it would cost you, but if you produce these things on a farm, they figure they don't cost you anything! Your labour, the use of machinery, gasoline, are worth nothing! Farmers have not had a fair break.

We never had a milking parlour – we had four rows of stalls – and new regulations came in that each stall had to allow a certain distance behind and in front of the cow. Well, when you've got a barn already set up that's got steel reinforcement in the cement, how can you change? I remember one day the inspector said, "You know, you don't have enough room for the cattle, and you should do away with one of those rows of gutters." Fill all the gutters and then dig three new gutters in cement reinforced with steel and do away with a row of cows! However, I had 4- by 8-foot sheet metal on the walls and scrubbed them every day, and because I was doing that, the inspector rated the premises grade A and we were allowed to continue as before. (Ironically, I had thought sheet metal on the walls would be easier to clean than enamel paint but it was twice as difficult.) If we had sold the farm, however, the buyer would have had to make the changes to the cattle barn. And anybody building new would have had to build to a certain standard. You never thought about these things in the old days.

The inspector hassled Rawleigh as well about his manure pile.

We had a four-foot manure bucket hanging from a track in the ceiling of the cow barn. You'd run the bucket out of the barn about forty feet and use a long pole to trip the chain and dump the manure. The inspector said the manure pile was too close to the barn. He wanted us to spread it on the field. It was summer. We used to spread it in the fall when the crop was off. You can't move manure once and then move it again! "What are you doing in your summer holidays?" I said. "How would you like to come and spread manure?" He didn't say any more. But when the milking parlours came in, the cows could lay down in their own mess and it was perfectly legal, so it never made sense to me.

Whichever way he looked at it, a dairy herd was unstimulating company, and Rawleigh took every opportunity to escape.

I liked being with people, and being with cows all day long.... I used to take night courses in different things just to keep my mind active and associate with people. I took a business administration course ... a Dale Carnegie course ... Toastmasters.... I joined every organization I could. I was thirty-nine when Kinsmen came to Armstrong and too old to become a member, but I wish I could have been; the other one I never joined was the Lions Club. [However], I was a founding member of the Rotary Club in Armstrong, and I was the first member to get the founder's award – a Paul Harris Fellowship. I'm #29 in the Co-op Society here, and I've been a member of the Legion for over forty years. (During the War and for a couple of years afterwards, I was a member of the Rocky Mountain Rangers – a reservist, as farming was important to the war effort.) I was active in the chamber of commerce for over thirty years, was president of the Dairy Improvement Association and a director of the cheese factory for several years, and I was interested in sports and president of the track and field club when my older son, Roy, belonged. I always regarded these activities as experience. I always figured your mind was like your muscles – if you don't exercise it, it gets slack.

Motivated by this belief, Rawleigh continued searching out ways to use his talents. *When Don MacDonald was reeve of Spallumcheen, I was on council for a term. I was on different committees – representative to the health board and the 'nuisance ground' – another name for the dump.* Novices got the lowly jobs. *For several years I was chairman of the Court of Revision, which received complaints from people that weren't happy with their tax assessment.*

His term on Spallumcheen Council led to further interest in politics.

Dad had an interest in Social Credit. He didn't drive. He had one of those original driver's licenses that had no date on it, so it was good for the rest of your life. When you needed to renew it, you were supposed to turn in your old one. He never bothered turning his in, but he also never bothered driving. There was a play or something on that I was going to attend, but Dad said, "There's a Social Credit meeting in Armstrong tonight – do you want to take me?" It was just a small gathering, and instead of saving money by not attending the play, we ended up having to pay the hall rental out of our own pocket, and they made me president of the group. Later I was also president of the provincial and federal constituencies.

Nowadays you get your news mainly from TV or the newspaper. In those days important announcements were given at public meetings. I chaired the first meeting that W.A.C. Bennett gave when he told the people of BC why he had walked across the floor of the legislature and joined the Social Credit party. He used to be a Conservative, then resigned and became an Independent. Then he made a trip across Canada and visited all the provinces, and the one whose government most impressed him was Alberta's Social Credit. He first told that story in Armstrong, and as president I chaired the meeting.

Later on I chaired quite a few others for the party. One time they used the movie theatre in Vernon – there must have been 1000 seats. Bennett had been in Prince George the night before, and his assistant had left Bennett's briefcase behind. I was the only one that knew Bennett had to get up before 1000 people and speak with no notes. I became quite familiar with Bennett and most of his cabinet ministers down through the years. I remember in the early '50s we elected a member to the legislature, and the whole campaign cost $800. It was a good education.

In 1948 Rawleigh was thirty years old and the new public

health nurse, Lydia Doris Penner, came to town. She and other family members had escaped from the Ukraine in Russia following the Communist Revolution in 1917.

Actually her dad and mother were German and well educated. Her father was a teacher and Mennonite lay minister. Her mother's people had a lot of land in Russia and they went there – he was the principal in a local school – but when the Communists took over they seized everything. The situation was chaotic. Lydia's father refused to renounce his faith and was removed from his principalship. *They just got out with their lives. They had to hide in the cornfields and sneak out of the country. They travelled at night by train for two weeks and reached Latvia, where they got a boat for England. They were sponsored by somebody in Canada and settled in Herbert, Saskatchewan. Lydia was just a little girl, but she vividly remembered being seasick for the entire voyage across the Atlantic.*

At Lydia's funeral service in Armstrong on December 30, 2003, her niece Patricia Field read several stories that Lydia's sister, Susan, had written about Lydia's early life. They included the following:

On their departure from the Ukraine, Lydia's mother had dressed her in a bright red jacket in the hope of pleasing the 'Red' guards, but Lydia had been terrified that she made a bright target and would be shot. Lydia's family arrived in Saskatchewan in 1923, the same year that Rawleigh's family moved to Armstrong from Nova Scotia.

Lydia and her brother Philip took teacher training in Saskatchewan and got jobs in local schools. Lydia wanted to save money to pay for her real goal – nurse's training. The Depression and Prairie drought were in full spate. Sandhills piled themselves against fence posts and Lydia's leather shoelaces disintegrated. One morning she was forced to tie up her oxfords with string, and she walked to school to discover the inspector had arrived for a visitation! She felt very embarrassed.

She taught for one year. Her brother stayed with it. I think that year he earned $225, later became an English professor at the University of British Columbia [UBC] and co-authored several textbooks. Lydia ended up with a ticket home, thirty-five cents in her pocket, and a second-hand washing machine. The local farmers didn't have money to pay the teacher. Someone in the community boarded them and they were lucky to get any pay at all. When Lydia entered nursing, she received her contractual thirty dollars a month in small increments from the school board until the debt was repaid in full.

Lydia took her training in the Winnipeg General Hospital and graduated a little over sixty years ago. They keep track of their graduates, and we were told [2003] to watch for their latest annual report, their 60th, as they were honouring two of their nurses. One was a woman who did missionary work in foreign countries most of her life, and the other was Lydia. The article discussed her nursing career and her ability as an artist. The picture of her that accompanied the tribute was taken at the class's 50th anniversary with the girl who was bridesmaid at our wedding.

Following graduation, Lydia joined her family, who had moved to Chilliwack. She worked in Chilliwack Hospital for a couple of years, then took a degree in public health at UBC. Armstrong was her first assignment. In the late '40s a woman with a university education and a career was sufficiently unusual to excite interest.

Did you ever see a donkey baseball game? The players have to ride a 'well-trained' donkey. You hit the ball, jump on a donkey, and the donkey stops mid-base and can't be made to move! Lydia was the new nurse and I was sitting behind her at the game. That was the first time I had seen her. The first time she saw me I was in a play. The United Church used to have an annual play as their big fundraiser, and down through the years I had roles in them. That particular Christmas I was playing an eccentric old miser trying to protect his money from gold diggers, and she wondered who he was. We met shortly afterwards at an old-time dance.

Plays – comedies, in particular – were a source of fun and a good way to meet and interact with others over a period of time. *Plays in the 1930s and '40s were a big thing, especially if you didn't have other entertainments. They were put on in the Rec. Hall by our young people's group, but we also took them around to the army camp in Vernon, to Grindrod, and other places. I was in a lot of plays. In one role I had to speak over 300 times. It was good experience. You met a lot of young people – schoolteachers, banktellers – a lot of people in their twenties were active in it. There was a young people's group in Vernon, Armstrong, Enderby, Salmon Arm, and Revelstoke. They used to have wonderful get-togethers – picnics at Mara Lake, socials and dances. It was a wonderful organization until sadly somebody scuttled it. Someone said, "Oh, we don't want these old people in our young people's group." These old people included Rawleigh. So the group fell apart. When the club failed in Armstrong, I think all the towns suffered.*

Rawleigh wasted no time in courting Lydia, the gentle, serious public health nurse.

We got married at her parents' place in Chilliwack on July 28, 1950. That was the first real wedding I ever attended – my own. So I didn't know what to do! My mother was down – Dad didn't come. He didn't take part in social events in later life. We stayed in Mission with the old Bird family – they once lived in Armstrong – Dad had introduced Donald and Grace Bird back in the early 1900s. Noland wasn't there because somebody had to stay home to milk but Chandler and my sister, Violet, came.

It's kind of a funny thing – I had a radio in the barn and every day I would listen to a certain program and hear an advertisement for suits – 'Two for the price of one!' So on our honeymoon we went down to Seattle, the first leg of our circle trip, and I went to that store looking for my two suits. "Oh, the sale was just over yesterday!" We continued on to Grand Coulee Dam and back up to the Okanagan. It was a five-day honeymoon. I couldn't be away too long from the herd and, besides, we didn't have much money to spend.

Rawleigh and his bride came home to live in the Boss family farmhouse. *Our farmhouse was the first house that Jim Leduc had built. We drew our own plans, then hired Jim and helped him put it up. It was quite large. It had two storeys, and about six bedrooms altogether. So we turned one upstairs bedroom into a little kitchen, and another into a living room, and made a small suite. But we also had the run of the house. The house was near the barn, and I had to be up at four o'clock in the morning and go back and forth, so I didn't want to be too far away.*

Their two sons were born in the Boss home: Roy in 1951 and Gary in 1956. Flora Bella and Rawleigh looked after the children while Lydia continued her career in public health. Her territory included Fintry, Falkland, Deep Creek, Spallumcheen, and Armstrong.

She was a career woman – over thirty-five years or so. The first public health office was a lean-to on the side of the Hassen building. Harvey Brown had a plumbing shop there, and the Armstrong Hospital secretary and Lydia shared the lean-to. Later the public health office was located on Railway Avenue. Next it was part of Pleasant Valley Manor on Patten Drive. The eye clinic is still there but the office itself has been moved to Enderby.

When Lydia retired from public health, the City and the Municipality joined together to give her a civic reception. She was highly respected. After Roy was born, she worked for a while in the Armstrong Hospital, and I remember Jim Hopkins saying one day that she was the only nurse who could give you a needle and you didn't feel it. There's a knack to it. Tributes at Lydia's funeral lauded her attitude of personal attention and her compassion for her clients.

It's kind of interesting. As a public health nurse Lydia's life was dealing with people's problems – so come the end of the day she liked to get away from people. But I would join anything to forget the cows! But actually we did take part in practically everything together because she soon realized that it took her mind off her work as well. We patronized just about everything that came along in the community.

Rawleigh himself continued his policy of community involvement. As the years passed, he joined the Masonic Order and the Royal Arch, the Shrine Club and Gizeh Temple – *they do a wonderful job for disabled children and burn victims* – and the Independent Order of Odd Fellows. Except for the Preceptory and the Shrine Club, in each of these organizations he progressed through the chairs of office to become the presiding officer. *I never went in for glory – they were useful experiences to broaden my mind, and my mind needed broadening! Twice I was district deputy grand master in the Odd Fellows. At Lydia's funeral there were three BC past grand masters.* They were honouring Rawleigh as well as Lydia.

When their son Roy began attending school, he displayed the same expertise in sport as Rawleigh had done. Rawleigh was determined Roy should have the support that he himself had lacked.

Roy was a very versatile athlete. He entered all the track classes. The first time he ran down a field of hurdles he set a western Canadian record. He went to a track meet in Vernon – I guess he was about 16 – so he went in the age 16 and under, and in the 18 and under Open event, and he came home with nine first-place ribbons. He was a good broad jumper too. His BC high-school broad jump record lasted for twenty-five years. He was in a Canadian champion indoor meet at Kelowna and got four firsts – two were Canadian records. The BC Junior Track and Field Meet is held annually in Nanaimo. Ironically, thirty years after I had been there, he won three gold and two silver medals, so he won the aggregate for BC in his age class. Now his kids are in track meets. This year or last [2002], his daughter set a new BC record there – three generations. Cabinets in Rawleigh's family room exhibit trophy cups, medals, and awards won at track meets – both Roy's and his own – while Gary's awards celebrate his success at bowling. A basket overflows with winners' ribbons.

When Roy became involved in track, we decided to build a house in town. It would be easier for Lydia to get to her job, and I could commute back and forth for a few years. We bought the property on Sage Crescent in 1963. We picked a lot where you could go out the basement at ground level and not have too many steps to reach the upper level. This area was the old Fulton farm – a little orchard. When we were kids, we used to come up here and pick apples and hide them in the schoolyard. It was one of the earlier subdivisions. I think at the time there was just Mat. Hassen and Bill Parker, and then Jack Allen built and it gradually filled up. Just as before, we drew our own plans and had Jim Leduc build the house, and we moved here in 1964. If we had to build it over again, we would make some changes. They say you have to build three houses before you get one you really like.

The new house played Rawleigh one unpleasant trick. *I've been a vegetarian for over fifty years and always took care of my health. I had a bit of emphysema from hay and grain dust, but it wasn't too bad. One day Lydia and I were looking for something in the basement, and she handed me a jar that was just sitting there in a cupboard and said, "What's that?" I took the lid off and sniffed and it just about knocked my hat off. We have a hot tub, but it wasn't the kind of chlorine you use in it – it was a very potent type – a tablespoonful in a swimming pool will kill all the algae – and I don't know why we had it. The next day I read the label*: 'Don't handle without rubber gloves. If you get it on your hands, hold them under running water for fifteen minutes. Go to the doctor immediately.' *Well, I didn't go to the doctor until the next day, and then I had to go for oxygen four times a day for about a week. That chlorine didn't harm my bronchial tubes but it singed my lungs.*

In 1972 the Boss family sold the farm and Rawleigh's servitude to the dairy herd ended. For the first time in several decades, he was free to choose other work. However, he also recognized certain limitations.

Property wasn't valuable and the sale price on the farm had to be divided four ways. *(Chandler had died in 1972.)* I was up against the question: "What am I going to do the rest of my life?" If I had my life to live over again, I think I'd be a schoolteacher – I liked kids and people. But in those early days a teacher got $840 a year – $84 a month for ten months, and $70 a month if you spread it over the twelve months. But how would I get the money to go to university? Times were tough.

I was in my mid-fifties and businesses don't usually want to hire someone that old. My lungs would make it hard for me to do physical work, and my hearing is partially impaired. You wouldn't think a little milking machine motor in a big barn would damage your ears. I was just reading in the paper the other day where this smart fellow put a $40,000 stereo in his car. The noise!! What's going to happen to his hearing in twenty years?

I applied for a job at the liquor store. The manager had retired and his replacement hired the first name on the list. Mine was the second name.

Then I thought about selling real estate. In real estate you meet a lot of very nice people, and you're usually on one-to-one, so hearing wouldn't be a problem. I felt under pretty heavy pressure, though, because one of Lydia's brothers was a university professor, her younger brother was a teacher, one of her brothers-in-law was a high school superintendent, and another was the national director of the Red Cross swimming programme. All those brains and me just a farmer starting out on a new career!

Besides feeling nervous about venturing into a new arena and being unfavourably compared to successful relatives, Rawleigh had several hurdles to overcome before he could begin to sell real estate, open his own office, and eventually obtain an agent's license.

The previous year, 532 people took the first correspondence course from UBC – twenty-six lessons split into two sections and a final exam – and only fifty-eight percent got through. In my year

900 applied, so how many of us were going to make it? Believe me, I was under pressure. You don't know before you start what the course involves. Was I going to flunk it and look stupid? So when I was told, "Congratulations, you have made the grade," I was grateful. We had sold the farm in 1972 in March. The course started in August. In January, 1973, I was selling real estate.

I got hired the first time over the phone. I had heard the Vernon company Star West was interested in opening a branch office in Armstrong. So I phoned them up, introduced myself, said I'd lived here most of my life, farmed, knew the area.... "You're hired." I stayed with that company all the way through although it changed hands about seven times in the twenty years. I won the best salesman award three years in a row. I knew Armstrong and was well known here. In 1979 I took the agent's course.

At that time Rawleigh was 61. His grandfather Boss was his model for challenging the phrase 'one's declining years.'

I hadn't seen my grandfather since I was five years old, but he wasn't in the prime of life until he was in his sixties – very agile and athletic. He turned handsprings when he was 60. Around 1979 I had my own company in Armstrong – R. Boss Realty. It was located in the office of the former Star West branch from Vernon next door to Hassen's. Sage and Pothecary, and Mat. Hassen and Son were the other real estate offices.

When you have your own company, you have to associate yourself with an agent. He's ultimately responsible for everything that goes on in that office. The salesman and the agent can both sell real estate, but the agent is responsible for the transactions – all the listings and the deals have to be vetted by him. If a salesman pulls a dirty deal on a client, the agent is on the carpet. I was paying an agent several hundred dollars a month for his piece of paper on the wall, and he'd come in about once a week. To run a company on my own required a full agent's license.

I don't know if I made a mistake attempting the agent's course because it took a huge toll – it almost cost me my health. The course at that time was thirty-eight lessons. Like many other programmes, the course may not be exactly relevant to your own situation. I finished the first half of the course, passed the final and started the second half – and the first question was one I just couldn't answer: 'Give the actual bookkeeping of a recent sale of two different apartments.' There were only two apartments in Armstrong, neither had been sold, and if I had asked to see their books, they would have told me where to go. I had nobody in Armstrong to turn to for help.

Then somebody suggested I go to the Coast and take the second half as a crash course at UBC. So I signed up. We stayed in the Gage apartments on campus for several weeks one summer. Our teacher seemed too young to be a professor – he was just a kid – and he told us to ignore the textbook: "I'm going to set the questions and mark the papers." That assurance sounded good but didn't match the reality.

One fellow in the course had owned a real estate company for twelve years and you'd think he'd learn enough there to write an exam. His sister had a couple of children and was going to quit because she couldn't keep up with the work, but we persuaded her to stick with it. She moved out of her home and stayed at Gage with the rest of us. She passed the exam and her brother failed it. Half the material on the exam had not been covered. We got more help from a Vernon schoolteacher taking the course.

One morning part way along I was at a coffee break complaining to a woman about the course: "It's so frustrating. I come down here to learn how to run a business and they throw a bunch of crap like this at you." "Oh," she says, "I'll tell them when I go upstairs." That was a shock! I'd thought she was one of the class! But she must have said something to somebody because before our course was over, we heard that the agent's course was going to be revised.

As an agent, Rawleigh now had full responsibility for his own real estate company and was a more valuable asset to the Vernon company with which he maintained a connection throughout his career. He retired around 1996.

I'd still be doing that work if Lydia's health hadn't gone. She broke her wrist and needed help. She was spending hours every day deciphering her uncle's letters and translating them into English for the family. They were all handwritten in German, and there were hundreds of pages. She insisted on doing it. She got bad headaches. That was the beginning of the deterioration in her health – she was overexerting herself. That's what brought on her stroke.

The real estate business went through crises – right now it's booming [November, 2003]. This year I got birthday cards from two real estate companies in Armstrong and one of them said, "Market's booming. Why don't you renew your license?" But I don't know anything about the computer. I'm too late now, but I'd still like to be in it. I was happy with my choice.

Rawleigh had carried his earlier experiences of community neighbourliness into his work in real estate. *In Depression days we had a wonderful farm neighbourhood down where we lived – we used to help each other back and forth – never a dollar crossed the way – and sometimes a neighbour would do more for us than we in return could do for him. If somebody finished his own haying, he'd come and help with ours, and we'd do the same for somebody else. I always thought that life was like that.*

So when we sold the farm and I went into real estate, in meeting people I thought, "Well, I can't help my neighbours any more, maybe I can help somebody else." Sometimes the reaction was "If he's stupid enough to do that, then let's take him for whatever we can." It's sad to see that. So I've had some unhappy experiences in trying to do what I feel was right.

Toward the end of his career, Rawleigh had an exceptionally good prospect for a large commission. *A fellow who had about five little properties in Langley wanted to move his dairy herd up here. I found him a nice 160 acres in the Salmon River area – three houses, a big barn and the Salmon River ran through the property – beautiful. The deal was subject to the sale of several of his parcels. They didn't sell, and when the Silver Creek fire swept through here in 1998, all those buildings were completely wiped out. So that could have been a disaster for him. I was glad he hadn't brought his cows up, but it would have been my biggest sale.*

Rawleigh sold real estate until he was nearing eighty years. On his 77th birthday he received a compliment. *I had a client and I happened to mention it was my birthday. "Oh," he says, "I was wondering how old you were." "How old do you think?" "You must be getting near 65." I looked at him. "Do I look that old?" He thought he'd insulted me. He was quite elated to find out my real age.*

Rawleigh sold the old Boss place on MacDonald Road for his uncle Ivan. *The property was listed with me and in the '80s I sold it to Redstone. He tore down our old house and built a log house there.* Subsequently, the log house became the property of Polterman, then of Prangley, and currently of Garraway.

While Rawleigh and Lydia were still on the farm, they gradually became aware that their younger son, baby Gary, had a disability. This knowledge propelled Lydia into a course of action that culminated in the formation of Kindale Developmental Association for the support of disabled persons in the area.

Gary has Down's syndrome. It is more likely to happen to a woman pregnant in her forties. I remember my dad holding Gary shortly before he died, and I didn't think anything of it at the time, but I wondered later if he had sensed something was wrong. Dr. Art Sovereign brought it to our attention when Gary was about five or six months old. Lydia was quite concerned about what my reaction would be, but he was given to us and that was all. We've supported him in every way that we could.

I think Gary was about four or five years old, and there were about seven or eight of those kiddies in the community between Armstrong and Enderby. Lydia saw a need for special training because they weren't acceptable in the school system. The Kinsmen were looking for a project and she approached them. They accepted the challenge and built the little school [now Armstrong Play School] on Rosedale by the railway tracks. And that's where Kindale got its name – from Kinsmen. I think Rona Leduc was the first teacher and Jean Lockhart taught for quite a while. When these kids grew up, they couldn't carry on as a school per se, so the programme switched to being a type of workshop. The location changed to the old Perry house above Centennial Hall [Kin RV Park], and when it was torn down, the Association bought the property on Patterson Avenue. Down through the years different leaders had different ideas for the programme. It's grown a lot since Henry Sundquist took over. He's done a wonderful job.

We were very fortunate that Gary is in the higher bracket of Down's syndrome and is more mentally capable than others in the lower bracket. He is [presently] the clientele representative on the Kindale board of directors. I wish that he could speak clearer, but he has some impediment that can't be improved. But we were very fortunate that he is as healthy as he is. He's as sharp as a pin – he's a good bowler and an excellent cribbage player.

I can't help but laugh…. The Odd Fellows Lodge has two cribbage tournaments a year. Don Still and I were on the team that won the Okanagan Valley championship: Vernon, Armstrong, Enderby, Salmon Arm, and Kamloops. I came home from there and played Gary two games. The first game he beat me by eight points and in the second game I needed thirty points to get to the Skunk Line. Sure brought me down to earth! So since then we've had him on the team at the Lodge, and in five tournaments we've won four times.

Actually, it's a wonderful experience raising a child like Gary… That may not be the right way to describe it…. It isn't something that you 'enjoy' in that sense. You go through the different stages with him.... *You hate to see it happen to the child, but it's an education that you don't regret, other than you regret that the person isn't as normal as others are. I think if you asked a lot of people they'd say the same thing. It's a learning experience for us. I wish he wasn't that way, but since he is that way, I'm glad we were able to do what we could for him. I think Gary has done quite well for himself.*

Connections between the BC and Maritime sections of the Boss and Beaton families continued from that first 1906 trek throughout the century. *Several of Dad's brothers were bachelors. Ivan, his youngest brother, came out in 1925. Joe, the second youngest, also came out in the '20s, worked on the Stepney Ranch near Enderby for a while and then returned to Nova Scotia to marry. When one of his kids was about 16, they sent him out – I guess his dad couldn't handle him. We had him a few months and mailed him back!*

I would have liked to see the Bay of Fundy. Ironically, both my kids have got to Halifax and I have never been there. Roy went down to a Canadian national track meet, and Gary belonged to the Kindale Boy Scouts troop and stopped in Halifax first before attending an international Scouts meeting in Newfoundland. When Lydia and I went back in 1975, a very nice cousin treated us like kings. He took us to Prince Edward Island and around the Cabot Trail on Cape Breton: one day to see the top half and another to see the bottom half. But I never did get to see Halifax or the Bay of Fundy!

It was kind of funny.... When I was in real estate, they were developing Rattlesnake Point at Vernon into lakeshore lots that cost $25,000. You'd need a 100-foot ladder to get down to the lake. When I was back in Nova Scotia, I said to my cousin, "Are there any ocean shore lots left?" "No, they're pretty scarce, but the price has just doubled – they've gone from $500 to $1000 apiece." "Well, if you can find me one, I'll give you $2000 for it!" One of Dad's old bachelor brothers owned several cottages along the shore. He left them to a married nephew who died shortly afterwards. His wife had no interest in Nova Scotia and I think let them go in a tax sale. I *wish I'd known. I would love to have salvaged that part of our family history.*

At eighty-five Rawleigh is tall and active, attends local functions and enjoys dancing. *I tuck my puffer in my pocket and slip into the washroom occasionally for a couple of breaths. Then I'm all right again. My hearing aid occasionally cuts in and out but it doesn't affect my tongue.*

When Roy got married, I wanted to wear a white suit to the wedding. I had a white suit and I wanted a chance to wear it. He wouldn't let me. "No way! Men don't wear a white suit to a wedding!" Every year while Bill Bennett was premier, I always got a Christmas card from him with a family picture. First his kids ... and then his kids growing up ... and then wedding pictures. Bill Bennett sent me a wedding picture of one of his sons and Bill was wearing a white suit! The premier can but I couldn't?

Above all else, Rawleigh remains true to his guiding principle:

You only live your life once. I always figured I'd sooner wear out than rust out.

Rawleigh Boss jumps 6 feet on July 1st, 1946, in Armstrong

Chapter Seven

Grit and Grace

Martin Houlding Meggait

Until the day she died, Brantford, Ontario was still "home." She lived here most of her life, but it was always "back home." Very few homes around here are as stately as hers was. They would be the first to have a washing machine on their road.

Martin's mother, Eva Leonore 'Leo' Houlding, grew up in a substantial, two-storey, red-brick house wrapped by a white verandah. *It had to be painted every year and the white picket fence all around the yard had to be painted every year.* The Houldings lived on a productive farm in a well-established part of Ontario.

They had a 90-acre farm – it was practically paid for off the Brantford Market – they could sell anything at that market from a load of hay to a dressed chicken. It was always a race in the spring to see who could produce the first dressed chickens, and Mother sold to those fancy people that came down with the butler carrying the basket – the Harrises, for example, from the Massey-Harris people of Brantford.

A great deal of their land was under-drained with tiles and that's where the best crop was. There was a picture came out in the paper of stooked grain – a field of oats – and the stooks were so close together that they backed the wagon in through the gate to start loading. There was no room to drive in the wagon.

Everything in Brantford was so green. When Mom and Dad came up the Okanagan, she was shocked when she saw Osoyoos and Penticton. It was the middle of August – hot – hot – and dry. "Is this your vaunted *Okanagan?" It was hard for women – especially those veteran women that came out after the First and Second Wars.*

It must have been a terrific shock to come from running water and heated homes to a sod cabin. Martin's mother did not come to a sod cabin, but the contrast between Brantford and Spallumcheen was still acute.

Leo Houlding and Bill Meggait had met as youngsters on the Houlding farm.

My father could tell some terrific history. He was born on September 28, 1888, in California from Ontario stock – there's an Ontario County in California. His father and mother were from around Brantford and went down to California and acquired a big farm, and they both died within a year of each other – his father with pneumonia, and his mother with TB. And he also lost two sisters within that eighteen-month period. So that just left him and his brother. Then when his brother was twenty-two, he died, and Dad was an orphan. An old aunt came down and moved him back to Ontario. And he was in and out of trouble because he hated the city, and so she farmed him out to my grandparents' place in Brantford. So he and my mother met and fought because he kept ferrets and she'd go down to see what he'd killed to feed his ferrets.

You see, he came out of California as a twelve year old, and he had lots of experience already with rough and tumble down there. It was a very fine family, but he had a vivid memory of his father shooting a big deer and grabbing the deer by the neck to cut its throat, and the deer lunged up – carrying him – with his father hanging in the horns and still cutting – likely cussing too.

The marriage of Leo Houlding to Bill Meggait seemed an unlikely possibility. Her sights were on an academic career – *she trained as a teacher and taught the Montessori Method* – an innovative and experiential system of education for young children. Bill, on the other hand, fretted under discipline – *her mother was very strict* – and pined for the west. Since California held nothing for him now, when he was old enough, he headed for Alberta. *He must have been somewhere around eighteen.*

He bought a little horse in Calgary and rode out to Red Deer – he must have had some connection – and he got on with a very good farmer and his wife. One of his first jobs that winter was feeding about 100 heifers every day in a nice set-up on a meadow. The hay had been put up in a stack yard – stacks of loose hay and a good corral around it so the cattle couldn't get at it, and a gate so he could take the team of horses into the corral and load the hay. There might have been a hundred tons stacked up there, and it kept him busy forking out for that many cattle. And he had a cabin and a collie dog [that] slept on the bed with him.

Often out there they were able to pasture into December, and then things would start closing in and he'd be there until March. It was the winter of 1906-07. It was a terrible winter on the prairie. It went down in history. Thousands of head of cattle were lost in the blizzards. And he was alone all that time feeding cattle, and nobody came to check on him. And he said if it wasn't for the collie, he might have frozen to death himself in the cabin, but the dog would start to whine when the fire went out. He said he never lost any cattle. The next spring my aunt, Mom's sister, came out to Calgary and she said it was devastating – there were cattle standing in fence lines – still standing where they had frozen to death. The snow was gone and they hadn't thawed out enough yet to fall over.

Canadian academic and historian Grant MacEwan specialized in the history of the Canadian west.

I met him. He was our 4H beef judge over in Kamloops. I can still remember him judging our calves. When I saw his book, Gerry sent for it: <u>Blazing the Old Cattle Trail</u>. When they couldn't get any farther on land, [MacEwan said] they'd load the cattle on a barge and transport them up the river – clear up to the Yukon. They were bringing up fresh meat for the miners – the best way to transport it – transport it fresh – and they'd slaughter them there. It tells about somebody moving 3000 sheep!

Bill remained with the couple in Red Deer for only a year or two. *They wanted him to stay and would have turned the farm over to him. The farmer was also raising purebred Percheron horses and was a terrific horseman, but Dad kept looking at the mountains, and finally the man said, "Well, you'd better go – you'd better head for those mountains because you're not going to be satisfied here on the prairie."*

He landed in Sicamous with a pack on his back and came down the valley, stopping and looking at every ranch along the Enderby Road. It was about 1908. He went into the Young Ranch because he saw a good-looking ranch there. It was a Sunday and Mrs. Frank Young senior [B.F. Young] was shelling peas. And he sat down and shelled peas with her, and she told him that the crew was all out at the Round Lake range tending cattle. They came back and Youngs hired him on.

At slack times he would leave the Ranch and work in logging at Mabel Lake. On one small three-man crew he did what they called 'shore logging.' They had a raft, and a boom, and a team of horses, and they would just log what they could fall into the water, practically all handwork. The raft was quite large – the camp was on it – the horses lived on it – and the boom was attached behind it. When they wanted to log farther along the shore, they'd put an anchor in a dinghy and row ahead to the end of the cable and drop the anchor. A horse walked in a circle on the raft to operate a winch that wound the cable around a drum and pulled the raft and boom up to the anchor.

He also worked on a twenty-man crew at a big camp on the Cottonwood Creek just across from Dolly Varden beaches. They logged away up on the mountain and shot the logs in a 600-foot log chute down to the lake. Then they'd boom them there and send them on the Shuswap River in spring down to the big sawmill in Enderby.

Dad was [part of] the 'clean-up crew' on three river drives. They trailed the logs down, walking along the river a lot of the time – rolling the logs back into the water that got beached, and trying to keep watch for a log-jam. They were big logs. One time they had a terrific jam at Shuswap Falls. They were bringing logs downriver from the Sugar Lake country by water all the way. They'd try to pick out the key log in the jam, and take powder down and attempt to blow it loose – and then scramble out of there before the fuse went. The odd man perished. His cork boots would be nailed to a tree close to where his body was found. Perhaps the game 'Pick-up Sticks,' played in the early days with wooden sticks, replicates the log-jam. Working to free a specially marked stick is the object of the game.

Dad spent years logging in the bush. Then he'd get a letter from Frank Young: "Come back, Bill; we need you." So he'd go back and spend time at the Youngs'. Their relatives – the McCleerys – owned a big dairy farm on the mainland across from Lulu Island in the Fraser River, and the Youngs [also] sent him down to work for them. The farm is now a golf course, I understand. Dad was below sea level because when he was ploughing in the back field, the boats on the river were above him. He had a deal with one of the Chinese fishermen there – in the morning he'd leave a dollar tied to a willow stick by the river, and at noon he'd go back and very often the dollar would be gone and a fish tied to the stick.

Horses would be brought out from Vancouver to the farm by order of the vet because their feet had gone lame on them and they were cripplin' around. So their shoes would be taken off and they'd be turned loose on the meadow, and their feet would heal up again on the soft walking on the grass. They'd be too good a horse to be put down – all they'd need was a rest from pounding the pavement.

Dad spent quite a bit of time around Kamloops too working on the Fruitland Ranch. Then he'd go up in the Cariboo. He was wandering and looking. He was looking for something like this place.

'This place' is the Meggait Farm, 1152 Mountain View Road, where Martin has lived most of his life. *It was a quarter section – 160 acres with the road allowance taken off.* The yard is a cluster of farm buildings including the original barn. *We've started to reclaim it but haven't got very far.* In front of the barn is a corral and behind it, the glimpse of another. The view from the porch is instantly calming – a large field thinly scattered with large shade trees that give it the look of a park. *The trees have grown a lot since Dad bought the place.* At the back the field rises gently toward the mountain. North of the house is a stand of bush which Martin's wife, Gerry, calls 'The Chapel.' *Our granddaughter is getting married there next summer.*

We had wonderful community picnics here when I was a kid – a Thursday afternoon when the stores in town were closed. It would be held between crops – the first hay crop would be off and we'd be waiting for the second – usually around July 1st, as nobody went any distance. They gathered and played horseshoes, and played baseball on a small ball diamond, and ate and ate and ate.

Gerry says the farm is more than a family property; it is a 'community centre.' Over the years the Meggaits senior and junior regularly hosted the Scout Movement's camps, as Martin and Gerry became leaders when their children were small. Early Scout leaders – Derek Pickering and Barry Maddocks – built a dining hall and kitchen at the foot of the mountain where the troops pitch their tents. *Derek did all the cement work. That was one of his trades.*

The last Cub camp for those boys entering Boy Scouts is called the Arrowhead camp. The participants camp on the farm and undergo a round robin of challenges. *We once had 200 Scouting boys back there set up in tents – all divided off into blocks. The leaders – the rascals! – have an on-going joke – practically a lie – that they tell the boys every year is one of the challenges. They say they have a long hike to Cherryville with full pack. And they take them away up into the canyon and back down again, and across a cable bridge that Scouts and their parents built, and back down the mountain, and they come taggin' in exhausted at the end of the day and camp just across the creek. They've never left our property but they've been all the way to Cherryville!*

Until 2002 the farm was also the base of a North American Indian Mission camp – *a type of Outward Bound – hikes into the Alpine country, each young person carrying a pack; canoeing on white water at the Skookumchuk Rapids on the Shuswap River near Mabel Lake; rock scaling with ropes in Ellison Park [Vernon]; trips to the Monashee. We had school groups out here – Girl Guides – church groups of several denominations. Young people still come out here and play ball.* Some of these functions continue. Others come and go as interests change.

Before he bought the property, Bill Meggait had had a good look elsewhere in British Columbia. Hilary Place's memoir, <u>Dog Creek, a place in the Cariboo</u>, contains a reference to 'Billy Meggot.' *My sister Ann went to the archives in California and photocopied half a dozen different ways the name was spelled. Dad only spelled it AIT.* In the Cariboo Bill had found a job driving a two-team stage from Ashcroft to Alkali Lake. On one occasion a young woman named Ada Halstead-Netherwood was a passenger destined for the Place Ranch at Dog Creek. Chapter two in her son's memoir records the challenges faced by the stage driver, and the excitement and dangers of the route:

> The [Ashcroft] hotel clerk, white shirt, red armbands and all, threw the suitcases into the back of the rig. The horses were restless, jumping around and pawing the ground. Somebody was holding the bridle: "Let 'er go!" Dust flying, dogs barking, chickens squawking, all the boys from the livery stable waving their hats and hollering, the wagon rolled down the street, around the corner and out across the bridge over the blue-green waters of the Thompson River, the horses galloping and shying, testing the skill of the driver to the limit.

Bill had his work cut out for him. The distance from Ashcroft to Dog Creek was 115 miles and took three days with stops for lunch and overnight. *You could drive it in an hour or so now.* A four-horse hitch hauled a democrat carrying passengers, supplies for the store at Dog Creek – rice, sugar, beans, hardware – and mailbags for the post offices at Jesmond, Canoe Creek, Hat Creek and Alkali Lake. Depending on road conditions, in the following days Bill had to transfer his horses, passengers, baggage, supplies and mailbags to a sleigh and later back again to a democrat, both of which had been left for him along the route.

About twenty miles was the run for a team of horses before they had to be changed. That's why there were so many stopping houses all up the Cariboo Road – like 100 Mile House, 150 Mile House. Some of the names stuck and some didn't. To today's traveller twenty miles translates as twenty minutes. *Often a stopping house was just a ranch that was on the highway and had some extra rooms, and was possibly at the right distance from the last one. Some of the pictures show the road going right through the centre of the yard – farm buildings on both sides of it.*

The Place memoir continues:

> The Canoe Creek Canyon was very narrow and seemed just wide enough for the wagon. The cliffs rose on both sides, solid rock. Billy whipped the horses through it at a good clip to give Ada an extra thrill, and he laughed while doing it.

Perhaps he was also giving himself some encouragement, since upon leaving Canoe Creek the team had to negotiate thirteen switchbacks up Canoe Creek Mountain to reach the plateau and then come back down again into Dog Creek. This final stage would be a heart-stopping climax to the journey:

> Billy had to use all his skill to keep the wagon on the road. The lead horses were obliged to go way out on the corners so that the wheelers would be able to keep the wagon on track around the turns.

The lead horses would seem to be leaning over the edge of the drop in order for the wheelers to have room to inch around each corner with the democrat. Bill needed steel nerves, and his passengers, a strong motivation to reach their destination:

> They stopped to rest the horses every little while, and Billy held the

wagon from running back down the mountain with a huge brake lever that he pushed with his foot. It was a tricky business.

Once at the top, the jolting trail was 'a maze of twists and turns, over rocks and roots, and through mud holes.' As Bill began the descent into Dog Creek Valley, the danger increased:

> The snow hadn't melted off the road. Instead it was packed down into six inches of solid ice. Billy was having a tough time handling the outfit. He did not have much experience in slippery conditions.

Apparently, it was only his second trip. At one place a spring crossed the road and ice had built up around the next turn for 100 yards. Bill stopped the horses and put on a 'rough lock.' *It's a chain wound around one of the spokes in a wheel and attached to the wagon so the wheel can't turn – it drags and acts like a brake.* Unfortunately, he attached it to a wheel on the wrong side of the wagon and was about to begin driving around the icy curve when two cowboys broke out of the bush on the side of the road and stopped him. They must have been waiting for him. If they hadn't, the ill-chosen stationary wheel would have sent the teams and wagon over the side of the mountain. *It was the same when I was grading logging roads. Coming off the Bolean midwinter, we left the top in winter conditions and by the time we got into Falkland, the water might be running. Dad was dropping about the same altitude.*

Mat. Hassen said to me on Saturday – only half the stories have been told of your dad's life in the Cariboo. There's a lot that have never been told – stories that even you *don't know.* He was called Wild Billy Meggait. As a daughter-in-law, however, Gerry remembers him as Gentle Bill. *In the Cariboo it wouldn't have been possible for him to be Gentle Bill.*

On the farm here it was part of the tradition of Easter Monday – the young people from the church would come, and after they had eaten and were all filled up, they'd get a campfire going and get Dad to come with a story. He'd have been thinking of what he was going to tell them. Mom used to be a little bit jealous of his popularity and she would say, "Well, you didn't tell it that way last time!" Well, maybe it didn't happen that way in his mind last time too!

In one of his stories he had a young team and was driving the extra mail. He was alone – no passengers and nobody riding up with him. He was coming along near a high-cut stump and a cougar was sitting on it. Horses are terrified of these animals. *Now he possibly had a rifle with him or a revolver, but they were such spooky young horses he daren't shoot. They would have bolted before he could get his hands off the reins long enough. He had such a time to keep those horses from jack-knifing the rig on him, turning and breaking the pole. The way he told it, they sat for two or three hours before that cougar finally moved or he was able to get a shot at it.*

On one trip Bill had a passenger with a mission. *He had a Chinese man riding with him who was going up to collect the bones of the buried Chinese and return them to their families in China. On another occasion it was the summertime – hot and dry and dusty – and he came upon this Chinese fellow walking and asked him if he'd like a ride. "No," he said, "I'm punishing this old body. I'm punishing these bones." He had worked and worked earning money to go back to China, and he had the money and got down into Vancouver and gambled it away – he was broke – so he was taking his old body and bones back and making them do it again. Dad said the man walked in the dust of the wagon – he wouldn't get in and ride.*

Another story he told was just unreal. *It was the fall of the year and it was still muddy. This character at a stopping house had sent out for a crock of whiskey – a gallon jug usually. In those days the whiskey was so strong you didn't have to cover it up – it could stay right on top of the load because it wouldn't freeze – there was no water left in it to freeze – it was pure alcohol. When he pulled up at the stopping house on his route, the guy came tearing out to get his crock. Up on top of the wagon he went, and coming down with it he slipped and cracked the jug on the wagon wheel. Down he went on his knees – and he was drinking right out of the ruts. "Dam her up,* boys, dam her up – I'm losing it all!" He was sucking it up – didn't even run and get a ladle!

During these long days driving stage and watching the antics of his fellows, Bill was searching for the perfect farm. *He was trying to get something for himself. He homesteaded Big Bar Lake. It's on the way into the Gang Ranch. When he went in the army, he sold this homestead to Harry Marriot and it's a resort now, I understand. Harry Marriot wrote a book and mentions 'My friend Billy Meggait.'*

Dad also proved up on homesteads that the Gang Ranch bought. He did it twice. The homestead would be a meadow away back, maybe twenty-five or fifty miles from any Gang Ranch territory. He 'proved up' on the meadow – put a cabin on it and a barn and maybe a corral and lived on it for at least six months and then he'd have title to it. Then he'd sell to the Gang Ranch. And then they were able to run lines and take in all the territory between that meadow and their boundary. They did those kinds of tricks in those days.

For someone with Bill Meggait's skills and temperament, the Cariboo was an adventure playground.

The Gang Ranch was such a vast country. It fronted for fifty miles on the Fraser River – a terrific gorge. There was a suspension bridge hanging on cables across the river – the only way for moving cattle into or off the Ranch – and it was a real bottleneck. To keep the bridge from swaying sideways, they'd move fifty head up to the centre and cowboys would hold them there. Then the next bunch of fifty would be brought up to them, and the first fifty would be moved ahead. If they tried to drive them all across at once, the bridge would start bouncing like a trapeze.

They didn't have to put up much feed for the cattle because the Gang Ranch had such a wonderful winter range, and they depended on it. When Dad worked there, if they had to feed three weeks in a winter, they were in trouble because they had so many thousands of head of cattle.

Old Wycott was an Englishman. He had married an Indian woman and they had ten children. She took good care of him and raised the kids. A cruel thing – some homesteaders, like Wycott, took Indian wives. Then they'd go back to England and bring out an old girlfriend and boot out the Indian woman and children. They might help them out and they might not. That went on in the Cariboo but Dad kept clear of that – he didn't want to get involved in any capers like that. Some of these children were terrific men and some were renegades. Wycott got old and his boys left him and he was alone, so he hadn't branded for ten or twelve years. And the Gang Ranch bought him out. He had ten-year-old steers on his place that had never been rounded up and taken to market.

Wild cattle were a potent and intractable force.

One old character in town, Dave Hill, was a cowboy – that was his life – he always wore a big Stetson. He had no teeth, and when he got to talking, his nose and chin would just about touch. He'd tell stories about working on a ranch in Osoyoos rounding up Black Angus cattle. He said they once had about fifty head to bring off the mountain in the fall, and he and a bunch of cowboys started down over the wild Osoyoos country with these fifty head. By the time they got to the bottom of the mountain, all they had was three deer! The cattle had just shot off along the sides and were gone!!

Not surprisingly then, one of the most challenging and exhilarating activities the Cariboo offered was a round-up.

That's what they were rounding up – these wild things – cattle and horses – out on the range. Dad rounded up wild horses in back of the Gang Ranch – possibly was on the crew. They'd have a breeding programme too but they'd be bringing in those wild ones and trying to make something out of them. I think there are some in pockets up there yet – just got away from the Spanish and drifted north out of Mexico and California – good quality horses too. Dad said he used to see some pacers. When they were running, the other horses would be galloping and these were pacing – they weren't breaking stride – and the guys would spot them. They make terrific driving horses if you ever got them broke.

You see, in those days everything had to go on its own feet. When you went to move animals, you had to drive them. They never even dreamed of trailers and trucks and cattle liners. Horses were essential, and wild ones were available if they could be caught.

The men went up on the plateau country and were six weeks getting ready for the horses. They picked a meadow usually because they didn't want them spreading out into the bush along the sides. They rode around and found where their trails were, and they built two corrals, one directly in front of the other, on their main trail a half mile from water. The two corrals were for sorting the horses later. There were no gates – just bars that they left lying on the ground beside the opening at each end. They even felled trees against the corrals so that if the horses piled up inside, they didn't smash them down. They were wild and dangerous – they'd climb right up on each other to get out. Then the cowboys left for a week or so, and somebody would ride up and check on how the horses behaved. And when he saw that the horses had settled down and weren't scared and were going through the corrals to water, they made plans for the big round-up.

Wild horses were a mixture of feral cunning and ferocity.

The men had to be good riders. On the big round-up day, they closed the far end of the corrals. They hung sheets of cheesecloth on the trees and made a Y on the edges of the meadow, and the horses would see the cheesecloth and veer in, and so they funnelled them into the corrals. At the entrance they had put up all the bars except the two middle ones. One bar lay across the bottom and two more were across the top. To the fleeing horses the space between the bars represented escape and they poured through the gap.

The men would ram their saddle horses right up tight to the corral, and as soon as the horses were inside, somebody would have to jump off his horse and shove those bars into place fast because that's all the time they had before the horses would hit the [closed] end of the second corral and start thundering back. And they'd have them trapped. And they'd mill around and mill around in there and try to jump out – wild!

Then what they did seems cruel. It was rough and ready. The old ones and the stallions were shot because the stallions in particular would be impossible to do anything with. The young ones were held in the corral for three days without feed or water, and then they were let go to water. And their jaws were locked up because of the fear and strain so they couldn't drink. They'd just duck their heads and suck in water through their teeth. And gradually as they got the water into their systems, their jaws would unlock. Then they were full of water and couldn't run so they'd rope them. They'd cut out the best ones and turn the rest loose. They'd snub a wild one up tight between two saddle horses – start the breaking. There were lots of ranches up there then who needed horses. They had a rodeo everyday!

Dad said some of the best horses came out of the round-up and some of the worst. You never knew. Some never became manageable. Every time they were saddled, they bucked. They'd kick and bite. They were saddled early so their backs were warm. They bucked a lot fiercer when you just slapped a saddle on cold and climbed on. They just exploded under you.

When World War One began, many of the locals enlisted.

From up in the Cariboo a number of them joined up. About half of them were Indians – they were terrific fighters – along with Dad and the Gottfriedsons, Howard Payne, and different names from up there. They were such a rang-a-tang bunch that the authorities said, "We'll never control these!" and they sent a few of them here and another few there. I imagine they had to go to Kamloops to enlist. Bill was twenty-six.

One story Dad told to explain the sort of fighters the Indian men were. One of them was operating a machine gun in the front lines in Europe, and when the men came up to him, they found him slumped over it, and lying all out in front of him were dead Germans. They thought he'd been shot, of course, but he was sleeping.

Dad was about four years in the army. He did a lot of guard duty at Vernon Army Camp – civilian prisoners brought in for their own protection – Germans. He went with a boatload of Chinese labourers over to England and then to France to dig trenches. After the war I think he made a trip with prisoners from Canada that were being taken back to Germany. How he got involved with that duty, I don't know. We were raised on World War One stories.

Bill was demobilized on January 29th, 1918. His Discharge Certificate from the Canadian Expeditionary Force, 1st Depot Battalion, lists the following details: age - 29 years; height - 5 feet 7 inches; complexion - fair; eyes - blue; hair - dark brown. A note under 'Marks or Scars' indicates a hernia 'well held in by truss.' *He was promised in the army that it would be repaired, but he lived his life with it and it was never fixed.* Following his discharge, Bill made a trip to Brantford. He had been gone for over twelve years. *He had property back in Ontario that was left to him and he needed to get back there and tend to it. He lost heavily on that property because he wasn't there paying attention to it, but he came out of it with enough money to buy* this *place.*

He also had enough money and grit to propose marriage to Leo Houlding. *He must have had his eye on her all those years.* She too must have been waiting for him. Born April 20, 1892, at the time of their wedding she was thirty-one and he would soon be thirty-five. While Bill had been blazing his own trail in the west, Leo had taught for a number of years in public schools *and at a school that must have been connected to the Conservatory. She talked about the students there – she played the cello.*

In her parents' home on Thursday afternoon the 7th of June, 1923, at 'one of the daintiest and most attractive weddings of this bridal month,' Eva Leonore Houlding married William Meggait. *His parents hadn't wasted any time giving him a middle name.* The newspaper clipping describing the wedding was found with other papers in an old dictionary at the Meggait house. It continues:

> The spacious rooms were most artistically arranged with roses, bridal wreath and lilies of the valley, and at 3 o'clock to the strains of Lohengrin's wedding march the bride with her father entered the drawing room. She was preceded by two fairylike three-year-old nieces ... in pink organdy, each carrying a basket of white lilacs and pink roses, while a [small] page in a suit of white performed the important office of ... carrying the ring on a velvet cushion....

Bill Meggait certainly held up his end of the affair:

> The groom's gift to the bride was a handsome ermine stole while the flower bearers received gold lockets; the page, cuff links; and the pianist, a silver mesh bag.

A photograph catches a happy, good-looking couple in wedding finery flanked by three small children in splendid costume. Another occasion registers a side view of Leo sitting at leisure in a straight-backed chair. Her satin evening dress is fitted with a matching stole that drapes casually to the floor. Her shoes are a dainty complement. *She was quite a lady.*

They bought a brand new 490 Chev and drove out here from Ontario, pretty well all through the States, as there were no connecting roads, no Trans-Canada Highway. Dad said they "detoured" out. They camped across the country because there were no motels – they toured Yellowstone [National] Park – it took them about three months.

They got into Armstrong and all she could smell was celery – the whole of Armstrong smelled of celery. You know, there were seven packing houses along the railroad tracks in Armstrong at one time. Poole's was across from the Machine Shop/Museum on the other side of the track beside the overpass, McDonald's was across from the [current] Pea Pod restaurant, and the one nearer the hotel was a big one – John Wilson's. He was a very fine man – a Presbyterian, and a leader in the church there. Wilson's could store tons and tons of potatoes and onions and so on for growers that didn't have any storage facilities. Even Wallace Patten had a little packing house on a siding in the meadow near where Mountain View Road joins the highway – I can still remember seeing the ramp going out to the [rail]car so they could load produce from out of that packing house.

Bill and Leo rented a house on Schubert Road and began looking for land that would suit them both. *They looked at a lot of farms. They looked at property all along Deep Creek. Every other property was for sale because somebody was sick. Mom used to say, "I don't know – how come there are so many people having to sell because of their health? There are a lot of sick people in this country." To her, Deep Creek was solid bush on both sides of the road. Now it's beautiful up there with all those great dairy farms.*

They decided on the farm that bordered on Mountain View Road and Back Enderby Road. *It was a long ways from town – you didn't run in for a loaf of bread.* But Leo raved over the view. She had an image of the farm as a park. She had flowers everywhere – beds all around the house. She was terrible to go walking with. She wanted every little scrap of wood picked up: "Clean up this!" "Clean up that!" The mountain at the back sold Bill. *That mountain is what Dad was looking for – he wouldn't have to make fence along there – the cattle could just range up on top. One year Dad and Chan Boss brought them down on the 23rd of December – it was a wide-open fall. The next day it snowed.*

I have a notion that Mat. S. Hassen's dad was the agent for the sale. Dad bought the farm from Patchett. George Patchett was a hardware merchant in Armstrong. He had three or four girls and one boy at least, George. One of his daughters married Mr. Cox and they lived just down the road from us. There was a frame house on the [Patchett] property and an old barn. A little strip across the creek north of the house was cleared as well as ten acres on the south side, but the rest of the quarter section was solid bush.

That same fall Bill and Leo moved onto the farm, and Leo experienced her first Spallumcheen winter.

The house wasn't very big. There was a pump in the kitchen that had to be thawed out in the morning. The old house was cold – poorly insulated. Martin points to a photograph. *You can tell how much insulation* wasn't *in the roof. The heat was just going right through it and melting the snow.* The house looks as if it has teeth. Icicles spiking thickly from every eave are up to a metre long. *And you didn't keep as comfortable as we are either. The kettle on the stove would be frozen in the morning.*

There was a lean-to porch at the back – we ate out there all summer long and right into the fall. We'd be out there and everybody visited there. Few would have used the front door underneath the small porch roof. A window looked from the kitchen on one side of the front door and from the parlour, or the front room, on the other. *Nobody went into the parlour except a special visitor or to lay out your dead or for something special. There were three upstairs bedrooms – Mom and Dad's, the boys' room and the girls' room.*

The children arrived to fill them – Lawrence (Lawrie) first, then Martin on March 9, 1927, Mary a little later, and finally Ann. Leo's teaching experience and her life in Brantford had honed her organizational and social skills. She knew how to raise children 'properly' and run a home. *She was strict* – no crude language – *she had to put up with it somewhat* – Bill had to go outside. She wore no makeup. *She sat very straight – never let her shoulders slump. We weren't allowed cards at all. That was taboo. Dad wasn't as strict because*

I'm sure he played cards in the logging camps to while the evenings away.

In the old house Leo placed reminders of her former life – among them a wicker chair upholstered on the seat and back and made by *Brantford Wicker Works,* a rectangular oak dining table with extra leaves, and two exquisitely painted china plates signed *E.L. Houlding* and dated 1923. A narrow, clear blue border encircles the rim of each one, a fine dark line hemming it in. Five small areas of delicate colour – gold, pale orange, and blue – curl towards the centre while the major portion of the plate fills the outline of a pale yellow, five-petalled flower. Her artistic talent is evident. These heirlooms are still in the house, but there were other treasures too. *We got the farm, so the other children got most of the contents.*

Leo Houlding lived to be ninety-seven years of age. What sustained her during a long and active life in Armstrong Spallumcheen? *Her church and the community. Our community was terrific back in those years – the community spirit was really strong. All the other women around the neighbourhood – they took her in and she took them in. She had some great people around her: Mrs. Biggs, Mrs. Fowler, Mrs. Thornton, Mrs. Boss, Mrs. Frank Marshall, Mrs. Nash. Even before them, Mrs. Frank Young senior [B.F. Young], and Mrs. Vance Young. Mr. and Mrs. Jack Hopkins were down on the bottom road [Stepney Road] and Mrs. Hopkins was a great friend. Mrs. Hopkins loved her garden, and Mom loved nature and her garden so they had a lot in common. The Coxes were down the road. Mrs. Sam McCallum, Rich McCallum's mom, was a fine seamstress. She sewed with a hand-crank sewing machine – one hand cranked the wheel and the other hand guided the material. She made suits for all the boys and dresses for the girls.* All of these women would have been a help to the young bride.

Many of them were in the same situation. Men came out here and sent for wives when they got established. The lady across the road came out before World War One so she was quite a bit older than my mom. We called her Auntie Watson – she was the great-

grandmother of Jim Maundrell. A fellow in Enderby – Lambert – had paid for her passage out to Canada, and she came across country by train all alone – didn't know the money – she'd hold the coins in her hand and the waiter would take what he needed. She was supposed to marry Lambert, but while he was away for some reason, old Ernie Watson started courting her and she fell for him. When he asked her to marry him, she said, "I can't marry you because I'm supposed to marry Lambert – I owe him the passage money." "Oh," he says, "forget about that! I lent him the money to bring you over and he's never paid it back!" She raised five or six children for good old Ernie. A photograph shows Auntie Watson holding baby Martin.

Often our front room was cluttered solid with a quilt. The neighbour women would come and do a quilting bee. They gave them to the Red Cross mainly during the War. Like the other women Leo had a hobby. She cut up coats or blankets into strips, dyed them, and hooked rugs on sturdy hemp backing – *she would look for gunny sacks. She worked on a heavy frame.* One rug that she made for Martin and Gerry's wedding is a combination of rich darks with paler squares interlocking in the centre and another in each of the corners. Keeping the family comfortable and fed consumed the rest of her time.

[Many of] the women had landed out here and times were really hard. I'm sure Mom's family in Ontario weren't feeling the hard times as they were here. But she dug her heels in and was actually proud of how well she was doing – to the extent that she would look over the table and there'd be three items on it that were boughten – salt, pepper, and sugar – and the rest was full of our own food. And Auntie Watson made our butter a lot of the time and Mom would trade for butter. She was very proud of how well we were doing. Oh, she was happy that she came – raised us kids.

Like his neighbours Bill was clearing his land and practising mixed farming.

We had a very fine horse and he drove single or double very

well – he got to be 30 or 35 years old – quite an age. At one time we had seven horses – draft horses that could [also] drive. The horses worked all week and then went to church on Sunday and any trips to town.

Lawrie, Dad and I did a lot of land clearing, but Dad didn't sell hardly any timber. People came and cut wood – he gave it away. He cut logs to build the new Baptist Church and they were milled right there in the canyon. Dan Popowich and Albert Haller brought in a portable mill powered by a big tractor, and Ernie Vliet hauled the lumber to the building site on Becker Street. The new church was dedicated in 1949.

My dad broke his arm on Larmer Hill. The Larmers were a pair of bachelors that lived on the corner of Back Enderby Road above the highway. Dad was going to town with a load of poles on the wagon – stovewood for the pastor – and the road wasn't good – frozen ruts – not sleighing weather yet. He was sitting on an apple box and the box collapsed and he fell off the load and his arm went under the wheel. He got the horses unhooked with one hand and turned around, and he went back up to Larmers'. And as he drove, he had enough power to hold the broken arm by the wrist so the bones didn't get away on him. Larmers had a car – a Model T – and took him to the doctor. The doctor had to X-ray to see the break because in the car Dad had held the broken arm between his knees and didn't let the bones slide around. There was survival training in the bush camps – he knew what could happen. You could still feel the lump where the break was.

Most days were not so damaging but just plain hard work.

Our main fields are over there across the creek and this one past my son's house was cleared already. It was not very productive but Dad worked hard to make it productive – grain and corn and hay. We had pigs and chickens and geese. At times we would milk ten cows. They were separating milk before I was born. Mom would take the cream – usually a five-gallon can – in the buggy down to the creamery [on Creamery Road]. Then she'd perhaps go on into town to shop. That was a very picturesque road especially in the winter. Gerry remembers driving it when she and Martin were courting. *It goes straight now across those gulches. Before, the road went down into the gulches and across the creek and wound its way up the side again. At this time of year with the leaves off, you should be able to see the old bridge that's still down there at the back of Fennell's property. I think you can still see the abutments.*

After the creamery burned, Nelson Griffith took the cream to Vernon. [He] had a well-kept, flatdeck truck with a canvas over the deck. It was a long trip around – wound its way in the hot days back to Vernon. Very often the cream was sour. Sour cream makes good butter, as far as I know, but we'd get docked for it. Gravel roads, of course. It would almost be butter when it arrived. *When the Armstrong Cheese Factory started up, we shipped whole milk there and quit shipping to Vernon. Ken Nash took the milk to Armstrong. It got there in a lot better condition.*

The absence of an adequate local market within driving distance was frustrating.

The sad part – Mother would have a pen of roosters all ready to slaughter and she'd go to Fred Murray, the only outlet, to sell them. "I can't take them this week," he'd say. "Somebody else owes a meat bill and I promised to take his." And there they were – having to be fed longer and developing more when it was time to be butchered. And it was the same for the cattle – when we had a beast to sell, we just couldn't move it.

Then Fred Murray started shipping every Tuesday through Robert Burns, and then we had an outlet for our pigs and cattle. You could take live animals into the stockyard – it was across from the Liquor Store in the Y of the track. There were scales, and holding yards, and loading chutes to load them. Cattle cars were dropped at the loading ramp every Tuesday – two cars in the big season and one car at other times. *A few years later Carlson's, another butcher shop, would take our sheep.*

We survived much *better than the town people. It was a struggle for them. We ate well, but much of what we ate was raised. There were fruit trees on the farm. One year we put away forty-six boxes of apples – I remember counting them and putting a number on each box. Sometimes Dad would wrap them in Eaton's catalogue to prevent spoilage.* Eaton's catalogue had many uses. *(That's what I used to love about Christmas – the tissue paper wrappers on the oranges. They were* made *for the toilet and they were really nice – they lasted for a week or so.)*

Martin motions towards the corral. *Out there in the bunch there's a beef animal slotted for the deep freeze. That's what Dad did. An animal was fed special for our own use. They'd get grain whereas the others didn't get any. We always tried to have grain for the milk cows – it was the only way you kept them milking.*

Martin's favourite photo finds him at age four standing triumphantly beside a small Hereford bull calf that has his head in a bucket.

Vance Young gave us the calf. It was so small it couldn't reach its mother's udder – that was the story he told – she might have refused it – but it was an orphan and he brought it over here. It became the herd sire for a number of years. We had a terrible time getting it to drink – you'd get them sucking your finger and then lead them down into the milk. It fought us and fought us. We didn't bottle-feed – on a farm they need to learn to drink. We did bottle-feed our orphan lambs – we used to bring them into the house sometimes. The oven door on the old woodstove was laid open and the lamb would lay on it in a box – warm them up and get them going.

Martin began school in 1933. *The little schools were all closed by then. There used to be one on Mountain View Road and another on Back Enderby Road. I went to the Brick School. Bill Biggs was our first driver.* In the photograph the bus consists of a canopy on the back of a truck. *Armstrong Machine Shop built some of them and some of the guys built their own. They bought a chassis and put a body on top of it. The bus was pretty rough. There were just benches along the side to sit on and another bench down the middle. The exhaust pipe came up and ran down the centre of the bus.* The temptation was too great. *The burning rubber would start to stink up the bus: "Get your feet off that!!" Winter or summer the truck went through. If it didn't, you stayed home.*

Our next driver was Irwin Trudel. He married Vi Boss. I don't know who built his bus but it was a beautiful blue. It was so much newer. He was such a fine man – so good. He would take the whole neighbourhood to hockey games in Vernon in the evening in his bus. No restrictions – no nothing – you didn't ask nobody – it was his bus. Twenty people would fit in. Irwin could supply a cheering section. *My dad would go along. The Vernon arena was brand new – it was built in 1936 – it's still standing.*

Mrs. Dimock was my first teacher. Miss Fowler was another grade 1 and 2 teacher – Terry Fowler's aunt. We see him at funerals. I was a farm kid – life on a farm, you farm! We didn't get to [play] hockey or lacrosse or ball or anything. My brother took guitar lessons for quite a while. He went after school and Mom would go and get him with the horse and buggy. She drove horse and buggy and the sleigh.

Horses were essential for farm work and transportation. Bill's extensive experience with horses and the hard times of the '20s and '30s led naturally to his raising and breaking his own colts. Martin was initiated early into this art.

We had a terrific team – not great to look at but they were well broke. They were our work team. We logged with them, drove them – they would do anything – very willing – and he broke them 'gentle break.' The corral was right where it is now in front of the old barn. It was built of poles. Dad would have a colt harnessed, and after school one of my jobs was to drive that colt round and round the corral, one way, then the other way, and then in figure eights. Then he'd put a pole down so as to make it step over the pole, as if it was being backed into a wagon, because one horse would have to step over the pole when you backed the team into the wagon and hooked them up. So we did that all spring – he had two colts going that spring – and then we'd take that colt in the barn and harness the other one and bring it out. This was done before we ever put them in the team.

'Gentle break' required time and patience – long, diligent hours tracing patterns in the old corral, the training progressing step by step.

The old style was to use a 'breaking horse,' a great big heavy horse. Over at Youngs' they had a mare and she was the breaking horse, and she sure knew her job. She weighed about 2200 pounds so she had no trouble. The colt weighed about half as much as she did. Its head was tied over to the hame ring on her collar on the left, and then the britchen was tied together so the colt couldn't swing away and she would teach it. She'd yank that colt around with her. That was the method.

But Dad – because he didn't have a big heavy horse – I was allowed to do the job. He did a lot himself too. You'd harness a bridle and a surcingle and maybe a collar and hames – they were halter-broke by then – they just needed to learn the bit. First off, he would put the bridle on with the bit in the mouth and turn them loose, and they played with the bit, chewing on it, and trying to spit it out. Finally they'd get used to the feel of it.

Then the checkrein was put on, and they'd have to get used to that. We drove all our horses with a checkrein – they didn't have freedom to drop their head to eat when you stopped. We didn't want that because they lost attention from what they were supposed to be doing. It was a second rein on the bridle and it hooked into the bit too. Some went up the side of the bridle into a little ring, but ours went on the hames. In a driving horse it hooked right through to the crouper, which was a strap underneath the tail.

The colt had more lessons to learn. *And then there was the britchen that hung right down; and the martingale was the strap that went around the neck yoke and back to the straps that came from the britchen, and that all hooked up between their front legs and in front of the hind legs. And that was their braking power. That was how the horses put the brakes on the wagon if the wagon had no mechanical brake. That's how a horse controlled the wagon to back it up – they were using that harness. The martingale would come up real tight (it hung loose when they were pulling forward) and as soon as the wagon run up on them, then all these straps – if they were set right – they all tightened up.*

And that took a lot of 'breaking.' You know, a lot of touching the horse so that when the britchen pulled up on them, they didn't kick it or spook. And when they were well broke, it was just natural – they expected *that britchen to tighten up to control the wagon or to back up the wagon or the mower or the hay rake or anything with a pole attached to it – a horse on each side of the pole, and a neck yoke with a big ring that the pole went through.*

Dad was a firm believer in preparing the colt – don't spoil it – don't wreck it – the same with riding. We had a lovely little Arab mare – an Arab cayuse – for a number of years. I raised her from a colt. She was a dark chocolate – very nearly black, but not. A beautiful disposition. We had her mother [first], and I rode her down to Vernon to a stallion. Latimer and his wife raised Arabs in Vernon for many, many years along BX Creek, I think it was. And she got a colt. And next spring Mom was trying to wash that morning – a Monday morning – and everybody was so excited about this colt coming that she couldn't get her wash done for watching for it. Punky would be the children's riding horse.

Well, when we broke her, I walked alongside her. I had her neckreining before we ever rode her. Put the saddle on her and walk her around the corral – round and round. She never did buck. She never ran away with anyone. I put my sister on first and led her, and then we started riding her. Finally, everybody grew up and nobody was riding her anymore and Vance Young offered to buy her. Then he gave her to Frank [his brother] and Frank had her for years after that. He rode her in the IPE Parade – quite a few times she led the parade – and she was well into her thirties when she died. He called her Scamp. He used to ride her into town to get the mail.

When Gerry came to Armstrong in 1950, she remembers the hitching rails behind the Co-op store. Farmers would tie up their horses there and carry out 100-pound sacks of feed to their wagons.

Frank and Harry Hope were great friends so Frank would have tied up over at Harry's blacksmith shop. One day when Frank was having a beer in the old Armstrong Hotel, some of the young rascals went and got his old mare. He was sitting in the bar and in she came: 'Time to go, Frank! I'm tired of waiting!' Can't you just see the face of the bartender? "Get that xxx horse out of here!!" People were always looking for a chance to have a bit of fun. *Jokes and teasing – oh, they got <u>miles</u> out of that story!*

Frank Young was a very mild-mannered man. Mrs. Young used to travel around the area selling insurance. She was patient and persistent and would out-wait or out-talk neighbours until they signed on. *Dad hid in the irrigation ditch because she was trying to sell him insurance. We bought some.*

Once Frank took a young salesman out to see Scamp. The salesman said, "You can't train a horse nothing!" Frank winked at Mrs. Young. "Scamp, is it bedtime yet?" And she nodded her head up and down. Then she went out of her corral and around the barn back to her own door where she waited for him to put her into her box stall. He went up to her and said, "Give me a kiss," and she nuzzled his cheek.

The Youngs had a reputation for good horsemanship. *Frank Young senior kept a barn in Vernon where he'd spend the night if he had business there. He had a driving horse that would whisk him down pretty fast – it would be a trotter that could really hit the road – and he gave Mom one of his retired trotting mares for going to town because it would be faster. I think they raised a colt from her here on the farm. The horse had a heart condition that finally took her. Then we had a lovely old white horse – Mom drove him too – and another one, Jean.*

Donovan Clemson, a neighbour on Schubert Road, was a talented photographer whose work was published nationally. Local subjects were his inspiration. *Our Belgian mare, Queen, was on the cover of the Family Herald [and Weekly Star] about three times – first when she was a colt and then when she was older. He took a lot of photographs of the place. He took that one of the house in summer with the mountain behind it.* In the album the Clemson photographs are unmistakable. *Donovan Clemson had so many pictures in the Family Herald that at times people would write to the paper: "Is Armstrong the only place in Canada?" But he was such a photographer and he kept them supplied. Donovan Clemson built his house across from Max Clemson on Schubert Road [4602]. It's Freeman's place now.*

In the mid-thirties Leo and her mother were reunited. Mrs. Houlding came to Spallumcheen to live with her daughter and son-in-law.

We only got to know Grandma Houlding in her last year, but she was always very important to us. At Easter time in 1937, Mom travelled back by train to Ontario and talked her mother into coming out here, and they packed her up. Grandma Houlding brought with her four goose eggs and she carried them in her lap the whole trip. As soon as they got here, Mom scoured the neighbourhood for a clucky hen. Auntie Watson had one, and they got that clucky hen over and she took to the eggs and hatched out four goslings. She was running loose with them and they'd go down to the creek and get in the water, and she would pace up and down ... up and down ... at the edge of the water, calling them back, and they wouldn't listen to her. Oh, it was a sight! It was our first introduction to geese.

Mrs. Houlding died that fall. *Grandma didn't like alcohol, but she kept it for her heart. Mom administered her teaspoon of brandy to get her up in the morning. She had a very slow heart – it finally took her. She died in her sixties – most of them dropped off in their sixties. She was buried here in Highland Park Cemetery. Mom had to promise not to take her back to Ontario, so she's not buried beside her husband. It was mainly the expense, and she wasn't so tied to Brantford. She'd say, "The Lord will find me where I am. I don't have to be beside my husband in Ontario."*

The geese and the down pillows and blankets, however, became an enduring legacy of Mrs. Houlding's stay with them. *Mother would set up down in the basement before Christmas, and Dad would butcher the geese and bring them in to her. She'd sit with a goose in her lap and take off all the guard feathers first, and they went in one bag, and then she'd start taking the down off, and it went into another bag. There'd be down in your nostrils and down floating about, but it was all preciously stowed away in bags. Her wedding gift to family members was a set of down pillows and to each grandchild, another one.* Babies were snuggled in down blankets.

When those geese were nesting, they would pull the down out of their fronts – I can see them bending their necks – and when they left the nest, they covered the eggs all over with down that they picked off the sides of the nest, and away they'd go with a squawk and a holler down to the water, and then come back. Ducks were bad because they would forget. You got a duck setting on eggs – they'd get playing around and forget to come back. But geese were very protective. I've seen the old gander tackle a horse! He grabbed the horse by the tail and the horse was running and he was holding on and floppin' and squawkin'!!

A tragedy that happened too often in these early days struck the Meggait farm in early summer, 1938.

The old home burned. It was the third of June. Us kids were all at school, even Ann. Mary had taken her because she was to start school in September. Lawrie seemed to know what had happened but the rest of us didn't. They'd contacted Irwin Trudel that he was to drop us off at the little Boss house up the road and that's where we lived at first. It wasn't the main Boss house – it was an old one on one of the properties he had bought.

It had been a dry, dry spring – it hadn't rained for the longest time. Dad was up in the bush working on the irrigation flume – trying to get water down to save the crops. A spark from the breakfast fire caught in a shingle on the roof.

Mom was here and a neighbour, Dave Lawson, came running to help. Dave was very, very Scotch – a beautiful brogue. Other neighbours came flocking but.... In fifteen minutes it was gone. Dad had to fall a tree beside the house because it was catching fire and was going to throw fire all over the country. He burned his shoe as he was cutting – the fire was that close – a crosscut saw – but they knew how to run it! They got quite a bit of stuff out from downstairs but nothing from upstairs. Just what us kids had on our backs. We had to start again.

The wicker chair was rescued from the fire, and the dining room table, but the extra leaves were destroyed. Many family treasures were gone. The irony was that Leo and Bill had just completed extensive renovations and had firm plans for more.

The previous fall they'd worked and worked, and they had it quite well insulated – it was a lot more comfortable – felt-papered the whole thing and then painted or papered over the felt-paper. They built a fireplace very like the fireplace that's in the front room now. The same man built it – Leslie Bird, Dorothy Bird Smith's father. When they put the fireplace in, they cut some arches, took doors out, opened the house up, and we lived in the parlour with the fireplace. I have good memories around the fireplace that winter. Over the summer they were planning to re-roof the house and have it wired. Marshalls got the power that year and the old Phillips house down at the corner – everybody was getting it. We had it only one winter and then it burned. I well remember the old house.

The fireplace was the only thing left standing. Some people said, "Oh, you can just build your house around it." But the insurance people said no, there'd been too much damage. And they had to dig under it and topple it over. Mom picked through and used some of the same stone. She chose every stone facing outwards on the fireplace. Her artistic sense dictated the result.

Luckily the Meggaits had the summer to build another house and willing hands to help. *Eugene designed it – the husband of Mom's cousin Gladys from the Coast. They came up and spent the summer here. He was the main carpenter. Pete Paras' father worked on the house too – his dad was just a farmer/carpenter. Mr. Paras got $3 a day and his meals. He did the corner cupboards in the dining room. Pete is 82 now [2003]. When he visited us recently, he was thrilled again to see his father's work. Leslie Bird redid the stonework too – the foundation and the chimney. The basement is stone, not cement.*

Poor Mom. She must have suffered. She was cooking in a shed for nine or ten people. They had moved a big army camp stove out from town. Mrs. Timberlake – her name was Mrs. Wilson at the time – she gave them the stove and they set it up out there. The flies! And four kids!! Dad often butchered a sheep for meat. And no refrigeration, of course, for the whole summer – just put some things down the well in the milk house to keep cool.

The living arrangements were patched together with help from the neighbours. *Mr. Fowler – Terry Fowler's dad – dragged the back end of an old school bus over here, and Lawrie and I slept in it. Mom and Dad slept in the old shed that she cooked in, and when Gladys and Eugene arrived, they slept in the Boss house with the girls. We started moving in when the house was all shiplap yet – before there were any cupboards or anything.* No wonder! *Dad worked on the house all winter on and off.*

Gerry can relate to the feelings of destitution and dislocation that the Meggaits must initially have felt. *In Manitoba my dad had a store and it burnt down completely. I was grown up and working in the next town, and I heard the rumour and I didn't know if it was true. I phoned home. In those days you got the operator, and she said, "Your store is burnt down." And it was* loaded *with Christmas merchandise that Dad had just got in. All those dainty little muffs that women wore to keep their hands warm. There was one counter full of muffs that had a doll on the front of them, and I could imagine those new doll muffs all burnt up. Fires are devastating.*

Martin, though, recalls a funny story about friends who fled from one of the several fires that plagued the commercial section of Armstrong. *It happened after the first renovations to the Co-op store, and the old block was still standing [1950]. That fire was so hot that it cracked some of the windows in the Armstrong Hotel across the street. There were living quarters above the Co-op, and when it burned, the man came running in to his wife: "You've got to get out!" "I can't leave," she argued. "My hair's in curlers!"*

The Meggaits never forgot the summer of 1938. *Everything dated from that time – "Oh, that was* before *the fire" or "Oh, that was* after *the fire."* But they adapted. The children were of an age to be good company for one another, and the daily and seasonal farm chores kept everyone well occupied.

Mary and I were real good chums and we played together a lot. Mom said that when I wore my 'Billy hat,' we were the best of kids! I imagine I gave it the name. I liked the name Bill. I would rather have been a Bill than a Martin. Martin looks like his father and has the same spare shape and ready smile. *I have a logging picture taken over in the bush of my brother and I and Dad, and if we didn't have* suspenders on, we couldn't hold our pants up – we looked so thin. But Dad liked his fat food.

Lawrie was three years older than me. He was into building things – tree houses – there are still parts of them in the trees up here. You climbed up and went through a hatch onto a platform. He also collected – scrounged – loaded cartridges – old .30-30 and .22 shells – all sizes. He had a great collection of those and he lost the whole collection in the fire – they just exploded – Bang! Bang! Bang! He had them mounted on heavy cardboard that he'd acquired somewhere – all pointing downwards. Chan Boss and Gordon Sidney helped him collect them and they would trade back and forth. He'd get in trouble at school for having live cartridges in his pockets.

The old prospector up here gave him bullets for his collection – we got to know him pretty well – Mr. Empey. He prospected in the canyon next to us – you can still see some of his holes. Gold! Just around the corner! The next stake he'd be rich! Guys would do that – they'd start a family and then the 'gold bug' got them and they'd take off. They couldn't hold down a job – or wouldn't – because they had to hunt for that gold. He was grubstaked by some of the men in Armstrong. They'd get a percentage if he found anything.

He was a character – slept on rawhides – bear and deer that he'd shot. You could get into his cabin and there'd be a block of wood to sit on – but if any other boys came with us, he never showed. He didn't run us off – but he wouldn't show. He was watching – I'm sure he was watching – so we soon learned, if we wanted to go visit him, we went on our own. And he smelled so wild and so bad that when he crossed through our yard here, or came to the house to see Dad for something, the cattle would react – their heads would be up in the air giving the signal that they were smelling a bear! He never washed. But we enjoyed him. Accused occasionally of poor hygiene, the boys could always be confident that the old man smelled worse.

He smelled too of that powder that he put in his miner's carbide lamp. You put a little water with this powder and it made a gas.

There was a striker on the lamp, and you cupped your hand over the shield, struck a flint, and the gas would ignite. After you got the light going, you shut the glass door in front of it. He would show us how to work it. He either carried it or wore it in his hat.

He was killed by a bus one Christmas outside the Chinese place. The Chinese place was straight across the railway tracks from the [present] Liquor Store – cross two tracks and get to it. There's still a big house standing there, a warehouse, and buildings. Quite a number of Chinese women and men were living there – we used to go in with the buggy and buy vegetables from them.

The buggy had once been the 490 Chev. Dad cut the top off the car and made a Bennett buggy. He used the chassis and built the box. We sold the motor to a cousin in Courtenay who had the car but not the motor, and he restored it and put it back in a 490 Chev. That car went into a lot of parades, I understand.

The Meggaits knew several of the local Chinese residents.

We got to know this Chinese man that came out here from Armstrong with large baskets of vegetables – celery, lettuce, and the like, that he had grown in his little plot of land in Armstrong. We never got a name on him. I used to know a lot of the others – Wong Duck and Yip Too – that farmed right around the same area. This was when the creek ran through the middle of the fairgrounds. It was all beautiful black soil in there then. His farm and little cabin sat where the horse stalls are now, right across from that old house on the corner of the [Highland Park] School property. One of the Hoovers lived there.

The little man – I bet he wasn't 4 foot 6 inches – would come out here with these two baskets on a pole across his shoulders – one basket ahead and one behind. He'd come to the door – he might knock or he might not – and he'd trot over and feel the kettle on the stove to see if it was hot because he wanted a cup of tea. He didn't have much English. And right from the start Mom would make him a cup of tea. She would make him a sandwich to take on the road with him or she'd feed him right here at the table. He was terrific, and we all became great friends with him. If he saw us on the street in Armstrong coming along with a team of horses, he'd hail us. My dad would stop right in the middle of traffic – there wasn't much – and he'd come over and Dad would talk to him. And the odd time we stopped at his little farm and bought vegetables from him.

This one time Mom had put a cup of tea on the table and a sandwich. Dad was sitting there too – it was in the old house before the fire. I don't remember him coming after the fire but I definitely remember him coming before the fire. Mom put a quart jar of plum jam on the table with a dish and a spoon. She thought he'd take jam out of the jar and put it on his plate. He took the whole quart jar over in front of him and began to eat out of it – chop, chop … chop, chop … and stir it up … and eat a little more … and he was sighing…. Finally he turned to Dad and said, "Too sweet! Too sweet! Mind if I leab?" That jam would have been half sugar, and that poor old boy wouldn't be used to it – he didn't eat a lot of sugar. He thought for good manners he was obliged to eat the whole quart. *And we never caught him again!* After that Mom would bring fruit over and ladle it out to him. Two spoonfuls and then: "Tha's 'nuff! Tha's 'nuff!" And he would eat a little bit, then trot out to his baskets and bring in another head of lettuce or a bunch of celery or radishes, new carrots…. He started coming as soon as he had new vegetables growing in his plot.

I wish I'd known his name. He was so much a part of our lives as kids. He walked from town. I don't know how much further he went, but it was a long way from Armstrong. How many times he stopped before he got here, I don't know. He'd land about noon, so he'd have left town pretty early. Gerry adds, *They were hard workers – their backs would be bowed down with carrying their loads. They were good people.*

The family made friends with the natives too.

Indians were mainly from Enderby, and we got to know them because they'd come as a whole family – aunts and uncles and children – to pick fruit up the road at the Cowley place, where they'd live in a bit of a cabin and tents. Mr. Cowley had raspberries, blackcurrants, and the like. And another family would camp in tents in our bush when they were picking for Mr. Les Bird – Cecil and Dorothy's father – just across the fence – presently Art Frederick's place. Mr. Bird had quite an acreage of strawberries, raspberries and blackcurrants which he would sell.

One time we stopped in at Cowley's, and there's this old Indian lady sitting beside an open fire with a big pot of raspberry jam that she was cooking. She was comfortably sitting there, stirring the pot – the mosquitoes and the smoke and the ash all got stirred in – and she said to Mom, "Dis da way to do it!" Mr. Cowley had given them the 'overripes' that he couldn't ship – they wouldn't have lasted to Armstrong before they were jam – and she could have those after they went through and picked the 'shippers' – the ones solid enough to ship.

There was one sweet old lady, Mrs. Dan Joe, and Mom and she would call each other 'sister': "And how's my sister today?" Many years later when we lived on Moray Street, Gerry took in three foster children, and they were her grandsons. The old grandmother is gone now. Gerry explains, *I had kept a six-year-old for her father for a year, and then I got the three brothers, and after they left, I got a four-year-old native boy with epilepsy. Then one of the boys came back and altogether he was with us for four years going to school. It was a busy life.*

The Meggaits had four boys of their own – Jim, Billy, Tony, and Gordon. Billy died of leukemia when he was nine. *That was the hardest time we ever went through.* Gerry says, *We've always called him Billy because we never grew him up. He planted that maple tree out there in his grandma's garden in 1962, the fall before he died. We call it Billy's tree.* The seedling has become a substantial maple shading the back door.

The Meggaits attended the First Baptist Church on Becker Street. Bill held the office of treasurer and was a deacon for many years. *Mother kept the treasurer's books at our church but she wouldn't let her name go on them. Her husband's name had to go on them.* Martin grins. *He'd never look at it. He had to sign the cheques – she kept him the head of the house. She was very clever – he was a doer – practical – but she was a very capable person – she did the accounting.* One suspects the pastor may have guessed the truth.

There was some collaboration in the area among the Protestant groups, both adults' and young people's groups. *Many Mennonites fellowshipped with us until they built their own place, Armstrong Bible Chapel – Abe Giesbrecht was one of the leaders. The Pentecostals used to worship with us too until they built a church on Patterson where the Senior Activity Centre is now.*

One Christmas Day became a lesson in the virtues of Christian charity and patience.

At that time Vance and Annie Young lived where Bob Paul is now – on the highway near the Fortune Creek bridge. After Vance's dad, Frank senior, died, for quite a while he and Annie ran the old ranch that Frank had homesteaded on Lansdowne Road. Then they sold it. I can vaguely remember the senior Youngs. They were gone by the time I was growing up.

We all had to go to church Christmas morning. And we hadn't had the tree yet. It was good sleighing then, and we were on our way home in the cutter. Vance walked out on the road with his little dog and said, "Come in! The wife's got lunch on." It didn't bother my brother and I too much, but my sisters were younger – and oh! all those presents waiting!! Dad went and put the horse away in the barn. Vance had a nice big barn there – it's still standing. It was a long afternoon. There was oyster soup – that was very special – but we didn't like it. Who likes oysters when you're a kid? But we enjoyed the Christmas cake.

In addition to her function as ghost accountant for her church, Leo kept meticulous records of farm income and expenses. The entries in her long, narrow ledgers are written finely in pen, each page sufficient to hold the transactions of a month. One ledger covered the period from 1948 to 1954. Below is a sample of credits and debits and Martin's comments.

I was reading Valley Auction's sale prices last week, and they are comparable to what Dad was receiving in those ledgers when he shipped an animal through Fred Murray on Tuesdays. Many people are in danger of going broke if this problem [borders closed to Canadian beef] doesn't shape up pretty quick.

May, 1948
	Eggs		$33.37
	Electric	3.67	
	Milk Check		111.30

The usual was eight cows.

	Butter	8.00	
4	4 bags of seed oats	16.00	

We'd get it at Hoover's.

	Family Allowance		8.00

I would be gone by that time – just Ann was left.

	Ann	8.00	
	Gloves	2.75	
	Hospital Insurance	2.50	
26	Dentist (Mary)	10.00	
	Dentist (Leo)	50.00	

June, 1948
	Egg Check		29.29
	Electric	3.51	
	Milk Check		99.71
	Butter	7.92	
	D.D.T.	.90	
4	Family Allowance		8.00
	Ann	8.00	
	Horseshoeing	5.00	

Hospital Insurance	2.50
Flood relief	1.00

That was the year Fortune Creek poured down and there was a lot of damage on the meadows here. It was [caused by] three days of rain, deep snow up top, and a late, late spring. The Marshalls lost 30 acres of potatoes – they'd just been planted and were up about six inches. They were hauling rock from our quarry to try to reinforce the banks of the creek. Mat. and Rose Hassen's farm was on the highway near the bridge a mile east of Armstrong. Their potato fields were all up, and the trucks were driving over their potatoes to get in and turned around.

Wood sawing	6.00

Herbie Bannister had a saw.

Dentist	2.50
Feed wheat (Thornton)	10.00

October, 1948

Egg Check		7.50
Offerings	8.00	
Telephone	2.54	
Milk Check		91.13
Butter	10.10	
Family Allowance		8.00
Ann	8.00	
Hardware bill	6.60	
Hospital Insurance	7.50	
Sulky plow	25.00	
To Mary	10.00	

November, 1948

November was always big – lots going on.

1	Egg check		23.01
	Electric bill	3.67	
3	Combining barley (Moller)	15.00	
15	Milk check		149.11
	Butter	9.70	
	Family Allowance		8.00
	Ann	8.00	

Flannelette and cotton	17.25

She was going to make pyjamas for all of us for Christmas.

Taxes	93.42
Telephone	2.06
Tablets	1.00
Account book	.35
Horseshoe nails	.50
Stamps	.50

Probably four cents at the most for a sealed letter.

Groceries	1.42
Thread and elastic	1.25
Cabbage	.75
Hospital insurance	7.50
Meat	1.50
Plowing	5.00

Joe Moller would come here with a tractor and plough. We had a horse plough but not the power.

Mending cement	52.00

We were trying to pass the requirements for shipping whole milk – upgrading the premises. But we were hand milking. In the early days pretty well everyone hand milked.

Underwear (B)	6.50
Comforter satin	8.80

She'd be making something for Christmas.

Pillow ticking	4.28
Sundries (Postage, tax, etc.)	1.65
Meat	1.10
Hog	46.51

We had some pigs. We shipped through Fred Murray to Burns. Then Frank Evans took over and shipped for a while.

Russian oil	.86

It was a laxative for people and cows.

Bell's Remedy	1.29

Dr. Bell's horse remedy – you put it on the tongue. We had a team of horses that were very prone to colic. We used it on cattle too for stomach problems.

To Martin	10.00

> *I was living and working here; starting to work out some.*

To Mary	5.00
Groceries	15.43

Ron Wiser's wife was a Bell and her mother was a Hoover. They found ledgers of the Hoover flour mill and Ron turned them over to the [Armstrong Spallumcheen] Museum. They were fabulous – what they paid for grain and supplies – but it was not much more than you get right in these ledgers. Hers is very detailed – every penny is accounted for.

In the spring of 1939, Martin celebrated his twelfth birthday. That fall World War Two began and the community became involved in the fight for 'King and Country.'

Our schoolyard had a pile of scrap iron we were bringing in. Every Monday we bought War Savings Stamps. All our teachers were very loyal to the cause. Lawrie finished his grade 12, but before he graduated, he and a number of his classmates left school and joined up – girls and all. It happened in hundreds of schools across the country. In no time at all they were taken in and gone – with or without their parents' permission, or lying about their age. Sam Abramenko and his brothers went to join up and their father said, "I risked my life to get you out of Russia to keep you out of the army, and here you're going into the army." He didn't understand it.

Floyd Bigsby was the only one who didn't get in. He went through with top marks – he had a withered arm and hid it – but he couldn't pass the medical. He went on to be a professor in Saskatoon. (The Bigsby family was a terrific family – at one time there were five of them going to UBC – two girls and three boys.) Lawrie stayed active in the air force – he put in years there. After the war he took his senior matriculation – grade 13 – and then his teacher training for one year in industrial arts. He went to summer school ten times to complete his certificate. He taught for forty-some years – built three different industrial arts shops – had all the boys building worktables and benches. His tree house experience had paid off.

The two girls also took further education. Mary trained in Vancouver as a nurse. Ann began nurse's training and then decided to become an X-ray technician. *At the end of grade 10, when I was sixteen, I quit school and went farming with Dad. Then I started working off the farm too – combining with Joe Moller.*

On the back of the photograph someone has written: 'The Silo Fillers, Sept/47.' *It was taken at Joe Moller's. He had the machine and the tractor that ran it.* Martin names off the crew: *Sam Abramenko, Mr. Penney, Charlie Brown (an uncle to Al Brown that has the machinery equipment business), Joe Moller, Roy Joslin, Bill Meggait (my dad, hiding in the back), Klaus Moller, Herb Graves and his little son Kenny, and me. Mr. Penney was a great guy – a Boer War veteran – he died at 99 or 100. Charlie Brown was very English – he was a character.* In the photo one can see a load of corn and an upright wooden silo. *This machine chipped the corn and then blew it up into the silo, and Dad's job was inside the silo spreading it around. Pearl Moller would have made the dinner. After Moller's was finished, they would come to this farm and then go over to Dave Hope's and put up silage. In earlier years it was Thorntons and Fowlers and Biggs that we put up silage for.*

Martin Meggait met Barbara Geraldine 'Gerry' Pouncy at church in Armstrong. The Pouncys had farmed in Ochre River and Dauphin, Manitoba, where the weather was extremely harsh and the family diet was on occasion reduced to milk and potatoes. Her father in 1948 relocated to Vernon and then to Armstrong, where he opened Terminal Motors on the site of the present Co-op garage. He asked Gerry to leave her job in New Westminster and come back to Armstrong to look after her mother, who was very ill. The only employment Gerry could find was at the Co-op grocery store. Having met earlier, she and Martin undertook a closer acquaintance.

We were in a young people's group – they used to put on month-

ly parties with the young people from the Enderby Baptist Church, the Church of the Nazarene, and us. We often met in homes. We'd play games and eat. The Church of the Nazarene was a small building on the corner of Wright Street and Rosedale Avenue.

Within a month of going out on dates together, she and Martin were engaged. *I guess we knew. You got married younger then. We were twenty-five and on the verge of getting old!* Gerry adds the details: *We were engaged in 1952 on Ann's birthday, January 19th and married on August 14th, a wildfire romance that has lasted 51 ½ years.*

Vance Young was both an old friend and a tease. When news of their engagement became public, he stalked into the Co-op general store one day, ignoring Gerry at the checkout counter and all the while muttering loudly: "She must have asked *him*. He's too *shy* to ask her. She must have asked *him* to marry her."

After the wedding Martin and Gerry lived upstairs in the Meggait home. Gerry recalls the experience: *I got pregnant within a month, and I made three dozen diapers. Martin's mom wouldn't let me wash them and hang them up on the line because the neighbours would see them and gossip. When Lawrie got married and the couple came for a visit, her daughter-in-law wanted to wear shorts, but she daren't wear them around here. [Leo] had to relent a little bit when her girls came along, but it was hard for her to give up her values.* Shorts were not considered decent attire for young women, and pregnancy was a private matter until nature revealed the fact. After their baby, Jim, was born, Gerry and Martin moved into town to a number of rental places. She acknowledges, *I'm sure it was hard on the old folks but it was best for us.*

Martin continued working part-time with Bill on the farm and holding down other jobs too. *Farming isn't that profitable and Dad encouraged me to get into trucking, and then when I went to the bush – well, that was work he'd done when he was a young man.* Martin drove the milk truck for Bert Fletcher, gathering up the milk cans from the farms and taking them to the cheese factory. On occasion Gerry rode with him: *I admired the quick way he could jump down and swing the heavy cans into the truck – he was very agile.* When milk vats in the barns replaced milk cans, and a tanker truck was introduced, Bert sold the truck and Martin drove for Len Wood's Motor Transfer, which was being run by Wood's son-in-law, Bud Gessner.

Then starting about 1955 I worked about five years with Ganzeveld's sawmill in Vernon. First I was building logging roads – a swamper. He's the gofer – the guy that does the fuelling up and the greasing. A mechanic? A much lower grade than that! He was the guy that pulled the line out when the CAT got stuck. Most of the CATs had a winch on the back of them – usually a one-inch line with a great big hook on it – you pulled the line out and hooked it onto a stump – staggering up to your knees in mud and snow. We did that by the hour. It was hard labour. Ganzeveld's laid out the roads themselves. The road took off from Back Enderby at the Luttmerding area – it's called Baker Road now – named after the guy who lived at the bottom of the hill – a private road that we had to grade through. We had to get lots of permissions – fences were up and gates were locked. Oh, we had to fight the fisheries department when we were logging: "That's a fish stream! Can't log here!" And it was a miserable little stream that no fish in his right mind would ever come up. I worked as well in the Ganzeveld planer mill sorting the finished boards into their various lengths. At that time logging work was seasonal. I'd get laid off every winter and at break-up time – sometime before Christmas – and Gerry would have to save and save for when I wasn't working.

Then I got on with Armstrong Sawmill – Smith's – and was back into the bush again with Fernie and Pierre Vandenborre – uncle and nephew. Pierre was the CAT driver. Fernie was the foreman and laid out the roads. He had to take the plan into the forestry department and they would pass it and come out and check his work. I worked with him laying out roads and then building them as we got the go-ahead.

In 1961 we were putting road into Proctor Lake – taking off from Powerhouse Road and into that country over there – and we'd come into some very rocky country and couldn't get through, so we were drilling and blasting. We had drilled twenty-five holes the day before and three of them hadn't gone off properly, so the next day there was quite a bump of rock in the road yet. We had the drilling outfit – a compressor and a hand drill on a trailer – and I was drilling. We didn't need the CAT at that point so Pierre was watching to help if I needed him. Fernie was standing beside me pointing and hollering where he wanted me to drill – "Drill here ... drill there ... drill there ..." and then – a lucky thing – he tapped me on the shoulder and said, "I'm going to go down and load those other holes."

So he took his pickup and drove down the road a hundred yards or so, and he was just getting out of the truck when he heard the KERPOW-W-W-W. I'd hit the powder from the day before. It broke my knee and my leg – we were blind for days from the rock because we were standing right over it. Fernie must have pretty near died right there himself from fright – he came back and gathered up the two of us – we were laid out unconscious. It was the third of November, the first snowfall of the year. *He started for Vernon on the highway and the truck spun around on the ice and was headed back toward Armstrong so he thought, "Okay, I'm closer to the Armstrong hospital." He was looking at us and thinking, "I don't think I'm going to get to Vernon in time."*

Gerry was enduring her own nightmare: *We were living on Rosedale, and I got a call from the hospital that Martin had been hurt. Tony wasn't fully dressed – I grabbed him up – stocking feet – and stepped over the fence into Alf Tooley's yard and put him in the door and said, "Look after him" and I ran the couple of blocks to the hospital. As I went in, here was the bush truck driver – Glen Maw – with his face as white as a ghost and a trail of blood all the way into the hospital and an aide mopping it up. It was our neighbour on Burns Avenue, Mrs. Smith, and she hadn't even recognized Martin when Fernie carried him in. Martin and Pierre were lying in the room, and Martin was so swollen – the tiny splinters of rock all*

355

in his face and his leg and his hand – so sore – I went to touch him and he said, "Don't touch me!" Then when the Compensation people came to investigate, they said to Martin, "You're lying!" "Why would you say that?" "Well, if you aren't lying, you'd be dead."

Martin agrees. *With three sticks of dynamite, you don't survive. Doris (Patten) Shiach was the bookkeeper and office worker at the sawmill office, and Fernie came in to report the accident. She said there was blood all the way down the front of his clothes – it was gruesome. Pierre was blinded in one eye and both jaws were broken – he was a mess. It was close ... it was close.... No two-way radio then, so nobody would have checked on us 'til too late. The boys wouldn't have had a dad at all.* If Fernie had been standing over the drill with the others, no one would have survived. *Fernie treated me like a son – even before that – but we became very close for years after. I felt so sorry for him. It wasn't the end of the job, but I never was involved with dynamite again.*

Gerry has a final vivid memory of the accident: *We were so poor in those days that the morning after Martin was hurt, I took his wool socks, which were all riddled with these minute pieces of rock and soaked with blood, and I put them in a pail of water to wash them out and save them. It was a gesture of defiance and faith. Some sort of tradesman came to the door and here I was wringing out what looked like pure blood. A dangerous woman indeed.* Martin smiles: *You washed the underwear too. They were heavy wool underwear – Stanfield's.*

At the time of his injury, Martin was only thirty-four. The accident coloured his life. His left leg was weakened and bowed. *I still have some of the rock pieces in my eyes. Whenever I go to a new eye doctor, he takes a look and says, "Whatever happened here??" and I have to explain. But I had a good career in the bush.*

I ran grader and built bridges and culverts – I worked with Doug Tucker – he was a great character – he married Moyreen McKechnie. Fernie is still alive but Pierre and Doug are both gone.

Fernie started me on running grader – a very rough start – he didn't show me nothing – steering, or anything else. The grader was parked at the shop – where they are rebuilding at Shepherd's [Wood Avenue at Mill Street]. He said, "You know how to start that thing?" We were logging at old lady Adler's property at 6 Mile. "Bring the grader out there." And he left me and went on out. I got out there a couple of hours after he did. That was my grader start. He coached me on a few things.

From there I went to a CAT 12 grader – it was a fine old piece of machinery – fairly big – and then to a 600 Champion, like the Municipality has now. I ran that for five years, and then Smith sold to Crown Zellerbach and they bought me a brand new 1980 CAT 14. It was a Cadillac – an absolutely beautiful machine – air-conditioning, a two-way radio – very comfortable. Martin didn't scratch his initials on it. But I had my picture taken on it a few times – a few write-ups.

My last ten years were the best – I wasn't doing any more swamping for the CAT. Before that, I used to run grader for two or three days and then I'd be off swamping. Finally one of the foremen was wanting a full-time grader operator – Doug Tucker had left to form his own logging crew with Pete Hornick. I'd had quite a bit of experience. I can remember it so clearly. I was servicing the grader in the shop – spring service – we drained all the oils and changed them and tested the antifreeze. He came to me and said, "You've got to make a choice – either drive the CAT or the grader." And I said I'd like the grader very much. And he said, "Okay, that's your job." That's all there was to it.

In winter Martin worked long hours plowing logging roads. I worked with different crews who were contractors at the mill. I usually started at 5 a.m. and worked twelve hours. Occasionally I was called out again near midnight to grade through 'til morning. But even then the logging trucks were ahead of me. It got worse and worse. In the summer when I was grading roads, they'd pull me off once in a while to help install a culvert – pick and shovel. Then

Fletcher Challenge came in, and then Riverside Forest Products at the last. They were very good people to work for. Through all the changes of ownership, Martin remained employed.

It appeared that Martin's dad had emptied out his sack of roving restlessness and was firmly settled on Mountain View Road. *After he came on the farm here, he never worked off it.* He hardly left the property – everybody had to come to him. It was his corner of the world. *I often wished I had pried him loose and taken him to the Cariboo – it's so short – an afternoon drive and you're there. We didn't do it and we should have.* Doubtless, every curve in the road would have resurrected a story.

In 1962 Leo decided to get her driver's license. She wanted her independence. And she and Bill had their combined old age pension to spend on gas.

One of her great accomplishments was getting her driver's license after she turned 70. That was a performance! I think she failed the test three or four times in Vernon – the guy wouldn't pass her. Jean Boss, as she was then – Jean Williamson – Jean McNair as a child – I went to school with her – Jean would drive Mom for these examinations, and Mom would just be in a sweat – she'd have white gloves on and they'd be soaked through. Finally Jean took her to an examiner in a different city and he passed her and they gave her a license. She had already bought a little green Volkswagon and she scooted around in it. Dad operated the brake. She would drive into town and buy vegetables at the Chinese warehouse.

More changes came quickly. In 1972 Bill died. He was nearly 84. After a couple of years on her own, Leo moved into a duplex behind Pioneer Square and Martin and Gerry took over the home place. Leo lived in town for roughly a dozen years. She walked everywhere and everyone knew her. *She'd go up the hill over the tracks on Bridge Street to get her mail and down the other side – she would – and she had a great time in town. She walked up to church*

– she'd given up driving by then – she wasn't a great ... well, we won't say.... She had got from A to B.

Gerry found what she calls her life work at Kindale Developmental Centre. First as a volunteer and then as a teacher of reading, cooking, and life skills, she developed the first personal programmes for Kindale clients and was an instructor for Okanagan College on the subject of teaching people with disabilities.

When Martin retired from road construction, he was able to enjoy the farm. This spring [2004] he is spending his days and nights birthing beef calves. He is expecting forty-three. *I wouldn't have this many except for the Mad Cow scare. I had Gerry buy batteries for my flashlight the other day special for looking for calves – their eyes shine at night when the light hits them. The cows go to calve on some bedding mounds because they get a little bit of heat and it's more comfortable. Last night I shone my flashlight and here's two little eyes down here and two big eyes up here. It was nice.*

Martin's love of farm life is built into his character. He remembers neighbours who were role models for him, particularly the Youngs and their hired man.

We called them Uncle Vance and Aunt Annie. They were very, very important to us. He laughs. *Vance bought real good underwear – very fine [weave], creamy coloured, with red trim on the cuffs. And his worn-out pairs would all be saved and washed – maybe some mending on them – but Mom would take the back off the legs and the tops – whatever was salvageable – and make underwear for us. And we wore this lovely, fine, very expensive underwear.*

[So] Vance Young I was just in love with, and Annie was very nice, but this character in the [2003] <u>Okanagan Historical Report</u> *was my idol – Harold Archibald Somerset. Somerset was the Youngs' hired man. Every summer when they still had the old ranch in Lansdowne, I used to get to spend a week, and I'd tag him around from the time I was a child. He was a great guy. He was just there*

– *and I was free to spend lots of time with him and he put up with me. From there he went to the Ellison Ranch at Oyama and gained his great reputation as a herdsman. He showed cattle at the IPE, and the CNE [Canadian National Exhibition] at Toronto. I didn't know he was into the collie dog-training too.*

The Meggaits' farm dog was always a border collie. Family photographs include the current pet. The collie presently sitting at the back door is Angus, who really belongs to Tony and Robin but spends a large part of his time with Martin and Gerry.

Angus is such a help. Yesterday I was separating out some cows that I thought were ready to calve. I'd got the one I wanted, and I was walking down the alleyway to open the gate to let the others out when I heard footsteps. I turned around and Angus was bringing the one I'd cut out. He thought she needed to go too. He's so eager – and I hadn't said, "Angus, just leave her." He ducked his head because he knew he had made a mistake. Angus (Robin, really) gave me a book on border collies for Christmas. It said: "Now, when you're talking to your border collie, talk sense. Don't talk gibberish." When we go to town, Gerry says, *I always say to him, "Now, Angus, we're going to town. We'll be home soon. You look after the place."*

For the last two years of her life, Leo moved back to the farm with Martin and Gerry and died in 1989, three years short of her hundredth birthday. Until the end she was a power in the home. Gerry remembers, *When Tony was just a little gaffer he said to Bill, "Grandpa, are you allowed to get in the fridge?" Tony was hungry but didn't know if Grandpa could help him out. Grandma had little Tinker Toys over in the corner of the kitchen, but the children couldn't play with them whenever they wanted. When she chose, the Tinker Toys came out, and when she chose, they were put away. Those were probably the only toys she had and all these kids wanting to play with them.*

The farm that Bill and Leo found and made their own continues to be a magnet for their grandchildren and great-grandchildren. *All the family – Martin's and mine – love this place. It's close to worship! All their heights are on the door frame. There used to be a bench and bookcases under the kitchen window, and as our family grew we took them out to make more room. We heard some objections: "But our diapers were changed on that bench!!"*

Martin wears a big grin: *At Christmas time [2003] we had five babies from one month to seventeen months including a set of twins. They were all in the front room on a big rug kickin' and crawlin' and squawkin.'* In a large coloured photograph in the kitchen, Martin cradles one of the newest babies. He still can put babies to sleep.

Gerry is mulling over the reasons the lives of Bill and Leo made an impact.

Grandpa and Grandma were very hospitable – that's one of the things that stand out for me. When they had a meal, even if it was only a family dinner, Grandpa would have the roast or the chicken or the turkey in front of him, and he would carve it and put the meat on the plate and pass it down to Grandma at the other end of the table, and she would put the vegetables on it. In spite of poverty there was a grace in the way they did things. They both had it. It seemed to come naturally.

Martin's parents are the bookends for his memories. His story began with Leo. It concludes with Bill.

Dad was a wonderful father – he was one of the best.

Four-year-old Martin Meggait and the Hereford calf that became a herd sire

Index

4H 14-15, 112, 283

A
Apples 14, 19, 25-26, 105, 147, 213-14, 333
Armstrong Cheese Factory 119, 288, 332
Armstrong Creamery 18, 20, 113, 230, 331-32
Armstrong Fair 9, 110-12, 236-37, 250, 283-84
Arts 3, 29-30, 110, 135, 146, 167-68, 174, 178-79, 200-01, 207-08, 227-28, 239-40, 329-30, 334, 338

B
Boer War 38-39, 207-09
Borrow pit 11
Brown, Kootenay 211-12

C
Cattle 19, 21-22, 110, 117, 120, 133, 146, 153, 185, 220-21, 236, 287-90, 313, 333, 359-60
Chickens 23-24, 52, 154, 187, 272
Child rearing 18-21, 133-34, 146, 183-84, 190, 199-200, 274
Chinese residents 73, 78, 88, 320, 344-45
City Dairy 74, 98
Cooking 18, 26-28, 52, 155, 171-172, 189, 330
Cowboys 36, 322-324
Commerce 34-35, 37, 47, 125, 149, 154, 178, 238

D
Depression 104-05, 189, 224, 254-55, 273, 279
Douglas Lake Ranch 22, 36-37, 254
Driving license 114, 358

E
Education 15-17, 35, 43, 100-01, 112-13, 154, 156-59, 187, 222-24, 228, 248-50, 274-75, 333-34, 359

F
Farming 12-14, 32-34, 46-47, 68, 102-03, 121, 123, 152-53, 155, 169, 182, 186, 220, 230-32, 251, 268, 272, 352

G
Geese 88, 338-39
Gang Ranch 321-22

H
Health 10, 19, 39-40, 99, 107-08, 161, 181-82, 187, 216-17, 219-220, 229, 250, 296, 346
Homesteading 149-51, 159-66, 194, 211-12, 214-15, 246, 321
Horses 30-31, 72, 103, 146-48, 169, 179, 213, 334-38

J
Japanese residents 53

K
Kalsomine 184
Kindale Developmental Association 134, 303-04

L

Logging 17, 131-32, 196, 215, 269, 314-15, 354

M

Market gardening 254-55, 283-86, 344, 346
Mining 343-44

N

Native people 322, 324-25, 346

P

Packing houses 26, 74, 87, 327
Pigs 13, 25, 103, 113, 127, 155, 186, 226, 250, 272, 331
Politics 135-36, 234, 237-38, 239-40, 250, 292
Potatoes 102, 122, 123, 169, 230-31, 251

R

Real estate 10, 48, 196, 299-303
Recreation 18, 28-30, 51-52, 109-10, 147, 167-68, 178-80, 251-53, 271, 294-95, 304, 334
Religion 30, 171, 208, 235, 268, 347
Roads 15, 17, 84, 122-23, 128-30, 181, 234, 282, 354-55
Rural electrification 115-17, 232-34, 255, 341

S

Sheep 186, 333
Sports 29, 110, 118, 275-80, 297
Springview Dairy 59-99, 106-08

T

Travel 16, 31, 43-45, 157, 179, 317-20, 326
Trucking 125-126, 133, 148, 332, 353-54

V

Valley Auction 133, 348

W

Water 69, 118, 150, 151, 154, 155-56, 165, 175, 225, 248, 273, 280-81, 340
Weather 16, 39-40, 108-09, 124, 155, 328
Women 86, 143, 146, 151, 154, 171-74, 176-77, 180, 185-86, 191-92, 215-16, 253, 254, 271, 284, 289, 328-29, 353
World Wars 38, 39-43, 46, 53, 89, 149, 217-18, 256-57, 324-25, 351

365

ISBN 1-4120-2466-8